T0213969

Communications in Computer and Information Science 1218

Commenced Publication in 2007
Founding and Former Series Editors:
Simone Diniz Junqueira Barbosa, Phoebe Chen, Alfredo Cuzzocrea,
Xiaoyong Du, Orhun Kara, Ting Liu, Krishna M. Sivalingam,
Dominik Ślęzak, Takashi Washio, Xiaokang Yang, and Junsong Yuan

More information about this series at http://www.springer.com/series/7899

Donald Ferguson · Víctor Méndez Muñoz ·
Claus Pahl · Markus Helfert (Eds.)

Cloud Computing and Services Science

9th International Conference, CLOSER 2019
Heraklion, Crete, Greece, May 2–4, 2019
Revised Selected Papers

 Springer

Editors
Donald Ferguson
Columbia University
New York, NY, USA

Víctor Méndez Muñoz
Escola d'Enginyeria
Bellaterra, Barcelona, Spain

Claus Pahl
Free University of Bozen-Bolzano
Bolzano, Bolzano, Italy

Markus Helfert
Dublin City University
Dublin, Ireland

ISSN 1865-0929   ISSN 1865-0937   (electronic)
Communications in Computer and Information Science
ISBN 978-3-030-49431-5   ISBN 978-3-030-49432-2   (eBook)
https://doi.org/10.1007/978-3-030-49432-2

This Springer imprint is published by the registered company Springer Nature Switzerland AG
The registered company address is: Gewerbestrasse 11, 6330 Cham, Switzerland

Preface

The present book includes extended and revised versions of a set of selected papers from the 9th International Conference on Cloud Computing and Services Science (CLOSER 2019), held in Heraklion, Crete, Greece, during May 2–4, 2019.

CLOSER 2019 received 102 paper submissions from 33 countries, of which 29% were included in this book. The papers were selected by the event chairs and their selection was based on a number of criteria that included the classifications and comments provided by the Program Committee members, the session chairs' assessment, and also the program chairs' global view of all papers included in the technical program. The authors of selected papers were then invited to submit a revised and extended version of their papers having at least 30% innovative material.

CLOSER focuses on the emerging area of Cloud Computing, inspired by some latest advances that concern the infrastructure, operations, and available services through the global network. Further, the conference considers as essential the link to Services Science, acknowledging the service-orientation in most current IT-driven collaborations. The conference is nevertheless not about the union of these two (already broad) fields, but about Cloud Computing where we are also interested in how Services Science can provide theory, methods, and techniques to design, analyze, manage, market, and study various aspects of Cloud Computing.

The papers selected to be included in this book contribute to the understanding of relevant trends of current research on Cloud Computing and Services Science. We can observe the classical centralized cloud processing to distribute out to the edge, towards fog, and Internet-of-Things applications. New platform and management solutions are required, but we also need to better understand how data is processed in these platforms. Even more fundamental concerns going deep into search and retrieval, security, but also self-adaptation principles need to be investigated. Furthermore, the organization and architecting of systems at service-level through microservice and container technologies is an open question. The papers presented here address these concerns, providing solutions to some of the urgent problems in this field.

We would like to thank all the authors for their contributions and also the reviewers who have helped to ensure the quality of this publication.

May 2019

Donald Ferguson
Víctor Méndez Muñoz
Claus Pahl
Markus Helfert

Organization

Conference Co-chairs

Markus Helfert   Maynooth University, Ireland
Claus Pahl   Free University of Bozen-Bolzano, Italy

Program Co-chairs

Víctor Méndez Muñoz   IUL, S.A. and Universitat Autònoma de Barcelona,
     Spain
Donald Ferguson   Columbia University, USA

Program Committee

Ahmed Alenezi   Northern Border University, Saudi Arabia
Vasilios Andrikopoulos   University of Groningen, The Netherlands
Claudio Ardagna   Università degli Studi di Milano, Italy
Danilo Ardagna   Politecnico di Milano, Italy
Marcos Barreto   Federal University of Bahia (UFBA), Brazil
Simona Bernardi   Universidad de Zaragoza, Spain
Nik Bessis   Edge Hill University, UK
Iris Braun   Dresden Technical University, Germany
Andrey Brito   Universidade Federal de Campina Grande, Brazil
Ralf Bruns   Hannover University of Applied Sciences and Arts,
     Germany
Anna Brunstrom   Karlstad University, Sweden
Rebecca Bulander   Pforzheim University of Applied Science, Germany
Tomas Bures   Charles University in Prague, Czech Republic
Matteo Camilli   Università degli Studi di Milano, Italy
Manuel Capel-Tuñón   University of Granada, Spain
Glauco Carneiro   Universidade Salvador (UNIFACS), Brazil
Eddy Caron   École Normale Supérieure de Lyon, France
John Cartlidge   University of Bristol, UK
Roy Cecil   IBM, Portugal
Rong Chang   IBM T. J. Watson Research Center, USA
Richard Chbeir   Université de Pau et des Pays de l'Adour (UPPA),
     France
Augusto Ciuffoletti   Università di Pisa, Italy
Daniela Claro   Universidade Federal da Bahia (UFBA), Brazil
Thierry Coupaye   Orange, France
Tommaso Cucinotta   Scuola Superiore Sant'Anna, Italy

Francesco Longo	Università degli Studi di Messina, Italy
Joseph Loyall	BBN Technologies, USA
Glenn Luecke	Iowa State University, USA
Shikharesh Majumdar	Carleton University, Canada
Mirco Marchetti	University of Modena and Reggio Emilia, Italy
Ioannis Mavridis	University of Macedonia, Greece
Andre Miede	Hochschule fuer Technik und Wirtschaft des Saarlandes, Germany
Monica Mordonini	University of Parma, Italy
Mirella Moro	Federal University of Minas Gerais (UFMG), Brazil
Kamran Munir	University of the West of England, UK
Víctor Méndez Muñoz	Universitat Autònoma de Barcelona, Spain
Hidemoto Nakada	National Institute of Advanced Industrial Science and Technology (AIST), Japan
Philippe Navaux	Federal University of Rio Grande Do Sul (UFRGS), Brazil
Mara Nikolaidou	Harokopio University of Athens, Greece
Emmanuel Ogunshile	University of the West of England, UK
Tolga Ovatman	Istanbul Technical University, Turkey
Claus Pahl	Free University of Bozen-Bolzano, Italy
Symeon Papavassiliou	National Technical University of Athens, Greece
Nikos Parlavantzas	IRISA, France
David Paul	University of New England, Australia
Dana Petcu	West University of Timisoara, Romania
Agostino Poggi	University of Parma, Italy
Antonio Puliafito	Università degli Studi di Messina, Italy
Francesco Quaglia	Sapienza Università di Roma, Italy
Arcot Rajasekar	University of North Carolina at Chapel Hill, USA
Manuel Ramos-Cabrer	University of Vigo, Spain
Christoph Reich	Furtwangen University, Germany
Pedro Rosa	Federal University of Uberlandia (UFU), Brazil
António Miguel Rosado da Cruz	Instituto Politécnico de Viana do Castelo, Portugal
Rizos Sakellariou	The University of Manchester, UK
Elena Sanchez-Nielsen	Universidad de La Laguna, Spain
Patrizia Scandurra	University of Bergamo, Italy
Erich Schikuta	Universität Wien, Austria
Lutz Schubert	Ulm University, Germany
Stefan Schulte	TU Darmstadt, Germany
Michael Schumacher	University of Applied Sciences and Arts Western Switzerland (HES-SO), Switzerland
Uwe Schwiegelshohn	TU Dortmund, Germany
Rami Sellami	CETIC, Belgium
Wael Sellami	ReDCAD Laboratory, University of Sfax, Tunisia
Carlos Serrão	Instituto Universitário de Lisboa, Portugal
Armin Shams	University of Limerick, Ireland

Keiichi Shima	IIJ Innovation Institute, Japan
Frank Siqueira	Federal University of Santa Catarina, Brazil
Ellis Solaiman	Newcastle University, UK
Cosmin Spahiu	University of Craiova, Romania
Josef Spillner	Zurich University of Applied Sciences, Switzerland
Yasuyuki Tahara	The University of Electro-Communications, Japan
Cedric Tedeschi	IRISA, University of Rennes 1, France
Gilbert Tekli	Nobatek, France
Guy Tel-Zur	Ben-Gurion University of the Negev (BGU), Israel
Rafael Tolosana-Calasanz	University of Zaragoza, Spain
Michele Tomaiuolo	University of Parma, Italy
Orazio Tomarchio	University of Catania, Italy
Slim Trabelsi	SAP, France
Francesco Tusa	University College London, UK
Bruno Volckaert	Ghent University, Belgium
Karoline Wild	University of Stuttgart, Germany
Bo Yang	University of Electronic Science and Technology of China, China
George Yee	Carleton University, Canada
Michael Zapf	Georg Simon Ohm University of Applied Sciences, Germany
Wolfgang Ziegler	Fraunhofer Institute SCAI, Germany

Additional Reviewers

Marios Avgeris	National Technical University of Athens, Greece
Belen Bermejo	University of the Balearic Islands, Spain
Dimitrios Dechouniotis	National Technical University of Athens, Greece
Athanasios Dimitriadis	University of Macedonia, Greece
Menelaos Katsantonis	University of Macedonia, Greece
Andrea Marchini	Politecnico di Milano, Italy
Tamas Pflanzner	University of Szeged, Hungary
Eduardo Roloff	UFRGS, Brazil
Dimitrios Spatharakis	National Technical University of Athens, Greece

Invited Speakers

Eleni Karatza	Aristotle University of Thessaloniki, Greece
Martin G. Jaatun	University of Stavanger, Norway
David Wallom	University of Oxford, UK

Contents

Human-Computer Systems for Decision Support: From Cloud to Self-organizing Environments

Alexander Smirnov, Nikolay Shilov, and Andrew Ponomarev$^{(\boxtimes)}$ (iD)

SPIIRAS, 14th Line 39, 199178 St. Petersburg, Russian Federation
{smir,nick,ponomarev}@iias.spb.su

Abstract. The paper describes conceptual and technological principles of the human-computer cloud, that allows to deploy and run human-based applications. It also presents two ways to build decision support services on top of the proposed cloud environment for problems where workflows are not (or cannot be) defined in advance. The first extension is represented by a decision support service leveraging task ontology to build the missing workflow, the second utilizes the idea of human-machine collective intelligence environment, where the workflow is defined in the process of a (sometimes, guided) collaboration of the participants.

Keywords: Human-computer cloud · Human-in-the-Loop · Crowdsourcing · Crowd computing · Human factors

1 Introduction

The widespread of information and communication technologies that allow people to access global networks from almost anywhere in the world brings joint and collective initiatives to a new level, which leads to an upsurge in crowd computing and crowdsourcing.

The applicability of systems that rely on human participation (including crowd-based ones) is limited by the fact that they usually require large numbers of contributors, while collecting the required number may require significant effort and time. This problem is partially alleviated by existing crowdsourcing platforms (like Amazon Mechanical Turk, Yandex.Toloka etc.) accumulating the "online workforce" and providing tools for requesters to post tasks and an interface for workers to accomplish these tasks. Existing platforms, however, bear two main disadvantages: a) most of them implement only 'pull' mode in distributing tasks, therefore not providing any guarantees to the requester that his/her tasks will be accomplished, b) they are usually designed for simple activities (like image/audio annotation). This paper presents a unified resource management environment, that could serve as a basis on which any human-based application could be deployed similar to the way cloud computing is used nowadays to decouple computing resource management issues from application software.

© Springer Nature Switzerland AG 2020
D. Ferguson et al. (Eds.): CLOSER 2019, CCIS 1218, pp. 1–22, 2020.
https://doi.org/10.1007/978-3-030-49432-2_1

This paper is an extended and revised version of [1]. In [1] a human-computer cloud (HCC) architecture was described. The proposed HCC includes: 1) an application platform, allowing to deploy and run in the cloud human-based applications (HBA), and 2) an ontology-based decision support service providing task decomposition mechanism in order to automatically build an execution plan for tasks in an *ad hoc* way (for decision support tasks, algorithms for which are not described in advance). However, historically attempts to build human-computer (crowd) information processing systems for complex tasks came to conclusion that no workflow (or, predefined coordination program) is able to account for all potential complications that might arise when dealing with complex tasks [2]. Therefore, any collaborative environment for dealing with complex tasks must support on the fly adaptation of the workflow and (to some extent) leverage self-organization potential of human collectives. The solution proposed earlier in [1] (the ontology-based DSS) only partly satisfies this requirement, as it relies on a task ontology where all possible tasks have to be described (but not algorithms for them). In this paper, we extend the earlier proposed approach by describing a concept of collective intelligence environment built on top of the HCC and supporting self-organization.

Together, the three proposed solutions allow to build human-computer decision support systems for all the spectrum of problems (on a complexity scale). For the most simple ones, where mere programming is enough, PaaS with HBA support should be used, for more complex ones, but studied and structured enough to build a task ontology, the ontology-based decision support service (*René*) is suitable, and finally, the most complex and underdeveloped ones, should be dealt with the help of the self-organization environment build on top of the cloud.

The rest of the paper is structured as follows. Section 2 briefly describes other developments aimed on building human-computer cloud environments and research on crowd support for complex tasks. Section 3 describes the organization of the platform layer of the proposed HCC with a focus on the digital contract concept. Section 4 describes ontology-based decision support service. Section 5 describes the concept of self-organization environment for human-machine collective intelligence. Sections 6 and 7 describe cloud platform implementation and evaluation respectively.

2   Related Work

2.1   Cloud with Humans

Generally, resources managed by cloud environments are hardware (CPU, storage) and software (cloud applications, platforms). There are, however, a number of attempts to extend the principles of cloud computing (first of all, on-demand elastic resource provisioning) to a wider spectrum of resource types. These attempts can be classified into two groups: 1) cloud sensing and actuation environments, and 2) cloud-managed human resource environments.

A very representative (and one of the earliest) examples of human-based cloud sensing and actuation environment was presented in papers [3] and [4]. Sensing resource is regarded there as a service that can be allocated and used a unified way independently of the application that needs access to the resource. The cloud system (called MCSaaS – Mobile CrowdSensing as a Service) provides an interface allowing any smartphone user to become a part of a cloud and allow to use his/her smartphone sensors for the benefit of cloud consumers.

The approach proposed in ClouT (Cloud+IoT) project [5] is aimed on providing enhanced solutions for smart cities by using cloud computing in the IoT domain. Both ClouT and MCSaaS approaches are highly relevant to the cloud environment presented in this paper. However, these solutions are focused mostly on sensing and the role played by human in these systems is very limited: human can provide an access to his/her smartphone and make some operations (i.e. point camera lens to some object and make a picture) requested by the application working on top of the infrastructure layer.

Solutions of the second group, earlier referred to as cloud-managed human resource environments, implement another perspective on managing member's skills and competencies in a standardized flexible way (e.g. [6, 7]). In these environments and systems human is regarded as a specific resource that can be allocated from a pool for performing some tasks (not necessary sensing). For example, in [6] the cloud consisting of human-based services and software-based services is considered. On the infrastructure layer, they define a human-computing unit, which is a resource capable of providing human-based services. Like hardware infrastructure is described in terms of some characteristics (CPU, memory, network bandwidth), human-computing unit in this model is described by the set of skills. The authors do not list the exact skills, leaving it to the application domain.

The human-computer cloud environment described in this paper stands more closely to the cloud-managed human resource environments (like [6]). It extends the existing works by an application platform based on a machine-processable specification of obligations in a form of a digital contract and a decision support service that is deployed on top of all resource-management services and can be used to solve *ad hoc* problems in some domain.

2.2 Human–Computer Programs for Complex Tasks

The overwhelming part of research in the field of human-machine computing (crowdsourcing, crowd computing) systems understands human participant as a special type of "computing device" that can process requests of a certain type. During the design time, the whole information processing workflow is build and operations requiring human processing are identified. In the run time the function of a human participant, is reduced to performing a specific task, proposed to him/her by the system, interacting with it in a strictly limited manner [8–11].

Although such a rigid division of roles (designer vs. participant of the system) and strict limitation of the participant's capabilities pay back in a wide range of tasks (mostly, simple ones like annotation, markup, etc.), the creative and organizational abilities of a person in such systems are discarded. It is also shown, that fixed predefined workflow is too limiting for complex tasks [2]. First attempts to build crowd systems, where participants could refine the workflow appeared in 2012 [12], but the problem is starting to receive the closest attention of the research community only nowadays. In particular, in recent years several studies have appeared on the limitations of systems based on the fixed flow of work [2] and proposing the formation of dynamic organizations from members of the crowd community (the so-called flash organizations [13]). We adopt main conclusions of these studies and integrate them with the earlier proposed HCC.

3 Human-Computer Cloud: Platform-as-a-Service

This section introduces platform-as-a-service (PaaS) functionality of the HCC, designed to enable development and deployment of human-based applications. The section enumerates main actors, interacting with the platform, major requirements that drive the design, information associated with applications and contributors, allowing to fulfill the requirements. The section finishes with main use cases presenting a general view of the platform.

All the actors of the proposed cloud platform can be divided into three main categories:

End users (application/service developers), who leverage the features of the platform to create and deploy applications requiring human effort.

Contributors, who may process requests issued by human-based applications running in the human-computer cloud environment.

System Administrators and Infrastructure Providers, who own and maintain the required computing infrastructure.

Primary requirements from the side of *End users* considered in the platform design are following:

- The platform must provide tools to deploy, run, and monitor applications that require human information processing.
- The platform must allow to specify what kind of human information processing is required for an application (as some human-based services, like, e.g., image tagging, require very common skills, while others, like tourism decision support, require at least local expertise in certain location).
- The platform must allow estimating human resources available for the application. This requirement, in particular, is different from conventional cloud infrastructures where resources are considered inexhaustible. Human resources are always limited, especially when it comes to people with some uncommon competencies and knowledge. Besides, the rewarding scheme of the application may be not able to collect the sufficient number of contributors. Therefore, having the information about the resource availability, an application developer is know what capacity is actually available to the application, and based on this information he/she may change the rewarding scheme, set up his/her own SLA (for his/her consumers) etc.

3.1 Application Description

The ultimate goal of the PaaS cloud service model is to streamline the development and deployment of the applications by providing specialized software libraries and tools that help developers to write code abstracting from many details of resource management. All the resource (and dependency) management operations are performed automatically by PaaS environment according to some description (declarative configuration) provided by the developer of the application being executed. The proposed human-computer cloud environment supports similar approach, however, with inevitable modifications caused by the necessity of working with human resources. To streamline the development of applications that require human actions (human-based applications, HBA), the platform allows both a developer to describe what kind of human resources are required for a particular application, and a contributor to describe what kind of activities he/she can be involved in and what competencies he/she possesses. Existing declarative specification means used in cloud systems allow to specify computing resource requirements and software dependencies of an application. However, they are insufficient for the purpose of human-computer cloud, first of all, because of variety of possible human skills and competencies. While virtual machine can be described with a very limited number of features (e.g. CPU, RAM, I/O capacity), human contributor's skills and abilities are highly multidimensional, they can be described in different levels of detail and be connected to a wide range of particular application areas. Moreover, the same skills can be described in different ways, and, finally, most of the skill descriptions in real world are incomplete (however, there might be a possibility to infer some skills that a human might possess from those that he/she explicitly declared).

Therefore, application deployed in the human-computer cloud environment must contain a descriptor that includes following components (we list all the components, but focus on those, that are relevant to human part):

- configuration parameters (e.g. environment variables controlling the behavior of the compiled code);
- software dependencies of the application (what platform services and/or other applications it relies on, e.g., database service, messaging service, etc.);
- human resource requirements, specifying contributors with what skills and competencies are needed for the application. Along with the software requirements, these requirements are resolved during the service deployment. In contrast to the software requirements, which are usually satisfied, these requirements may be harder to satisfy (resolving these requirements employs ontology matching which may result in some tradeoffs, besides, human resources are usually limited), therefore, the status and details of the requirements resolution are available to the developer and can be browsed via the management console. Human resource requirements specification may describe several types of human resources with different profiles of requirements. For example, an itinerary planning application may require people with significant local expertise as well as people with shallow local expertise but good language skills. These two categories of contributors may be declared as two types of resources;
- digital contract template for each type of human resources. Digital contract defines measurable and machine understandable/checkable specification of contributor's involvement, his/her obligations (e.g., number of requests, reaction time) and rewarding.

For a formal specification of requirements the proposed environment leverages the apparatus of formal ontologies. Specifically, arbitrary ontology concepts may be used to describe skills or knowledge areas. Main benefit of using ontologies is that they allow to discover resources described with related, similar but not exact terms. This is done either by using existing public mappings between ontologies (stating equivalence between concepts of different ontologies), or by ontology inference. We do not fix any particular set of ontologies to describe competencies. It allows tourist applications deployed on the platform to use public cultural, historical, and geographical ontologies, whereas, e.g., applications, that employ human-based information processing in the area of medicine or biology use the ontologies of the respective domain. The only restriction is that these ontologies have to be encoded in OWL 2.

Another important feature of the approach is the concept of digital contract, representing an agreement between contributor and platform about terms of work, quality management principles and rewarding. Terms of the digital contract are essential for estimating the amount of resources available for a service and its capacity (including time perspective of the capacity). The necessity of this digital contract is caused by the fact that human resources are limited. In case of ordinary hardware, the cloud infrastructure provider can buy as many computers as needed, human participation is less controllable due to free will, therefore, attracting and retaining contributors can be a complex task. As a result, the abstraction of inexhaustible resource pool that is exploited in the provider-consumer relationship of current cloud environments turns out to be inadequate for human-computer cloud. A consumer (*end user*) should be informed about the human capacity available for his/her application to make an informed decision about revising digital contracts (for example, making contribution to this application more appealing), or updating their own service level agreements. This creates a competition between consumers for the available resources and finally will create a kind of job market where different digital contract statements will have its own price.

3.2 Contributor Description

To support semantic human resource discovery and task allocation, human resources have to be described with ontology terms. Besides, they have to specify their preferences about task types, availability time etc. Therefore, when a contributor joins the cloud platform he/she provides two main types of information, that are very similar to the respective pieces of application descriptor. Namely, the description of competencies and working conditions. The competencies are described in terms of any ontology familiar to the contributor. For the contributors who cannot use ontologies the description is built iteratively via the analysis of contributors' text description followed by ontology-based term disambiguation. In any case, internally, each contributor is described by skills, knowledge and attitude, associated with the concepts of some shared ontology.

Moreover, the contributor's competency description is multi-layered. The first layer is provided by a contributor him-/herself, further layers are added by applications in which the contributor takes part. For this purpose, a human resource management API available for the application code allows to manage application-specific skills and qualifications, which can also be described in some ontology (application-specific or not). Therefore, despite initial description of competencies may be rather short, during the contributor's participation in various applications running on the platform it becomes richer. This facilitates further human resource discovery.

Working conditions include preferred skills, as well as payment threshold, reactivity and availability limitations. These parameters are also similar to those included in digital contract template in the application descriptor. During application enquiry and application deployment its contract template is matched against contributors' work conditions. Moreover, this matching touches not only contributor's declared work conditions and one application contract (of the deployed application) but also other applications which contracts this contributor has already accepted, controlling overall responsibilities that are taken by the contributor and resolving possible conflicts.

3.3   Main Functions of the Platform

Each category of users (identified earlier as actors) has unique purpose of using the environment. Main functions of the environment are the ones that allow users of each category to accomplish their primary goal.

Main functions exposed to application/service developers are application deployment (which initiates advertisement process to identify human resources available to this application), editing digital contracts, monitoring, and deleting applications. Editing digital contracts is important, for example, when the developer of the application competes for human resources with other application developers by offering higher rewards. Changing the contract produces a new version of the deployed application descriptor and leads to a new wave of advertisements. Application monitoring is a general name for a number of functions like reading usage statistics, logs, that are necessary for application developer and are common to many current PaaS. This also includes monitoring of the available human resources by each requirement type as well its prediction.

Contributors can edit their competence profiles (providing an initial version and updating it), browse application advertisements addressed to them (compatible with his/her competence profile and work conditions) optionally accepting some of them by signing digital contract and attaching to the respective application. Contributors can also execute application-specific tasks and detach from application (possibility of detachment in a particular moment and the effect of it might be affected by the digital contract).

System administrators can monitor the status of the platform (usage of hardware/human resources, communication channels throughput, platform services' health) and tune the platform parameters (e.g., edit ontology mappings used by the platform during identification of compatible resources (contributors) for advertising applications).

3.4   Application Deployment

A newly registered contributor is not automatically available for requests of all human-based applications running on the environment. However, he/she starts to receive the so-called *advertisements* from applications based on the similarity of a declared competence profile (including additional layers created by applications a contributor participates) and applications' competence requests as well as the correspondence of the declared working conditions and applications' digital contract templates. These *advertisements* describe the intent of the application, required kind of human involvement, rewarding scheme etc. Based on the information contained in the *advertisement*, a contributor can decide to attach to the application, which means that he/she will then receive tasks from this application. In other words, if a registered contributor agrees to contribute to the particular application a digital contract is signed specifying the intensity of task flow, the rewarding and penalty details and quality measurement strategy. In general, there is many-to-many relation between applications and platform contributors, i.e., one contributor may sign digital contracts with several applications.

Upon signing of a digital contract with an application (via platform mechanisms), the contributor starts to receive requests (tasks) from this application. The application issues mostly non-personalized requests, and it is the platform that routes requests to the contributors, ensuring that load of each contributor conforms the terms of the contract. A contributor also can detach from an application (however, the mechanism and terms of this detaching can also be a part of digital contract to ensure the application provider can react to it accordingly).

4   Ontology-Based Decision Support Service

The decision support service (named *René*) is an application, running on top of the human-computer cloud infrastructure, leveraging some features of the platform (e.g., resource management and provisioning), and provided to end users according to SaaS model. Users of *René* are decision-makers who pass task specifications to the application. The API of *René* accepts ontology-based structured representation of the task specification. The problem of creating such specification (for example, as a result of text analysis) is out of the scope both of this paper and of *René* functions. The core principle behind *René* is that it builds an on-the-fly network of resources (human and software) capable of performing the specified task.

In order to build the network, *René* decomposes the task into smaller tasks (subtasks) using a problem-specific task ontology, where domain tasks and their input and output parameters are described. After performing the decomposition *René* tries to distribute the elementary subtasks among the available resources. The list of available resources is retrieved via an API from underlying layers of the environment, which monitor all the contributor's connections and disconnections and software resource registrations. The resource management service under the hood treats human and software resources differently. Human resources (contributors) describe their competencies with a help of ontology and receive advertisements to join human-based applications if their requirements are compatible to the declared competencies of the user. *René* is basically one of human-based applications and may only distribute subtasks among contributors who agreed to work with it (attached to it by signing a digital contract). Software services are made available to *René* by their developers and maintainers by placing a special section into the application deployment descriptor. Task assignment is also done with a help of interfaces of resource management layer, aware of the status and load of the resources and terms of their digital contracts.

As contributors may go offline, *René* monitors the availability of the resources (via the underlying resource management) during execution of the subtasks and rebuilds the assignment if some of the resources fail or become unavailable to keep the bigger task (received from the end user) accomplishable.

4.1 Task Decomposition

Task decomposition is the first step to building the resource network. The goal of this process is to build a network of smaller (and simpler) tasks connected by input/output parameters, such that this network is equivalent to the original task given by the user. Therefore, in some sense, the process of task decomposition is actually driven by task composition (particularly, to searching a composition, equivalent to the original task). The proposed approach is based on the fact that there is an ontology of tasks. This task ontology should consist of a set of tasks and subtasks, sets of input and output parameters of task, set of valid values of parameters, as well as the set of restrictions describing the relations between tasks/subtasks and parameters and between parameters and their valid values:

$$O = (T, \ IP, \ OP, \ I, \ E) \tag{1}$$

where T is set of tasks and subtasks, IP – set of input task parameters, OP – set of output task parameters, I – set of valid parameter values, E – restrictions on the parameters of the task and parameter domain.

Unlike existing task ontologies (e.g., [14]) that usually contain relationships between task and their subtasks in explicit form, in the proposed task composition ontology these relationships are implicit. This allows, on the one hand, to specify tasks and subtasks in the same axiomatic form and, on the other hand, to derive task composition structure by reasoning tools. Therefore, the proposed ontology opens the possibility to describe a number of different tasks in the same form and dynamically construct their possible compositions using appropriate criteria.

The task composition ontology is developed in OWL 2. The ontology is expressed by ALC description logic, which is decidable and has PSpace-complete complexity of concept satisfiability and ABox consistency [15] in the case when TBox is acyclic. In addition, SWRL-rules are defined for deriving composition chains. The main concepts of the ontology are "Task" and "Parameter". The concept "Parameter" is used to describe semantics of a task via its inputs and outputs. The main requirement for TBox definition is that it shouldn't contain cyclic and multiple definitions, and must contain only concept definitions specified by class equivalence.

Each task should have at least one input and at least one output parameter. The taxonomy of parameters is presented by a number of subclasses of the class "Parameter". The type of parameters related to their input or output role are defined by appropriate role construct. In the ontology, the appropriate object properties are "hasInputParameter" and "hasOutputParameter". The domain of the properties is

"Task" and the range – "Parameter". Thereby the parameter could be input parameter of one task and output parameter of another. The task definition is expressed formally as follows:

$$T \equiv (\exists R.IP_1 \sqcap \exists R IP_2 \ldots \sqcap \exists R.IP_N) \sqcap$$
$$\sqcap (\exists R.OP_1 \sqcap \exists R.OP_2 \ldots \sqcap \exists R.OP_N) \qquad (2)$$

where T is the task, IP_i – the input parameter subclass, OP_i – the input parameter subclass, R – the appropriate role. In other words, the task is defined solely by its input and output parameters.

Task composition process is based on the fact that in a composition output parameters of one task are input for another. This relationship is utilized (and formalized) by an SWRL rule that infers the order of tasks. The rule specifies input and output parameter match condition in the antecedent and if the antecedent condition is satisfied, infers the relationship "nextTask" between the respective tasks. This relationship means that one task can be done only after another. This relationship is encoded as an object property binding two tasks (both domain and range of the property are "Task" instances). The rule of task composition can be expressed as follows:

$$hasInputParameter(?ta, ?p)hasOutputParameter(?tb, ?p) \rightarrow nextTask(?tb, ?ta) \quad (3)$$

where *hasInputParameter*, *hasOutputParameter*, *nextTask* are the mentioned object properties, *ta* – the next task, *tb* – the previous task, *p* – the parameter.

The proposed rule (3) allows to derive all task connections by the object property "nextTask". The example of task composition is presented in Fig. 1. For example, relationship "nextTask" is inferred between tasks "Task 1" and "Task 3" because parameter p6 is input for "Task 3" and output for "Task 1", meaning that "Task 3" can only be executed after "Task 1".

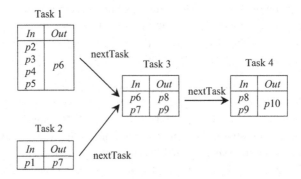

Fig. 1. Task composition structure (adopted from [1]).

The advantages of the described approach is that it allows to simplify task description (in comparison to the approaches where task/subtask relations are explicit) and to derive task compositions dynamically. The shortcomings are the possible deriving complexity and the lack of the support of alternative task compositions.

4.2   Subtask Distribution

In cloud computing systems, the number of interchangeable computing resources is usually very high [16, 17]. The decision support service distributes the specialized tasks that require certain competencies, therefore, a) the distribution algorithm has to take into account the competencies, b) not all resources are interchangeable for the assignment and the number of appropriate resources may be lower. Therefore, typical algorithms used in cloud computing cannot be directly applied.

In the areas with similar task characteristics (e.g., distribution of tasks among the robots or agents) the most common approach is instant distribution of tasks (instantaneous task allocation) [18, 19]. This approach involves assigning tasks to resources that currently provide the maximum "benefit" according to the given priorities. It does not take into account that at some point all resources with the required competencies may be occupied. Thus, it is usually supplemented by some heuristics specific to a particular application area.

Let, A – is a task, which contains several subtasks a_i:

$$A = \{a_i\}, i \in \{1, \ldots, n\} \tag{4}$$

Let, O – is the vocabulary of competencies:

$$O = \{o_1, o_2, \ldots, o_m\} \tag{5}$$

Thus, the matrix of competencies required to accomplish subtasks can be defined as:

$$\left(ao_{i,j} \in \{0, 1, \ldots, 100\}\right), i \in \{1, \ldots, n\}, j \in \{1, \ldots, m\} \tag{6}$$

The set of human-computer cloud resources R is defined as:

$$R = \{r_1, r_2, \ldots, r_k\} \tag{7}$$

The set of resource characteristics (speed, cost, etc.) C is defined as:

$$C = \{c_1, c_2, \ldots, c_l\} \tag{8}$$

Thus, each resource r_i is described by the following pair of competencies and characteristics vectors:

$$r_i = \left(\left(ro_{i,1}, \ldots, ro_{i,m} \right), \left(rc_{i,1}, \ldots, rc_{i,1} \right) \right) \tag{9}$$

where $i \in \{1, \ldots, n\}$, $ro_{i,j} \in \{0, \ldots, 100\}$ – is the value of competency j of the resource i, and $rc_{i,j}$ is the value of the characteristic j of the resource i.

The solution of the task A describes the distribution of work among system resources and is defined as:

$$S_A = \left(s_{i,j} \right), i \in \{1, \ldots, n\}, j \in \{1, \ldots, k\} \tag{10}$$

where $s_{i,j} = 1$, if the resource j is used for solving subtask i, and $s_{i,j} = 0$ otherwise.

The objective function, which also performs normalization of various characteristics, is defined as follows:

$$\begin{aligned} F(S_A) = & f\big(F_1\left(s_{1,1}, s_{2,1}, \ldots, s_{n,1}\right), \\ & F_2\left(s_{1,2}, s_{2,2}, \ldots, s_{n,2}\right), \ldots, \\ & F_k\left(s_{1,k}, s_{2,k}, \ldots, s_{n,k}\right)\big) \to min \end{aligned} \tag{11}$$

Specific formulas for calculating partial assignment efficiency (F_i) can use values of resource characteristics (e.g., speed or cost) $rc_{i,j}$, as well as competence values of both resources ($ro_{i,j}$) and subtasks ($ao_{i,j}$).

The minimization must be performed with respect to the following constraints. First, each subtask must be assigned to some resource:

$$\forall i = \sum_{j=1}^{k} S_{i,j} \geq 1 \tag{12}$$

Second, assignment can only be done if the competency values of the resource are not less than the required competency values of the subtask:

$$\forall i, j, q : \left(\left(s_{ij} = 1 \right) \to \left(ro_{j,q} \geq ao_{i,q} \right) \right) \tag{13}$$

Instantaneous Distribution of Tasks Algorithm
In general, the specified problem is NP-complete, therefore, it is not possible to solve it by an exhaustive search method in a reasonable time (provided that a real-world problem is solved). Based on the analysis of existing methods it is proposed to use the approach of instantaneous task allocation. The algorithm based on the approach of instantaneous distribution of tasks is defined as follows:

1. Take the first subtask from the existing ai, and exclude it from the set of subtasks A;
2. Select such resource j from the available resources to satisfy all conditions and $F(S_A) \to min$, where $S_A = (s_{1,1} = 0, \ldots, s_{1,j} = 1, \ldots, s_{1,k} = 0)$;

3. If a suitable resource is not found, assume that the problem is unsolvable (the system does not have a resource that meets the required competencies);
4. Repeat steps starting from step 4 until set A is empty (i.e. all tasks are assigned to resources).

Multi-agent Distribution of Tasks

There are two types of agents that are used to perform multi-agent modeling: the customer agent that is responsible for generating jobs and making the final decision, and the execution agents that represent the resources of the cloud environment and perform on-premises optimization for each resource. In the optimization process, agents form coalitions that change from step to step to improve the values of the objective function.

In the process of negotiations, an agent can play one of the following roles: a coalition member (an agent belonging to the coalition), a coalition leader (an agent negotiating on behalf of the coalition) and an applicant (an agent who can become a member of the coalition).

First, each agent forms a separate coalition (SC, which has the structure of the *SA* solution), and becomes its leader. Suggestions of agents (tabular representation $F(s_{1,1}, s_{2,1}, ..., s_{n,1})$) are published on the blackboard (information exchange entity available to all agents). At each stage of the negotiations, the agents analyze the proposals of other agents, and choose those whose proposals can improve the coalition: to solve a larger number of subtasks or the same number of subtasks but with a better value of the objective function ($F(SC) > F(SC')$, where SC is the current coalition, SC' – possible coalition). Coalition leaders make appropriate proposals to agents, and the latter decide whether to stay in the current coalition or move to the proposed one. The transition to the proposed coalition is considered if one of the above conditions is met: the proposed coalition can solve more subtasks than the current one, or the same number of subtasks, but with a better value of the objective function.

The negotiations process is terminated if one of the following conditions is met: a) there are no changes in the composition of coalitions at some stage, b) timeout, and c) the permissible value of the objective function is reached.

5 Self-organizing Environment

This section describes the concept of self-organization environment for human-machine collective intelligence, which is built on top of the HCC (e.g., leveraging the resource discovery and communication facilities of the cloud). In this way, the self-organizing environment is another specific application that may be deployed on the HCC.

The proposed environment aims at supporting the process of making complex decisions and/or making decisions in complex problem domains. The complexity of making such decisions generally stems from problem uncertainty in many levels and the lack of relevant data at decision maker's disposal. Hence, while in the upper level the methodology of decision-making stays quite definite (identification of the alternatives, identification of the criteria, evaluation of the alternatives etc.), the exact steps required to collect all the needed data, analyze it and present to the decision maker may be unclear. That is why decision support requires *ad hoc* planning of the low-level activities and should leverage self-organizing capabilities of the participants of the decision support process. Besides, currently most of the complex decisions are based not only on human intuition or expertise, but also on the problem-relevant data of various types and sources (starting from IoT-generated, to high-level Linked Data), processed in different ways. In other words, decision support is in fact human-machine activity, and the environment just offers a set mechanisms and tools to mitigate this activity.

There are several typical roles in the decision support process. *Decision-makers* are responsible for the analysis of a situation and making a decision. In some cases, where the uncertainty associated with the situation is too high, the decision-maker requires some additional expertise that may be provided by participants of a human-machine collective intelligence environment. Bearing in mind, that using collective expertise is usually rather expensive and can be justified only for important problems, the decision-maker is usually a middle-to-top level manager in terms of typical business hierarchy. After the decision-maker posts the problem to the collective intelligence, he/she may oversee the process of solution and guide it in some way.

Experts possess problem-specific knowledge and may contribute into decision support process in several ways. First, they can propose procedures of obtaining relevant judgments, constructing in an *ad hoc* way elements of the whole workflow. This can be done not only in a direct manner, but also indirectly, by posting various incentives for other participants. Second, they can use their expertise by providing data as well as processing it to come to some problem-related conclusions. In general, an expert can be anyone – within or without the organization boundary, the difference is mostly in the incentives important for the particular expert.

Service providers design and maintain various software tools, services and datasets that can be used for decision support. Their goal is to receive remuneration for the use of these tools, that is why they are interested in making these services available for other participants of the environment.

The environment should provide means and mechanisms using which participants of different nature (human and machine) could be able to communicate and decide on the particular steps of decision support process, perform these steps and exchange results, motivated by some external or internal mechanisms, making the whole environment profitable for all parties.

The rest of the section introduces foundational technologies and enablers for the proposed environment.

Meeting Collective Intelligence and Artificial Intelligence. Methods of collective intelligence (construed as methods for making people to work together to solve problems) and methods of artificial intelligence are two complementary (in some industries even competing) methods of decision support. Mostly, these approaches are considered as alternative (some tasks due to their nature turn out to be more "convenient" for artificial intelligence methods, and others – for collective), however, the scientists are currently tending to speak about possibility of their joint usage and the potential that human-machine technologies have [20–22].

In the proposed environment artificial and collective intelligence are meeting in the following way. The environment itself provides possibility of communication and coordination of agents while working on solving the problem (collective part). Software services have to "understand" common goal and build their strategy (AI part). Besides, some agents can provide application level AI methods.

There are four types of intelligent software services that take part in the functioning of the environment (Fig. 2):

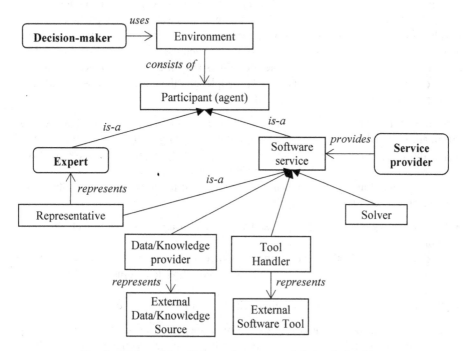

Fig. 2. Main entities of the environment and their relationships.

- Solver. A software code that can transform a task description in some way, enriching it with some derived knowledge.
- Data/knowledge provider. Interface-wise similar to the previous type, however, only provides some problem-specific information.
- Tool handler. A utility agent that manages human access to some software tools (with GUI). In many cases, certain data processing routines required for decision-making can be implemented with some software (or, SaaS). It is not practical to re-implement it in a new way, however, granting an access to such tools might be useful for all the involved parties.
- Representative. Allowing expert to communicate with other services.

Self-organization Protocols Taking into Account both Human and Machine Agents. One of the distinguishing features of the proposed approach is to overcome the preprogrammed workflows that rigidly govern interaction of participants during decision support and to allow the participants (human and machine agents) to dynamically decide on the details of the workflow unleashing creative potential of humans. Therefore, agents should be able to coordinate and decide on task distribution, roles etc., in other words a group of agents should be able to self-organize.

The protocols of self-organization in such environment have to respect both machine and human requirements. The latter means that widely used models of bio-inspired self-organization turn out to have less potential to be applied, as they are taken mostly from the analysis of primitive behaviors (e.g., of insects). On the other hand, market (or, economics) based models best of all match the assumed business model (on demand service provisioning). Another possible source are socio-inspired mechanisms and protocols, which are totally natural for people, and there are already some attempts to adapt them for artificial systems [23].

Interoperability of Agents. To sustain various coordination processes, as well as information flow during decision-making multilevel interoperability has to be provided inside the collaborative environment. This is especially acute in the case of mixed collectives, consisting of human and machine agents.

To implement any self-organization protocols, the participants of the system have to exchange several types of knowledge:

- Domain knowledge. What object and what relationships between objects are in the problem area.
- Task knowledge. Both goal description, and possible conceptualization of the active decision support task, e.g., mapping some concepts to alternatives, functions to criteria.
- Protocol knowledge. Terms of interaction, incentives, roles etc.

It is proposed to use ontologies as the main means ensuring the interoperability. The key role of the ontology model is in its ability to support semantic interoperability as the information represented by ontology can be interpreted both by humans and machines. Potentially, ontology-based information representation can provide the interoperability for all kinds of possible interactions (human-human, human-machine, machine-human). Taking into account the heterogeneity of the participants of the human-machine collective intelligence systems and the multidimensionality of the decision support activities, it is proposed to use multi-aspect ontologies. The multi-aspect ontologies will avoid the need for standardization of all services of environment through providing one aspect (some viewpoint on the domain) to services of one collective (services of one producer, services that jointly solve a certain task, etc.) for the service collaboration.

Soft Guidance in Collective Action. Though the execution process in the proposed environment is self-orchestrated and driven by negotiation protocols, human participants, however, will need intelligent assistance when communicating with other agents in the environment. The role of this assistance is to offer viable organization structures and incentive mechanisms based on current goals. An important aspect during the soft guidance is mapping actions defined by decision-making methodologies to human-computer collaboration scenarios. It means that the environment (or representative service) uses the existing knowledge on decision making process to offer agents viable collaboration structures.

6 Implementation

The implemented research prototype of the cloud environment contains two parts: platform-as-a-service (PaaS) and software-as-a-service (SaaS). The platform provides the developers of applications that require human knowledge and skills with a set of tools for designing, deploying, executing and monitoring such applications. The SaaS model is represented by an intelligent decision support service (referred to as *René*) that organizes (human-computer) resource networks for on-the-fly tasks through ontology-based task decomposition and subtasks distribution among the resources (human participants and software services).

The prototype environment comprises several components: 1) a server-side code that performs all the resource management activities and provides a set of application program interfaces (APIs), 2) a set of command line utilities that run on the computers of appropriate categories of users (platform administrator, developer, administrator of IDSS) and by accessing the API, enable to implement the main scenarios necessary for these users, 3) Web-applications for participants and decision makers. Also, it is possible to implement the interface of the participant for an Android-based mobile device.

To build and refine a participant competence profile the prototype environment interacts with social networks (ResearchGate, LinkedIn). It also exposes several APIs to the applications deployed on it, providing them basic services (for instance, request human-participants, data warehouses, etc.).

To support the processes of scalable software deployment (which is necessary for the PaaS, but peripheral to the main contributions of our work) the open source platform Flynn[1] is used. The capabilities of the platform has been extended by special functions (registration of participants, an ontological-oriented search for participants, and a mechanism for supporting digital contracts).

The intelligent decision support service (IDSS) is an application deployed in the human-computer cloud environment and using the functions provided by the environment (for instance, to organize interactions with participants). Main functions of the IDSS are: 1) decomposition of the task that the decision maker deals with into subtasks using the task ontology and inference engine that supports OWL ontology language and SWRL-rules (for instance, Pellet, HermiT, etc.); 2) allocation of the subtasks to participants based on coalition games. The IDSS provides REST API to interact with the platform.

---

[1] http://flynn.com.

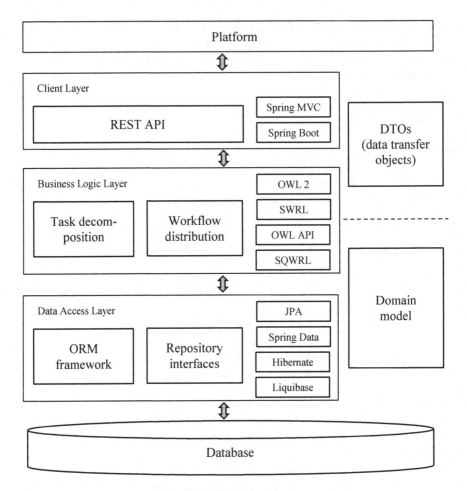

Fig. 3. IDSS implementation.

The architecture of IDSS (Fig. 3), in its turn, can be divided into several logical layers:

- The Data Access Layer is a series of DAO abstractions that use the JPA standard for object-relational mapping of data model classes (Domain model) that perform the simplest CRUD operations using ORM Hibernate and implemented using Spring Data.
- The Business Logic Layer of the application is represented by two main services: the task decomposition service and the workflow distribution service. The task decomposition service operates with an ontology, described using the ontology description language OWL 2, which includes rules in SWRL and SQWRL. Knowledge output (task decomposition) is carried out using inference engines (Pellet, HermiT, and others). To extract data from ontology, Jena APIs are used for ontologies recorded using OWL/RDF syntax using the SPARQL query language

and OWL API for other ontology scenarios (changing ontology structure, managing individuals, logical inference). The workflow building service provides support for the coalition game of agents of the human-machine computing platform agents.

- At the Client Layer, REST API services are implemented for interacting with the platform, providing an interface for interacting with the platform and indirect user interaction.

7 Evaluation

An experimental evaluation of the research prototype has been carried out. As the functionality of the application of the problem-oriented IDSS built according to the proposed approach is determined by the task ontology (namely, the basic tasks represented in this ontology and their input and output parameters), a task ontology for the e-tourism domain has been developed (specifically, for building tourist itineraries). In the experiments, dynamic task networks (for building tourist itineraries) did actually organize, and their execution resulted in valid lists of itineraries.

The developed software was deployed at the computing nodes of the local network of the research laboratory (an access to the server components from the Internet was also provided). 34 people were registered as participants available for task assignment. An ontology to describe the competences of resources (and the requirements for competences of deployable applications requiring human participation) representing 46 basic competences was used. With the experimental parameters (performance of hardware resources, number of participants, size of the competence ontology), the application deployment time differed from the application deployment time in the Flynn core cloud environment slightly (by 3–7%). The increase in time is inevitable, because during the application deployment process, in addition to creating Docker containers, compiling and launching an application (performed by Flynn), the semantic search of participants and the comparison of digital contracts are carried out. However, in exchange for this slight increase in application deployment time, the applications in the implemented cloud environment receive an opportunity to access human resources. In the future, most of the operations related to the resolution of application dependencies on human resources can be performed in the background, which will save the deployment time at the level of the cloud environment.

For testing the IDSS a task ontology of the electronic tourism domain, represented in the OWL 2 language corresponding to the description logic of ALCR (D) and containing 293 axioms and 40 classes, was used. The scenario for the load testing was to build a network of resources for the task of building a tourist route (the network assumes the fulfillment of 6 subtasks). The time of task decomposition and network construction obtained as a result of averaging over 25 tests is, 1157 ms (994 ms takes the task decomposition, 163 ms takes the allocation of the subtasks to resources). It should be noted that this time only takes into account the task decomposition and the resource network organization, and does not take into account the time spent by the software services and participants on solving the subtasks assigned to them.

8 Conclusions

The paper addresses the problem of building decision support systems, that leverage not only computing power of modern hardware and software, but also rely on the expertise of human participants (allocated from a big pool).

The paper describes a spectrum of solutions for this problem, tailored for slightly different situations.

The first proposed solution is an application platform (or, Platform-as-a-Service) for the development of human-based application. The platform is intended for the use cases when a user can specify the exact information processing workflow and this workflow includes operations that has to be performed by human experts. The platform provides tools for deploying and running such application and manages human resources based on semantic descriptions and digital contracts.

The second is a decision support service based on ontological task representation and processing. This service is intended for the use cases where exact information workflow cannot be specified in advance, but there are a number of information processing tasks in the problem domain that can be used to automatically construct the workflow required by the end user (decision-maker) in an ad hoc way. The service decomposes the task into subtasks based on the task ontology and then distribute the subtasks among resources (human and software).

Finally, the paper presents an extension of the human-computer cloud, allowing to address complex problems for which it is hard to design a workflow in advance, and/or there is no detailed task ontology. This extension is represented by the concept of human-machine collective intelligence environment, created on top of the cloud resource management facilities. The distinctive features of the proposed environment are: a) support for human and software participants who can build coalitions in order to solve problems and collectively decide on the required workflow, b) support for natural self-organization processes in the community of participants.

Experiments with a research prototype have shown the viability of the proposed models and methods.

Overall, the proposed set of tools allow to build human-machine decision support systems for problems of varying complexity in variety of domains (e.g., smart city, business management, e-tourism, etc.).

Acknowledgements. The research was funded by the Russian Science Foundation. The HCC architecture, PaaS and ontology-based decision support service based on task decomposition were developed as a part of project # 16-11-10253, the self-organizing environment for collective human-machine intelligence is being developed as a part of project # 19-11-00126.

References

1. Smirnov, A., Shilov, N., Ponomarev, A., Schekotov, M.: Human-computer cloud: application platform and dynamic decision support. In: Proceedings of the 9th International Conference on Cloud Computing and Services Science - Volume 1: CLOSER, pp. 120–131 (2019)
2. Retelny, D., Bernstein, M.S., Valentine, M.A.: No workflow can ever be enough: how crowdsourcing workflows constrain complex work. Proc. ACM Hum.-Comput. Interact. **1**, Article 89 (2017)
3. Distefano, S., Merlino, G., Puliafito, A.: SAaaS: a framework for volunteer-based sensing clouds. Parallel Cloud Comput. **1**(2), 21–33 (2012)
4. Merlino, G., Arkoulis, S., Distefano, S., Papagianni, C., Puliafito, A., Papavassiliou, S.: Mobile crowdsensing as a service: a platform for applications on top of sensing clouds. Future Gen. Comput. Syst. **56**, 623–639 (2016)
5. Formisano, C., Pavia, D., Gurgen, L., et al.: The advantages of IoT and cloud applied to smart cities. In: 3rd International Conference Future Internet of Things and Cloud, Rome, pp. 325–332 (2015)
6. Dustdar, S., Bhattacharya, K.: The social compute unit. IEEE Internet Comput. **15**(3), 64–69 (2011)
7. Sengupta, B., Jain, A., Bhattacharya, K., Truong, H.-L., Dustdar, S.: Collective problem solving using social compute units. Int. J. Coop. Inf. Syst. **22**(4), 1341002 (2013
8. Kulkarni, A.P., Can, M., Hartmann, B.: Turkomatic: automatic recursive task and workflow design for mechanical turk. In: CHI 2011 Extended Abstracts on Human Factors in Computing Systems. CHI EA 2011, pp. 2053–2058. ACM (2011)
9. Ahmad, S., Battle, A., Malkani, Z., Kamvar, S.: The jabberwocky programming environment for structured social computing. In: Proceedings of the 24th Annual ACM Symposium on User Interface Software and Technology (UIST 2011), pp. 53–64. ACM (2011)
10. Minder, P., Bernstein, A.: *CrowdLang*: a programming language for the systematic exploration of human computation systems. In: Aberer, K., Flache, A., Jager, W., Liu, L., Tang, J., Guéret, C. (eds.) SocInfo 2012. LNCS, vol. 7710, pp. 124–137. Springer, Heidelberg (2012). https://doi.org/10.1007/978-3-642-35386-4_10
11. Tranquillini, S., Daniel, F., Kucherbaev, P., Casati, F.: Modeling, enacting, and integrating custom crowdsourcing processes. ACM Trans. Web **9**(2), 7:1–7:43 (2015)
12. Kulkarni, A., Can, M., Hartmann, B.: Collaboratively crowdsourcing workflows with turkomatic. In: Proceedings of the ACM 2012 Conference on Computer Supported Cooperative Work. Seattle, Washington, USA (2012)
13. Valentine, M.A., et al.: Flash organizations. In: 2017 CHI Conference on Human Factors in Computing Systems – CHI 2017, pp. 3523–3537. ACM Press, New York (2017)
14. Ko, R.K.L., Lee, E.W., Lee, S.G.: BusinessOWL (BOWL) - a hierarchical task network ontology for dynamic business process decomposition and formulation. IEEE Trans. Serv. Comput. **5**(2), 246–259 (2012)
15. Baader, F., Milicic, M., Lutz, C., Sattler, U., Wolter, F.: Integrating description logics and action formalisms for reasoning about web services, LTCS-Report 05-02, Chair for Automata Theory, Institute for Theoretical Computer Science, Dresden University of Technology, Germany (2005). http://lat.inf.tu-dresden.de/research/reports.html
16. Ergu, D., et al.: The analytic hierarchy process: task scheduling and resource allocation in cloud computing environment. J. Supercomputing **64**(3), 835–848 (2013)

17. Kong, Y., Zhang, M., Ye, D.: A belief propagation-based method for task allocation in open and dynamic cloud environments. Knowl.-Based Syst. **115**, 123–132 (2017)
18. Sujit, P., George, G., Beard, R.: Multiple UAV coalition formation. In: Proceedings of the American Control Conference, pp. 2010–2015 (2008)
19. Kim, M.H., Baik, H., Lee, S.: Resource welfare based task allocation for UAV team with resource constraints. J. Intell. Robot. Syst. **77**(3-4), 611–627 (2015)
20. Kamar, E.: Directions in hybrid intelligence: complementing AI systems with human intelligence. IJCAI Invited Talk: Early Career Spotlight Track. (2016)
21. Nushi, B., Kamar, E., Horvitz, E., Kossmann, D.: On human intellect and machine failures: troubleshooting integrative machine learning systems. In: 31st AAAI Conference on Artificial Intelligence, pp. 1017–1025 (2017)
22. Verhulst, S.G.: AI Soc. **33**(2), 293–297 (2018)
23. Smirnov, A., Shilov, N.: Service-based socio-cyberphysical network modeling for guided self-organization. Procedia Comput. Sci. **64**, 290–297 (2015)

Designing an IoT-Cloud Gateway
for the Internet of Living Things

Tamas Pflanzner[1], Miklos Hovari[2], Imre Vass[2], and Attila Kertesz[1](✉)(iD)

[1] Software Engineering Department, University of Szeged,
Dugonics ter 13, Szeged 6720, Hungary
{tampfla,keratt}@inf.u-szeged.hu
[2] Institute of Plant Biology, Biological Research Centre, Szeged, Hungary
{hovari.miklos,vass.imre}@brc.mta.hu

Abstract. Cloud Computing and the Internet of Things (IoT) have started to revolutionize traditional systems to be smart. Smart farming is an example of this process, that aims to respond to predictions and provisions of population growth by providing smart solutions in agriculture to improve productivity and reduce waste. Plant phenotyping is an important research field related to smart farming by providing means for complex monitoring of development and stress responses of plants. The current phenotyping platforms for greenhouses are very expensive limiting their widepread use. The recent advances in ICT technologies with the appearance of low cost sensors and computing solutions have led to affordable phenotyping solutions, which can be applied in standard greenhouse conditions. In this paper we propose a low cost plant phenotyping platform for small sized plants called the IoLT Smart Pot. It is capable of monitoring environmental parameters by sensors connected to a Raspberry Pi board of the smart pot. We developed an IoT-Cloud gateway for receiving, storing and visualizing the monitored environmental parameters sent by the pot devices. It is also able to perform image processing on the pictures of the plants to track plant growth. We have performed a detailed evaluation of our proposed platform by means of simulation, and exemplified real world utilization.

Keywords: Cloud computing · Internet of Things · Plant phenotyping · Gateway

The research leading to these results was supported by the Hungarian Government and the European Regional Development Fund under the grant number GINOP-2.3.2–15-2016-00037 ("Internet of Living Things"). This paper is a revised and extended version of the conference paper presented in [28].

D. Ferguson et al. (Eds.): CLOSER 2019, CCIS 1218, pp. 23–41, 2020.
https://doi.org/10.1007/978-3-030-49432-2_2

1   Introduction

According to recent reports in the field of the Internet of Things (IoT) (e.g. [1]), there will be 25 billion connected things by 2021. These estimations call for smart solutions that provide means to connect, manage and control these devices efficiently. IoT can be envisioned as a dynamic network with self-configuring capabilities, in which devices (that are called as things) can interact and communicate among themselves and with the environment by exchanging sensor data. Such systems can be utilized in many application areas, thus they may have very different properties.

Smart farming is also a rapidly growing area within smart systems, that need to respond to great challenges of the near future. By 2050, it is expected that global population will grow to 9.6 billion as the United Nations Food and Agriculture Organisation predicts. A recent Beecham Research report [2] also states that food production have to respond to this growth to increase it with 70% till 2050. This report also states that agriculture is responsible for a fifth of greenhouse gas emissions and for 70% of the world's fresh water usage, which strives for a reform. IoT supported by cloud services has the potential to implement the required changes [3].

Plant phenotyping [4] also evolves rapidly and provides high throughput approaches for monitoring the growth, physiological parameters, and stress responses of plants with high spatial and temporal resolution. Recent advances use the combination of various remote sensing methods that can exploit IoT and cloud technologies. In the past typical plant phenotyping platforms used very expensive instrumentation to monitor several hundreds, even few thousands of plants. Although these large infrastructures are very powerful, they have high cost ranging to a few mEUR per platform, which limits their widespread, everyday use. Due to recent ICT developments we can apply novel sensor and IoT technologies to provide a promising alternative, called affordable phenotyping. Our research goals also point to this direction, and in this paper we propose a low cost plant phenotyping platform for small sized plants, which enables the remote monitoring of plant growth in a standard greenhouse environment. In an earlier work we introduced the first prototype of our IoLT Smart Pot [28]. In this work we discuss its extension for leaf area calculations, and present a detailed evaluation of it.

The main contributions of this paper are the design and implementation of the IoLT Smart Pot Gateway for managing smart pot clusters by monitoring their environmental parameters. This IoT-Cloud platform is capable of collecting, storing and visualizing sensor data, as well as performing leaf area calculations with image processing to allow plant growth tracking. We also evaluate the proposed solution with scalable simulations, and exemplify real world utilization.

The remainder of this paper is as follows: Sect. 2 introduces related approaches for smart farming and plant monitoring, and Sect. 3 highlights our research aims and discusses the proposed smart pot solution. Section 4 presents a detailed evaluation of our gateway framework by means of simulation, and Sect. 5 shows real world utilization. Finally, we conclude the paper in Sect. 6.

2   Related Work

Smart system design and development have started to flourish. Smart farming is also getting very popular, there are many commercial solutions and products in household areas.

Concerning indoor plant monitoring, many tools are available for monitoring temperature, humidity, light, water level and salt content of the plant soil, and are able to communicate with nearby devices. Some advanced systems are capable of automatic watering or provide notifications or even remote control through mobile applications. Table 1 shows a comparison of the available solutions, and we briefly introduce them in the following.

Table 1. Comparison of commercial smart pot solutions.

Product	Main features	No. of plants	Price (EUR)
Xiaomi Flora	Indicator board, salt content mon	1	40
Parrot pot	Self-watering system, 4 sensors	1	50
sPlant	Light supplement	4	90
PlantRay	Soil moisture, color change, beep	1	19
Tregren	Control light, water and nutrients	3–6–12	90
Odyseed	Automatic irrigation and lighting	2	70
Click & Grow	Water plants automatically, LEDs	3–9	100–200
CitySens	Self-watering, app	3–5	176
LeGrow	Modular	1+	40
AeroGarden	LEDs, Amazon Echo	2–24	40–450
SmartPot	Many sensor prototype	1	NA
Lua	15 different universal animated emotions	1	100
TOKQI	Pet plant to play music, bluetooth speaker	1	12
HEXA	AI robot moving to sunshine	1	950

PlantRay [8] is a really basic smart pot, it has a soil moisture sensor, and it changes color and beeps if watering is required. The battery may last for a year. AeroGarden [9] has many different size products, able to hold from two to 24 plants. They have LED lights, but only the bigger ones have automatic LED control. The most advanced one can be connected with Amazon Echo.

Xiaomi Flora [5] has an indicator board for providing information coming from the sensors, and it has a dedicated application for remote controlling the management of the pot. It is able to monitor the moisture and salt content of the soil. GAIAA [7] is a solution from sPlant, which is able to manage four plants at a time. It also has a remote app control, and provides automatic watering, light supplement, and WiFi communication with a cloud server. Tregren [11] produces 3 different size products, they can handle 3, 6 or even 12 plants. The watering and the light control are automatic, usually it can be leaved alone for

21 days. The SmartPot [15] is just a prototype, but it has temperature, humidity, light, soil moisture sensors and a water pump. It can be controlled by a mobile application. The Parrot pot [6] includes a self-watering system and four built-in sensors. Unfortunately, its production has been suspended. Click & Grow [12] has two similar products, they only differ in size. The smaller one is for three plants, the bigger one can handle 9 plants. CitySens [13] is a vertical pot system with auto-watering and variable pot numbers with an option to communicate with a mobile application via wifi. LeGrow [14] creates modules for a smart pot system. Currently they sell lamp, humidifier, power and pot modules. Odyseed [10] is a smart pot solution that uses time schedules for automatic irrigation and lighting.

There are some other interesting products, like Lua [16] the flowerpot with 15 different animated emotions. The emotions representing the status of the plant based on the moisture, light and temperature sensors. The Vincross [18] company has an AI robot called HEXA, and it can move the plant to get enough sunshine. The TOKQI [17] smart pot can detect if the user pets the plant and starts playing music. It is a decorative item with RGB lighting and it can be used as a regular bluetooth speaker too.

For professional usage, there are only very few commercially available platforms for affordable phenotyping (e.g. PhenoBox [19]).

Concerning generic IoT gateways, Kang et al. [20] introduced the main types and features of IoT gateways in a detailed study, which presents the state-of-the-art and research directions in this field. This solution is also too generic for our needs.

Focusing on the development of a smart farming environment, Dagar et al. [21] proposed a model of a simple smart farming architecture of IoT sensors capable of collecting information on environmental data and sending them to a server using wireless connection. There are also generic solutions to monitor agriculture applications using IoT systems, such as the Kaa IoT Platform [22]. It is a commercial product that is able to perform sensor-based field and remote crop monitoring. It also has an open source version called the Kaa Community Edition. Such generic toolkits are quite complex and heavy-weight, so they are not well suited to specific needs.

In contrast to these solutions, our approach aims to provide a low-cost solution using the latest IoT and Cloud techniques to enable a robust and scalable solution to be used for groups of plants with user friendly management.

3   The Design of a Smart Pot for the IoLT Project

The Internet of Living Things (IoLT) project was started in 2017 with the aims to integrate IoT technological research with applied biological research, and to develop IoT applications for three target fields: complex plant phenotyping, actigraphy for psychosocial treatments, and Lab-on-a-chip systems for microfluidic diagnostics. IoLT is also forming a Network of Excellence of researchers of corresponding disciplines working at the University of Szeged and the Biological

Research Centre of the Hungarian Academy of Sciences. An opensource IoLT platform is under development to enable the execution of applications on cheap, low capacity IoT devices providing easy to use programming interfaces based on Javascript.

In the research field of plant phenotyping we planned to design and develop a scalable, low-cost automation system called IoLT Smart Pot using IoT and cloud technologies, to monitor the effect of various stress factors of plants (drought, nutrition, salt, heavy metals, etc.), as well as behavior of various mutant lines. For the first prototype depicted in Fig. 1, the biologists designed a hardware for hosting 12 small sized plant pots (for Arabidopsis plants) organized in a 4×3 matrix. To monitor plant growth an RGB camera and a LED-based illumination system for additional lighting are installed above the plant cluster. The relevant environmental parameters are light intensity, air and leaf temperature, relative air and soil humidity, which are monitored by sensors placed above and into the pots. To govern the monitoring processes, a Raspberry Pi board is placed

Fig. 1. IoLT Smart Pot prototype (left), and one pot of the cluster (right).

beside the cluster. The monitored sensor data is stored locally on the board, and accessible through a wired connection on the same network. The initial configuration for performing periodical monitoring was set to 5 min concerning the sensor readings, and 1 h to take pictures of the cluster of pots.

3.1 Implementation of the IoLT Smart Pot Gateway

The architecture of our initially proposed IoLT Smart Pot Gateway [28] can be seen in Fig. 2. It has a modular setup, it consists of three microservices, and its source code can be found on GitHub [27]. The microservices are realized by Docker containers [25], which are composed together to form the gateway application deployable to a virtual machine (VM) of a cloud provider. Special monitoring scripts are used to track and log the resource utilization of the containers for performance measurements. The users can access the gateway through a web interface provided by a Node.js portal application. It can be used to group and manage pots and users with projects created by administrators. Projects need to have start and finish dates, associated users and a short description. Pots can also be registered by them and linked to projects. In this way, registered and connected smart pots can send sensor data to them, which can be visualized in the portal. A sample view of such a portal web interface can be seen in Fig. 3. It displays a project named *Real BRC Smartpot test (1 week)* managing a smart

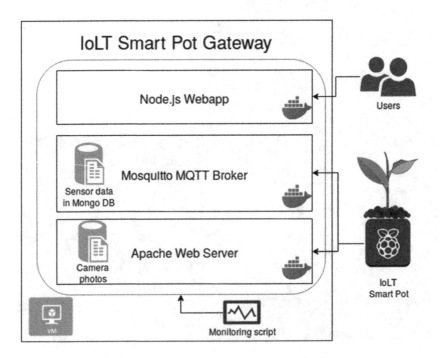

Fig. 2. The architecture of the IoLT Smart Pot Gateway as shown in [28].

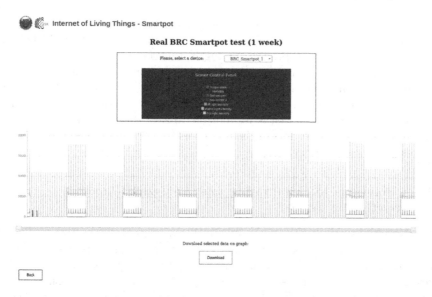

Fig. 3. Historical sensor data visualization in the IoLT Smart Pot Gateway as shown in [28].

Fig. 4. Real and segmented pictures of the Smart Pot cluster taken at 2019.01.01.

pot registered as *BRC_Smartpot_1*. The chart depicts values (y axis) of seven sensor types with timestamps (X axis) for a week of utilization. On the chart interface a user can tick or untick certain sensors, and change the time interval below the chart using a sliding bar. Once a setup is done, the depicted sensor datasets can be downloaded (in CSV format) by clicking on the "Download" button.

The Node.js portal application is built upon two other microservices. In the middle of the architecture in Fig. 2 we can find the Mosquitto MQTT Broker service, which is built on the open-source Mosquitto tool [23] to store the received sensor values of the pots using a MongoDB [24] database. The monitored seven sensor types of a pot are described by a JSON document (see later in Fig. 9), which should be regularly updated and sent in a message by an MQTT client of a smart pot to the MQTT broker running in this service. The sensor readings on the Raspberry Pi board are performed by a python script using an MQTT client package configured with a pot identifier, sensor value sampling frequencies and picture taking frequencies. The third microservice on the bottom is called the Apache Web Server, which is responsible to save the pictures of the plants of the pots. The python scripts of the boards use SFTP file transfers to send the pictures stored by this service.

3.2   A Solutions for Monitoring and Analyzing Plant Growth over Time

After the initial version of the gateway portal was released, the biologists started to use it for monitoring Arabidopsis plants. As mentioned in the previous section, the gateway stores regularly updated sensor values, and periodically taken pictures of the smart pot cluster. The portal can be used to query, visualize and download a set of sensor values for a certain period, and the created pictures.

Besides viewing these monitored results, the biologists had to perform postprocessing tasks of the monitored data by downloading them from the gateway portal. One of these tasks is to calculate the growth speed of the plants, which is generally performed by calculating the projected leaf area visible on the taken pictures, and filing them to a time series document, later depicting them in diagrams. Such a task had to be done manually, taking valuable time from the researchers.

By responding to their need, we extended the gateway with a new functionality. After a new picture is uploaded to the gateway, a python script is triggered to perform the segmentation of the picture. The segmented pictures are also stored in the gateway server in a subfolder to allow verification from the researchers. After segmentation the projected leaf area is calculated for all 12 plants visible on the segmented picture (also with image-processing algorithms in a python script), then saved to the database of the gateway in the format shown in Fig. 5 (in cm2).

```
{
Time:"2019-06-01 15:46:30",Slot_1:8.37,Slot_2:11.76,Slot_3:9.57,
Slot_4:11.54,Slot_5:10.73,Slot_6:16.39,Slot_7:23.87,Slot_8:22.39,
Slot_9:1.88,Slot_10:21.33,Slot_11:20.02,Slot_12:20.69
}
```

Fig. 5. Projected leaf area values to be stored in the database of the gateway.

Sensor data query

You can request measured data through this page.

It currently saves every data that has been measured on the project.

Name of the project:

| BRC_Smartpot_Real_2 ▾ |

| From: | Until: |
| 2018/12/19 16:15 | 2019/04/04 16:13 |

| Query |

Fig. 6. The gateway screen for querying detailed leaf area values.

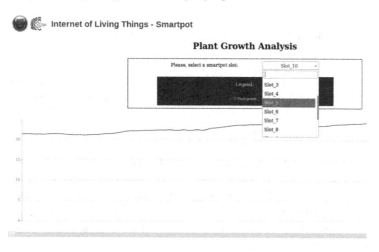

Fig. 7. Selection of a pot from the cluster.

In order to access the results, a researcher should log in to the portal web interface of the gateway, and select a registered project with a time interval, as shown in Fig. 6. For the next step, one can select one of the plants (represented with a slot id) of the smart pot cluster associated to the given project (as depicted by Fig. 7). Finally, as Fig. 8 shows, we can see the chart of the calculated values that represent a time course of the projected leaf area of the selected plant in a pot of the cluster. The curve nicely reveals a cirkadian oscillation pattern due to periodic leaf movement (flattening in the dark and erection in the light period).

4   Evaluation of the Smart Pot Gateway

In order to evaluate our proposed solution, we instantiated an IoLT Smart Pot Gateway service in the MTA Cloud [26] with a small VM flavor with a single virtual CPU core and two GB memory. The MTA Cloud is an OpenStack-based,

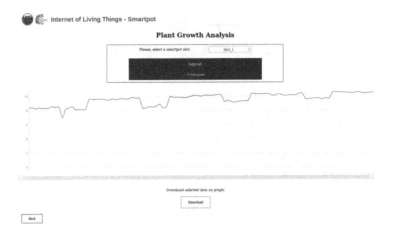

Fig. 8. Detailed leaf area values over time for a pot.

national community cloud financed by the Hungarian Academy of Sciences for providing cloud infrastructure services for scientists from the academy.

4.1   Simulations with a Python Tool

First, we performed a throughout evaluation by means of simulation. After executing some initial measurements, we found out the exact, real data value ranges for the installed sensors of the smart pot. Based on these values, we designed a simulated smart pot represented by python scripts capable of sending generated sensor data via the MQTT protocol. Figure 9 depicts a generated sample JSON file for the revealed sensor types.

```
{
    "Project": "SampleProject",
    "Soil-sensor II": "434.437",
    "Full light intensity [lux]": 16901.38,
    "Time": "2019-01-14 14:02:56",
    "Humidity [%]": "41.1",
    "Soil-sensor I": "594.940",
    "IR light intensity [lux]": 15865.80,
    "Temperature [C]": "21.8",
    "Visible light intensity [lux]": 1035.58
}
```

Fig. 9. Sample JSON message of seven sensor values of a pot as shown in [28].

First, we created 250 simulated pots with scripts that sent generated sensor data to our IoLT Smart Pot Gateway service (runing at MTA Cloud) for 30 min. We divided the total experiment time-frame to the following periods:

- in the first 10 min we applied sensor data generation frequency of 30 s (which means that each pot sent a message of 7 sensor values every 30 s);
- in the second 10 min we applied sensor data generation frequency of 10 s;
- in the following 5 min we applied sensor data generation frequency of 2 s;
- and in the last 5 min we applied sensor data generation frequency of 10 s, again.

We also developed a special monitoring script for the gateway (as shown in Fig. 2) to track its resource consumption. The resource usage sampling of the script was set to 10 s. They queried CPU, memory, network and input/output (I/O) resource utilization for all containers, and we summed these values to get the total resource consumption of the composed service (running in a VM). We can see the measurement results for this initial round simulating 250 pots in Fig. 10 and Fig. 11. The x axis denotes the timestamps of resource usage monitoring, while the y axis denotes the resource usage values (in percentage or in kB or MB). We can see that there are some spikes in the resource usage percentages after the first 10 min, when we start to send more messages, and from the 20th minute the utilization has an increasing trend. Nevertheless, we have to mention that the resource using sampling is less frequent than the arrival rate of the messages, which results in an incomplete curve (the resource utilization is not tracked between the sampling intervals). The network and I/O utilization was visible only for the first 10 min, possibly due to the initialization phase of the script.

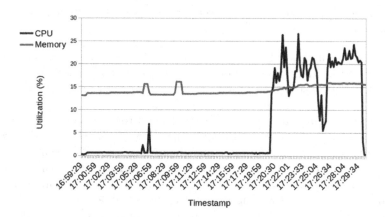

Fig. 10. CPU and memory usage measurement results for 250 pots.

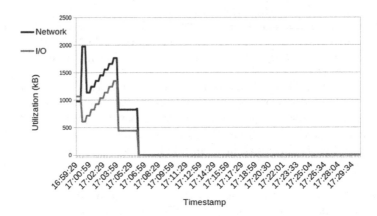

Fig. 11. Network and I/O usage measurement results for 250 pots.

Next, we set the simulation parameters in a way to mimic future, real world utilization. Our proposed IoLT Smart Pot is basically a cluster of 12 pots, as shown in Fig. 1. To evaluate the scalability of our gateway solution, we performed three simulation measurements with 50, 100 and 250 clusters (composed of 600, 1200 and 3000 pots respectively). In all cases we performed the measurements for 30 min, and the simulated smart pot platform sent sensor values with the following setup:

- in the first 10 min we applied sensor data generation frequency of 5 min (which means that each pot sent a message of 7 sensor values every 5 min: resulting 2 messages in this period per pot);
- in the second 10 min we applied sensor data generation frequency of 1 min;
- and in the last 10 min we applied sensor data generation frequency of 5 min, again.

In the first simulation for 50 clusters we set the sampling of resource usage (processor and memory usage) in every 10 s, while for the second and the third one (100 and 250 clusters) we set it to 2 s (to have a better resolution of resource loads).

We can see the measurement results for the first round simulating 50 clusters with 600 pots in Fig. 12 and Fig. 13 for 30 min. Here we can see that the average CPU load varies between 1 and 2%, and the memory usage fluctuates between 15 and 19%. The network and I/O utilization are slowly, but constantly growing. In this experiment we also observed that the time of an actual data processing (receiving a message and writing its contents to the database) and the time of the resource usage sampling are rarely matched. One matching example can be seen right after the 3rd minute in Fig. 12, which shows a spike with almost 14% of CPU utilization.

For the second round we doubled the number of clusters to 100, and performed the simulation only for 5 min with detailed resource usage sampling of

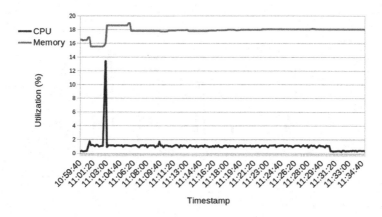

Fig. 12. CPU and memory usage measurement results for 50 pot clusters.

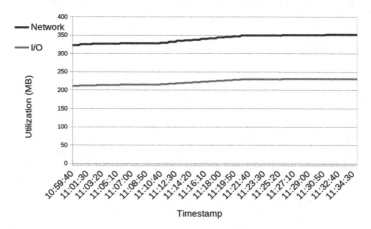

Fig. 13. Network and I/O usage measurement results for 50 pot clusters.

2 s. We can see the measurement results for this round simulating 100 clusters with 1200 pots. In Fig. 14 we can see that the results reveal a periodic resource usage fluctuation denoting the data processing activities. For the network and I/O utilization shown in Fig. 15 we can still see a constant grow.

Finally, for the largest experiment we further increased the number of pot clusters to 250 arriving to a total number of 3000 simulated pots. For this third round, we performed the simulation for 30 min, again, with the same periods as defined for the first round (of 50 clusters). We can see the measurement results in Fig. 16 and Fig. 17. If we take a look at the middle 10 min period we can see the periodic resource usage spikes for CPU and memory, as in the previous round. And we can also observe the utilization growth in network and I/O data transfers.

To summarize our investigations, Table 2 compares the average and maximum resource utilization values measured during the experiments. We can see that

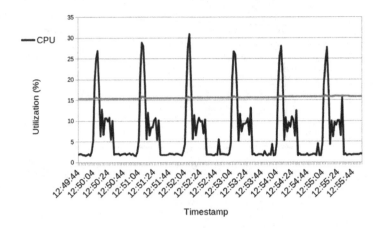

Fig. 14. CPU and memory usage measurement results for 100 pot clusters.

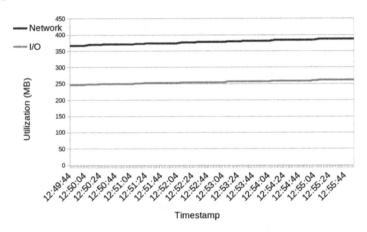

Fig. 15. Network and I/O usage measurement results for 100 pot clusters.

by increasing the number of pots to be managed by the gateway service, the utilization also increases. As expected, the CPU utilization was the highest in the third round for managing 3000 pots at the same time with almost 40%. The memory utilization is also the highest in this case with almost 25%. Table 3 shows a detailed comparison for the longest experiments denoting the different phases of the measurements. This table highlights that the CPU utilization generally reaches its maximum in the first phase, then it generally drops, while memory utilization shows a quite balanced load all over the three phases. Finally, we can state that these results prove that we can easily serve numerous phenotyping projects monitoring up to thousands of pots with a single gateway instance in a Cloud.

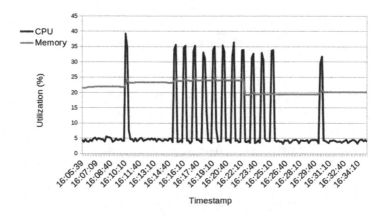

Fig. 16. CPU and memory usage measurement results for 250 pot clusters.

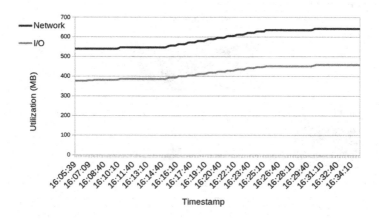

Fig. 17. Network and I/O usage measurement results for 250 pot clusters.

Table 2. Comparison of the four evaluation rounds.

No. of pots		250	600	1200	3000
CPU	AVG	6.22	1.19	7.06	8.65
CPU	MAX	26.64	13.42	30.91	39.29
MEM	AVG	14.28	17.79	15.55	21.72
MEM	MAX	16.14	18.94	15.95	24.73

Table 3. Comparison of the 30 min. evaluation rounds.

No. of pots			600	3000
CPU	AVG	0:00–0:10	1.37	6.65
		0:10–0:20	1.09	14.11
		0:20–0:30	1.11	5.01
CPU	MAX	0:00–0:10	13.42	39.29
		0:10–0:20	1.25	36.43
		0:20–0:30	1.27	31.78
MEM	AVG	0:00–0:10	17.44	22.67
		0:10–0:20	17.88	22.60
		0:20–0:30	18.05	19.81
MEM	MAX	0:00–0:10	18.94	24.47
		0:10–0:20	18.00	24.73
		0:20–0:30	18.11	20.74

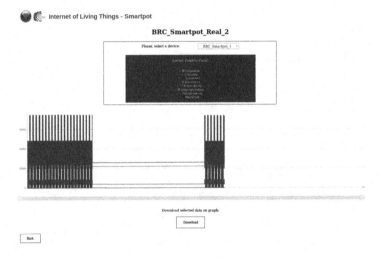

Fig. 18. Data visualization of a real world measurement in the IoLT Smart Pot Gateway.

5   Real World Measurements

We have seen in the previous section that our gateway service is scalable enough to manage a few thousands of pots in a single cloud VM. To exemplify real world utilization, we connected the gateway to the IoLT Smart Pot prototype. It is able to hold 12 Arabidopsis plants in small pots organized to a cluster (as shown in Fig. 1). We configured the python scripts of a Raspberry Pi board placed beside the pot cluster to perform sensor readings periodically, and send the

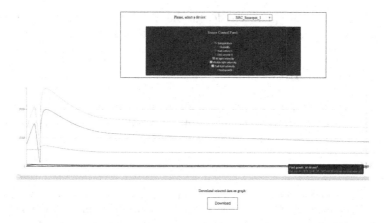

Fig. 19. Sensor data of a day in the IoLT Smart Pot Gateway.

environmental values to the IoT-Cloud gateway service. The wiring of the smart pot cluster formed a single IoT device with a camera and 7 sensors (attached to some of the 12 pots).

We performed the monitoring of the growth of Arabidopsis plants under standard greenhouse conditions for several periods, taking up around 2–3 months in total. RGB image taking was performed every hour, and the sensor sampling frequency was set to 5 min (to generate a JSON message). Figure 18 depicts a query at the gateway portal resulting in a chart of the sensor and leaf area values for over a month of monitoring. As we can see from the chart, the smart pot was disconnected for a certain period after around 20 days). If we zoom in by using the bar below the chart, we can view detailed results. Figure 19 shows the sensor values of a day of utilization of the smart pot cluster.

6 Conclusions

Smart farming approaches are meant to revolutionize agriculture to improve productivity and reduce waste by exploiting the latest ICT technologies and trends. Affordable phenotyping has the goal to provide low cost and easily scalable solutions to create greenhouses of the future.

In this paper we aimed to contribute to this field by proposing the IoLT Smart Pot Platform and Gateway that can be used to manage smart pot clusters by monitoring environmental parameters. This solution is capable of collecting, storing and visualizing sensor data, as well as performing leaf area calculations with image processing to allow plant growth analysis. We also evaluated the proposed solution with scalable simulations, and exemplified real world utilization in standard greenhouse conditions.

In our future work we plan to redesign the smart pot with a solar cell system to enable portable installations and remote monitoring at outdoor location.

Software availability

Its source code of the proposed cloud gateway is open and available at the following website: https://github.com/sed-inf-u-szeged/IoLT-Smart-Pot-Gateway

References

1. Jones, N.: Top Strategic IoT Trends and Technologies Through 2023, Gartner report, September 2018. https://www.gartner.com/en/documents/3890506
2. Beecham Research: Smart Farming. Smart Farming Sales Brochure (2017). http://www.beechamresearch.com/files/Beecham%20Research%20%C2%BB%20Smart%20Farming%20(sales)%202017%20.pdf
3. Botta, A., De Donato, W., Persico, V., Pescapé, A.: Integration of cloud computing and Internet of Things: a survey. Future Gener. Comput. Syst. **56**, 684–700 (2016)
4. Reynolds, M., Schurr, U.: The 4th international plant phenotyping symposium. Plant Sci. **282**, 1 (2019)
5. Sharma, P.: Xiaomi Smart Flower Pot Flora Review (2018). https://www.xiaomitoday.com/xiaomi-smart-flower-pot-flora-review/. Accessed June 2019
6. Parrot Pot, June 2019. https://www.parrot.com/global/connected-garden/parrot-pot
7. GAIAA sPlant smart pot, June 2019. http://www.splant.com.cn/en/index.php?m=Cpzs&a=show&id=14
8. PlantRay, June 2019. https://www.plantray.com
9. AeroGarden, June 2019. https://www.aerogarden.com
10. Odyseed, June 2019. https://www.odyseed.com
11. Tregren, June 2019. https://www.tregren.com/
12. Click & Grow, June 2019. https://www.clickandgrow.com
13. CitySens, June 2019. https://www.citysens.com
14. LeGrow, June 2019. https://www.legrow.co/
15. SmartPot, June 2019. https://www.smart-pot.net/
16. Lua, June 2019. https://www.indiegogo.com/projects/lua-the-smart-planter-with-feelings/
17. TOKQI, June 2019. https://www.tokqismartflowerpot.com
18. Vincross HEXA, June 2019. https://mymodernmet.com/little-robot-smart-planter/
19. Czedik-Eysenberg, A., et al.: The 'PhenoBox', a flexible, automated, open-source plant phenotyping solution. New Phytol. **219**, 808–823 (2018)
20. Kang, B., Kim, D., Choo, H.: Internet of everything: a large-scale autonomic IoT gateway. IEEE Trans. Multi-Scale Comput. Syst. **3**(3), 206–214 (2017)
21. Dagar, R., Som, S., Khatri, S.K.: Smart farming - IoT in agriculture. In: International Conference on Inventive Research in Computing Applications (ICIRCA), Coimbatore, India, pp. 1052–1056 (2018)
22. Kaa project website, January 2019. https://www.kaaproject.org/documentation/
23. Mosquitto website, June 2019. https://mosquitto.org/
24. MongoDB website, June 2019. https://www.mongodb.com/what-is-mongodb

25. Docker Container Environment, June 2019. https://www.docker.com/
26. MTA Cloud service, June 2019. https://sztaki.cloud.mta.hu
27. IoLT Smart Pot Gateway on GitHub, June 2019. https://github.com/sed-inf-u-szeged/IoLT-Smart-Pot-Gateway
28. Hadabas, J., Hovari, M., Vass, I., Kertesz, A.: IoLT smart pot: an IoT-cloud solution for monitoring plant growth in greenhouses. In: Proceedings of the 9th International Conference on Cloud Computing and Services Science, CLOSER, vol. 1, pp. 144–152 (2009)

Development and Operation of Elastic Parallel Tree Search Applications Using TASKWORK

Stefan Kehrer[(✉)] and Wolfgang Blochinger

Parallel and Distributed Computing Group, Reutlingen University,
Alteburgstrasse 150, 72762 Reutlingen, Germany
{stefan.kehrer,wolfgang.blochinger}@reutlingen-university.de

Abstract. Cloud resources can be dynamically provisioned according to application-specific requirements and are payed on a per-use basis. This gives rise to a new concept for parallel processing: Elastic parallel computations. However, it is still an open research question to which extent parallel applications can benefit from elastic scaling, which requires resource adaptation at runtime and corresponding coordination mechanisms. In this work, we analyze how to address these system-level challenges in the context of developing and operating elastic parallel tree search applications. Based on our findings, we discuss the design and implementation of TASKWORK, a cloud-aware runtime system specifically designed for elastic parallel tree search, which enables the implementation of elastic applications by means of higher-level development frameworks. We show how to implement an elastic parallel branch-and-bound application based on an exemplary development framework and report on our experimental evaluation that also considers several benchmarks for parallel tree search.

Keywords: Cloud computing · Parallel computing · Task parallelism · Elasticity · Branch-and-bound

1 Introduction

Many cloud providers, including Amazon Web Services (AWS)[1] and Microsoft Azure[2], introduced new cloud offerings optimized for High Performance Computing (HPC) workloads. Whereas traditional HPC clusters are based on static resource assignment and job scheduling, cloud environments provide attractive benefits for parallel applications such as on-demand access to compute resources, pay-per-use, and elasticity [12,31]. Specifically, elasticity, i.e., the ability to provision and decommission compute resources at runtime, introduces a new concept: Fine-grained cost control per application run by means of elastic parallel computations [11,12,19,24,36]. This fundamentally new concept in parallel computing

---

[1] https://aws.amazon.com.
[2] https://azure.microsoft.com.

© Springer Nature Switzerland AG 2020
D. Ferguson et al. (Eds.): CLOSER 2019, CCIS 1218, pp. 42–65, 2020.
https://doi.org/10.1007/978-3-030-49432-2_3

leads to new opportunities and challenges thus stimulating new research efforts and approaches. For instance, processing time and/or the quality of results can be related to costs, allowing versatile optimizations at runtime [19,24,36].

During the last years, there has been a growing interest to make parallel applications cloud-aware [11,15,17,27,37]. In particular, applications have to cope with the effects of virtualization and resource pooling causing fluctuations in processing times [17]. Existing research also studies how to employ elasticity for applications with simple communication and coordination patterns (e.g., iterative-parallel workloads) [11,37]. In these cases, problems are decomposed into a set of independent tasks, which can be farmed out for distributed computation. However, it is still an open research question to which extent other parallel application classes can benefit from cloud-specific properties, how to leverage elasticity in these cases, and how to ensure cloud-aware coordination of distributed compute resources.

In this work, we discuss how to tackle these challenges for parallel tree search applications. These applications are less sensitive to heterogeneous processing speeds when compared to data-parallel, tightly-coupled applications [15,16], but comprise unstructured interaction patterns and complex coordination requirements. Prominent meta-algorithms based on the parallel tree search processing technique include branch-and-bound and backtracking search with many applications in biochemistry, electronic design automation, financial portfolio optimization, production planning and scheduling, as well as fleet and vehicle scheduling. We discuss the challenges that have to be addressed to make these applications cloud-aware and present TASKWORK - a cloud-aware runtime system that provides a comprehensive foundation for implementing and operating elastic parallel tree search applications in cloud environments. In particular, we make the following contributions: (1) We discuss how to construct a cloud-aware runtime system for parallel tree search applications. (2) We describe the design and implementation of TASKWORK, an integrated runtime system based on our findings and solve corresponding coordination problems based on Apache ZooKeeper[3]. (3) We present a development framework for elastic parallel branch-and-bound applications, which aims to minimize programming effort. (4) We employ a canonical branch-and-bound application as well as several benchmarks to evaluate the performance of TASKWORK in our OpenStack-based private cloud environment.

This work is based on previous research contributions that have been published in the paper *TASKWORK: A Cloud-aware Runtime System for Elastic Task-parallel HPC Applications* [28], which has been presented at the *9th International Conference on Cloud Computing and Services Science*. We extend our former work by discussing the applicability of the presented concepts in the context of parallel tree search applications. Moreover, we provide an extensive evaluation of TASKWORK based on several benchmarks, which are commonly employed to evaluate architectures designed for parallel tree search.

---

[3] https://zookeeper.apache.org.

This work is structured as follows. In Sect. 2, we discuss the characteristics of parallel tree search applications as well as ZooKeeper and related work. Section 3 describes the conceptualization of a cloud-aware runtime system for elastic parallel tree search in the cloud. In Sect. 4, we present TASKWORK - our integrated runtime system for elastic parallel tree search applications. We elaborate on an elastic branch-and-bound development framework and describe its use in Sect. 5. The results of our extensive experimental evaluation are presented in Sect. 6. Section 7 concludes this work.

2   Fundamentals and Related Work

In this section, we examine the characteristics of parallel tree search applications, describe ZooKeeper, and discuss existing research closely related to our work.

2.1   Parallel Tree Search

We specifically focus on parallel tree search processing technique. Commonly employed meta-algorithms based on parallel tree search include branch-and-bound and backtracking search. They are typically used to solve enumeration, decision, and optimization problems - including boolean satisfiability, constraint satisfaction, and graph search problems - with many applications in fields such as biochemistry, electronic design automation, financial portfolio optimization, production planning and scheduling, as well as fleet and vehicle scheduling. These algorithms search solutions in very large state spaces and employ advanced branching and pruning operations/backtracking mechanisms to make the search procedure for problem instances of practical relevance efficient.

Parallel execution is most often accomplished by splitting the state space tree into tasks that can be executed independently of each other by searching a solution in the corresponding subtree. This approach is also called exploratory parallelism (or space splitting [13]). However, because the shape and size of the search tree (and its subtrees) are highly influenced by branching and pruning operations, these applications exhibit a high degree of irregularity. Thus, to exploit a large number of (potentially distributed) compute resources efficiently, task generation has to be executed in a dynamic manner by creating new tasks at runtime. Additionally, these newly generated tasks have to be distributed among compute nodes to avoid idling processing units. This procedure is also called dynamic task mapping (or task scheduling).

The high degree of irregularity constitutes the major source of parallel overhead and thus affects the performance and scaling behavior of parallel tree search applications. Moreover, additional communication requirements stem from knowledge sharing mechanisms that are required to implement meta-algorithms such as branch-and-bound and backtracking search. In this context, knowledge sharing often means communicating bounds [13] or lemmas [38] across tasks at runtime to make the search procedure more efficient by avoiding the exploration of specific subtrees.

Due to the dynamic exploration of the search space combined with problem-specific branching and pruning operations/backtracking mechanisms, resource requirements of parallel tree search applications are not known in advance. This makes them an ideal candidate for cloud adoption as cloud environments provide on-demand access to resources and enable an application to scale elastically. Moreover, they are less sensitive to heterogeneous processing speeds when compared to data-parallel, tightly-coupled applications [15, 16].

2.2   ZooKeeper

ZooKeeper has been designed to ease the implementation of coordination, data distribution, synchronization, and meta data management in distributed systems [20]. Many prominent software projects rely on ZooKeeper including the Apache projects Hadoop[4] and Kafka[5]. It provides an interface that enables clients to read from and write to a tree-based data structure consisting of data registers called *znodes*. Internally, data is replicated across a set of ZooKeeper servers. Each ZooKeeper server accepts client connections and executes requests in FIFO order per client session. A feature called *watches* enables clients to register for notifications of changes without periodic polling. Each server answers read operations locally resulting in eventual consistency. On the other hand, ZooKeeper guarantees writes to be atomic [20]. ZooKeeper's design principles ensure both high availability of stored data and high-performance data access by providing a synchronous and an asynchronous API.

Specifically in cloud environments, coordination primitives such as leader election and group membership are essentially required to deal with a varying number of compute nodes. Based on ZooKeeper, leader election and group membership can be implemented in a straightforward manner [21]. However, specific challenges arise in the context of parallel tree search applications: Global variables have to be synchronized across tasks, which imposes additional dependencies, and as tasks can be generated at each node, a termination detection mechanism is required to detect when the computation has been completed. We show how to employ ZooKeeper to tackle these challenges.

2.3   Related Work

In the past, researchers mainly investigated how to make cloud environments HPC-aware [30]. By exploiting HPC-aware cloud offerings, many parallel applications benefit from an on-demand provisioned execution environment that can be payed on a per-use basis and individual configuration of compute resources, without any modifications to the application itself. This is specifically attractive for applications implemented based on the Single Program Multiple Data (SPMD) model (especially supported by MPI) [27]. However, we can also see a growing interest to make parallel applications cloud-aware [11, 15–17, 37] with

---

[4] http://hadoop.apache.org.
[5] https://kafka.apache.org.

the motivation to exploit either low-cost standard cloud offerings or to make use of advanced cloud features beyond a simple copy & paste migration approach [27]. Existing research discusses how to adapt parallel applications and parallel system architectures to make them cloud-aware. The authors of [12] propose the development of new frameworks for building parallel applications optimized for cloud environments and discuss the importance of application support with respect to elasticity. We follow this approach by presenting a runtime system that does most of the heavy lifting to implement elastic parallel applications.

The authors of [15] present an in-depth performance analysis of different applications. Based on their measurements, the authors describe several strategies to make both parallel applications cloud-aware and cloud environments HPC-aware. A major issue to make parallel applications cloud-aware is the specification of the optimal task size to balance various sources of overhead. In [17], the problem of fluctuations in processing times is addressed, which specifically affects tightly-coupled parallel applications. The authors introduce a dynamic load balancing mechanism that monitors the load of each vCPU and reacts to a measured imbalance. Whereas this approach is based on task overdecomposition to ensure dynamic load balancing, our runtime system actively controls the logical parallelism of an application to minimize task management overhead. However, it is still an open research question if applications without dynamic task parallelism can benefit from such an approach.

The authors of [37] employ the Work Queue framework to develop elastic parallel applications. The Work Queue framework is designed for scientific ensemble applications and provides a master/worker architecture with an elastic pool of workers. The presented case study considers a parallel application for replica exchange molecular dynamics (REMD), which can be considered to be iterative-parallel. The authors of [11] present an approach to enable elasticity for iterative-parallel applications by employing a master/worker architecture. They make use of an asynchronous elasticity mechanism, which employs non-blocking scaling operations. Whereas we specifically consider parallel tree search applications, TASKWORK also makes use of asynchronous scaling operations that do not block the computation.

Task-based parallelism was originally designed to exploit shared memory architectures and used by systems such as Cilk [7]. A major characteristic of task-parallel approaches is that tasks can be assigned dynamically to worker threads, which ensures load balancing and thus effectively reduces idle time. This approach also provides attractive advantages beyond shared memory architectures and has been adopted for different environments including compute clusters [2,5,6] and grids [1]. As a result, the distributed task pool model has attracted considerable research interest. The authors of [33] present a skeleton for C++, which supports distributed memory parallelism for branch-and-bound applications. Their skeleton uses MPI communication mechanisms and is not designed to be cloud-aware. The authors of [9] present a distributed task pool implementation based on the parallel programming language X10, which follows the Partitioned Global Address Space (PGAS) programming model. COHE-

SION is a microkernel-based platform for desktop grid computing [4,39]. It has been designed with an emphasis on task-parallel problems that require dynamic problem decomposition and also provides an abstraction layer for developers based on its system core. Whereas COHESION supports similar applications, it is designed to tackle the challenges of desktop grids such as limited connectivity and control as well as high resource volatility. In contrast to desktop grids, cloud resources can be configured to consider application-specific requirements and controlled by employing an elasticity controller [24]. Moreover, compute resources are billed by a cloud provider, whereas desktop grids make use of available resources donated by contributors.

3   Constructing a Cloud-Aware Runtime System

To particularly benefit from cloud-specific characteristics, developing elastic parallel applications is a fundamental problem that has to be solved [12]. At the core of this problem lies the required dynamic adaptation of parallelism. At all times, the degree of logical parallelism of the application has to fit the physical parallelism given by the number of processing units to achieve maximum efficiency. Traditionally, the number of processing units has been considered as static. In cloud environments, however, the number of processing units can be scaled at runtime by employing an elasticity controller. As a result, applications have to dynamically adapt the degree of logical parallelism based on a dynamically changing physical parallelism. At the same time, adapting the logical parallelism and mapping the logical parallelism to the physical parallelism incurs overhead (in form of excess computation, communication, and idle time). Consequently, elastic parallel applications have to continuously consider a trade-off between the perfect fit of logical and physical parallelism on the one side and minimizing overhead resulting from the adaptation of logical parallelism and its mapping to the physical parallelism on the other. Hence, enabling elastic parallel computations leads to many system-level challenges that have to be addressed to ensure a high efficiency.

Because we specifically focus on parallel tree search applications, which require dynamic task parallelism, the degree of logical parallelism can be defined as the current number of tasks. We argue that a cloud-aware runtime system is required that transparently controls the parallelism of an application to ensure elastic scaling. Figure 1 shows our conceptualization of such a runtime system. It allows developers to mark parallelism in the program, automatically adapts the logical parallelism by generating tasks whenever required, and exploits available processing units with maximum efficiency by mapping the logical parallelism to the physical parallelism. An application based on such a runtime system is elastically scalable: Newly added compute nodes automatically receive tasks by means of dynamic decomposition and load balancing. A task migration mechanism releases compute nodes that have been selected for decommissioning (cf. Fig. 1). Our approach is not limited to any specific cloud management approach or tooling: An elasticity controller may comprise any kind of external

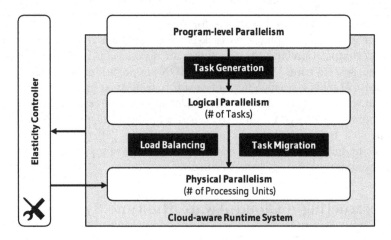

Fig. 1. The described cloud-aware runtime system adapts the logical parallelism by generating tasks dynamically, handles load balancing and task migration, and thus enables elastic parallel computations [28].

decision making logic (e.g., based on execution time, the quality of results, or monetary costs) that finally adapts the number of processing units (i.e., the physical parallelism). An example for such an elasticity controller is given in [19], where monetary costs are considered to control the physical parallelism. In this work, we focus on elastic parallel computations and address related system-level challenges.

Besides elasticity, the characteristics of cloud environments lead to new architectural requirements that have to be considered by parallel applications [25]. Due to virtualization and resource pooling (leading to CPU timesharing and memory overcommitment), fluctuations in processing times of individual processing units can often be observed [15]. Thus, in cloud environments, tasks should be coupled in a loosely manner by employing asynchronous communication methods. Similarly, inter-node synchronization should be loosely coupled while guaranteeing individual progress. A runtime system built for the cloud has to provide such asynchronous communication and synchronization mechanisms thus releasing developers from dealing with these low-level complexities.

4   Design and Implementation of TASKWORK

In this section, we describe the design and implementation of TASKWORK, a cloud-aware runtime system specifically designed for parallel tree search applications according to the principles discussed in Sect. 3. TASKWORK comprises several components that enable elastic parallel computations (cf. **A**, Fig. 2) and solve coordination problems based on ZooKeeper (cf. **B**, Fig. 2). Based on these system-level foundations, higher-level development frameworks and programming models can be built (cf. **C**, Fig. 2), which facilitate the implementa-

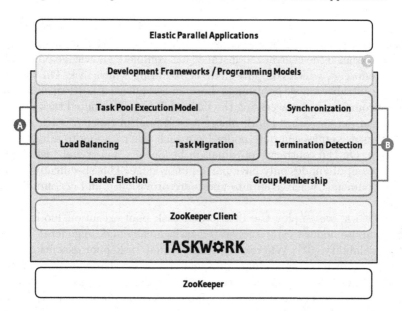

Fig. 2. The components of TASKWORK enable elastic parallel computations based on the task pool execution model, solve coordination problems based on ZooKeeper, and support the construction of higher-level development frameworks and programming models [28].

tion of elastic parallel applications. TASKWORK enables distributed memory parallelism by coordinating a set of distributed compute nodes based on the task pool execution model. Our research prototype is implemented in Java.

In this section, we briefly describe the well-known task pool execution model that we use to manage tasks, before the components of TASKWORK are described in detail.

4.1   Task Pool Execution Model

The task pool execution model [14] decouples task generation and task processing by providing a data structure that can be used to store dynamically generated tasks and to fetch these tasks later for processing. It has been extensively used in the context of parallel tree search applications [33,38,39]. We employ the task pool execution model as a foundation to enable elastic parallel computations according to the concepts depicted in Fig. 1: The task pool manages tasks generated at runtime (defining the logical parallelism) and provides an appropriate interface for load balancing and task migration mechanisms that enable elastic parallel computations.

The task pool execution model can be implemented in a centralized or a distributed manner. The centralized task pool execution model refers to a task pool located at a single compute node that is accessed by all other compute nodes to store and fetch tasks. In the context of distributed memory parallelism, this means that tasks always have to be transferred over the network, e.g., for load balancing purposes. The centralized task pool execution model is easy to implement because the centralized instance has complete knowledge on the state of the system, e.g., which compute node is executing which task. On the other hand, the centralized task pool might become a sequential bottleneck for large number of compute nodes accessing the task pool. The distributed task pool execution model, on the other hand, places a task pool instance at each compute node. It thus decouples compute nodes from each other leading to a highly scalable system. On the contrary, coordination becomes a non-trivial task because individual compute nodes only have partial knowledge. This specifically holds in cloud environments, where compute nodes are provisioned and decommissioned at runtime.

In this work, we employ the distributed task pool execution model, which enables compute nodes to store generated tasks locally and, in general, provides a better scalability [33]. Whereas the distributed task pool execution model leads to an asynchronous system, thus matching the characteristics of cloud environments, one has to deal with the aforementioned challenges. To deal with these drawbacks, we enhance it with scalable coordination and synchronization mechanisms based on ZooKeeper.

4.2   Leader Election

TASKWORK implements ZooKeeper-based leader election to designate a single coordinator among the participating compute nodes. This coordinator takes care of submitting jobs to the system, processes the final result, and controls cloud-related coordination operations such as termination detection. ZooKeeper renders leader election a rather trivial task [21]. Therefore, each node tries to write its endpoint information to the */coordinator* znode. If the write operation succeeds, the node becomes the coordinator. Otherwise, if the */coordinator* znode exists, the node participates as compute node.

4.3   Group Membership

As compute nodes might be added or removed at runtime by means of elastic scaling, cloud-based systems are highly dynamic. Thus, a group membership component is required, which provides up-to-date views on the instance model, i.e., the list of all currently available compute nodes. To this end, compute nodes automatically register themselves during startup by creating an ephemeral child znode under the */computeNodes* znode containing their endpoint information. The creation of the child znode makes use of ZooKeeper's *sequential* flag that creates a unique name assignment [20]. Changes in group membership are obtained by all other compute nodes by watching the */computeNodes* znode.

4.4   Load Balancing

Load balancing is a fundamental aspect in cloud environments to exploit newly added compute resources efficiently. Moreover, it is a strong requirement of parallel tree search applications due to dynamic problem decomposition. Load balancing can be accomplished by either sending tasks to other compute nodes (work sharing) or by fetching tasks from other nodes (work stealing) [7]. Because sending tasks leads to overhead, we favor work (task) stealing because communication is only required when a compute node runs idle. Load balancing is accomplished by observing changes in the local task pool. Whenever the local task pool is empty and all worker threads are idle, *task stealing* is initiated. Task stealing is an approach where idle nodes send work requests to other nodes in the cluster. These nodes answer the request by sending a task from their local task pool to the remote node.

Because the distributed task pool execution model lacks knowledge about which compute nodes are busy and which are idling, we employ randomized task stealing [8]. To deal with a changing number of compute nodes over time, up-to-date information on the currently available compute nodes is required. This information is provided by the group membership component (cf. Sect. 4.3).

4.5   Task Migration

To enable the decommissioning of compute resources at runtime, unfinished work has to be sent to remaining compute nodes. This is ensured by TASKWORK's task migration component. Compute nodes that have been selected for decommissioning store the current state of tasks being executed, stop their worker threads, and send all local tasks to remaining compute nodes. Technically, the task migration component registers for the POSIX SIGTERM signal. This signal is triggered by Unix-like operating systems upon termination, which allows TASKWORK to react to a requested termination without being bound to specific cloud management tooling but instead relying on operating system mechanisms. Also note that POSIX signals are supported by state-of-the-art container runtime environments such as Kubernetes[6], where they are used to enable graceful shutdown procedures. As a result, TASKWORK can be controlled by any cloud management tool (provided by a specific cloud provider or open source) and hence enables a best-of-breed tool selection. Furthermore, this approach ensures that TASKWORK can be deployed on any operating system that supports POSIX signals and the Java Runtime Environment (JRE), thus ensuring a high degree of portability.

Application developers simply have to specify an optimal interruption point in their program to support task migration. The `migrate` operation can be used to check if a task should be migrated (for an example see Sect. 5.2). TASKWORK employs weak migration of tasks. This means that a serialized state generated

---

[6] https://kubernetes.io.

from a task object is transferred across the network. To facilitate the migration process, application-specific snapshotting mechanisms can be provided by developers.

4.6   Termination Detection

Traditionally, distributed algorithms for termination detection (wave-based or based on parental responsibility) have been preferred due to their superior scalability characteristics [14]. However, maintaining a ring (wave-based) or tree (parental responsibility) structure across compute nodes in the context of an elastically scaled distributed system imposes significant overhead. To deal with this issue, TASKWORK employs ZooKeeper-based termination detection, which has been described in [28]. In summary, this approach maintains a tree-based task dependency structure stored in ZooKeeper, which is dynamically updated at runtime.

4.7   Synchronization of Global Variables

As discussed in Sect. 2.1, many meta-algorithms such as branch-and-bound rely on knowledge sharing across tasks at runtime to make the search procedure more efficient by avoiding the exploration of specific subtrees. TASKWORK supports knowledge sharing in form of global variables that are automatically synchronized across tasks. Global variables can be used to build application-specific development frameworks or programming models. The process of synchronization considers three hierarchy levels: (1) task-level variables, which are updated for each task executed by a worker thread, (2) node-level variables, which are updated on each compute node, and (3) global variables. Task-level variables are typically updated by the implemented program and thus managed by the application developer. To synchronize node-level variables, we provide two operations: getVar for obtaining node-level variables and setVar for setting node-level variables. Whenever a node-level variable changes its value, we employ ZooKeeper to update this variable globally, which enables synchronization across all distributed compute nodes. These generic operations allow developers to address application-specific synchronization requirements, while TASKWORK handles the process of synchronization.

By following this approach, small-sized variables can be synchronized across the distributed system. However, frequent data synchronization leads to overhead and should be used carefully and only for small data.

4.8   Development Frameworks and Programming Models

TASKWORK enables the construction of higher-level development frameworks and programming models based on a generic task abstraction that allows the specification of custom task definitions. The essential idea is that, as outlined in Sect. 3, developers only mark program-level parallelism while task generation, load balancing, and task migration are handled automatically thus ensuring elastic parallel computations. To define program-level parallelism, application developers specify an application-specific `split` operation based on the generic task abstraction to split work from an existing task. Afterwards, this `split` operation can be used for implementing any application program that dynamically creates tasks (for an example see Sect. 5.2).

Two execution modes for the splitting mechanism are provided: *Definite* and *potential splitting*. Whereas definite splitting directly creates new tasks by means of the `split` operation, potential splitting adapts the logical parallelism (number of tasks) in an automated manner. By following the second approach, application developers also implement the `split` operation in an application-specific manner, but only specify a potential splitting point in their application program with the `potentialSplit` operation. In line with the conceptualization discussed in Sect. 3, the `potentialSplit` operation is used to mark program-level parallelism and TASKWORK decides at runtime whether to create new tasks or not depending on the current system load. Thus, potential splitting automatically adapts the number of tasks generated and thus controls the logical parallelism of the application (cf. Fig. 1). As a result, TASKWORK manages the trade-off between perfect fit of logical and physical parallelism and minimizing overhead resulting from task generation and task mapping as discussed in Sect. 3. Different policies can be supplied to configure how this trade-off is handled. For example, tasks can be generated on-demand, i.e., when another compute node requests a task by means of work stealing (cf. Sect. 4.4). Alternatively, tasks can be generated when the number of tasks in the local task pool drops below a configurable threshold. By default, TASKWORK uses the on-demand task generation policy. We recognized that on-demand task generation is, in many cases, more efficient because formerly generated tasks might contain a subtree that has already been proven to be obsolete. Thus, threshold-based task generation often results in unnecessary transferal of tasks over the network, leading to additional overhead.

5   Elastic Branch-and-Bound Development Framework

In this section, we describe a development framework for elastic parallel branch-and-bound applications based on TASKWORK's generic task abstraction. Branch-and-bound is a well-known meta-algorithm for search procedures. It is considered to be one of the major computational patterns for parallel processing [3]. In the following, we briefly explain the branch-and-bound approach and show how to employ our framework to develop an example application.

5.1   Branch-and-Bound Applications

We explain the branch-and-bound approach by employing the Traveling Salesman Problem (TSP) as canonical example application. The TSP states that a salesman has to make a tour visiting n cities exactly once while finishing at the city he starts from. The problem can be modeled as a complete graph with n

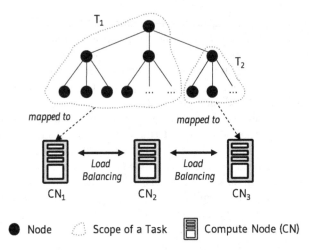

Fig. 3. To enable parallel processing, the state space tree is cut into several tasks, each capturing a subproblem of the initial problem. Note that tasks have to be created at runtime to avoid load imbalance.

vertices, where each vertex represents a city and each edge a path between two cities. A nonnegative cost $c(i, j)$ occurs to travel from city i to city j. The optimization goal is to find a tour whose total cost, i.e., the sum of individual costs along the paths, is minimum [10].

All feasible tours can be explored systematically by employing a *state space tree* that enumerates all states of the problem. The initial node (the root node of the state space tree) represents the city the salesman starts from. From this and all following cities, the salesman can follow any path to travel to one of the unvisited cities, which is represented as a new node in the state space tree. At some point, all cities have been visited thus leading to a leaf node in the state space tree, which represents a tour. Each node can be evaluated with respect to its cost by summing up the individual costs of all paths taken. This also holds for leaf nodes in the state space tree representing a tour. A search procedure can be applied that dynamically explores the complete state space tree and finally finds a tour with minimum cost. However, brute force search cannot be applied to large state space trees efficiently. Instead of enumerating all possible states, branch-and-bound makes use of existing knowledge to search many paths in the state space tree only implicitly. We describe the underlying principles, which make the search procedure efficient, in the following.

If the current node is not a leaf node, the next level of child nodes is generated by visiting all unvisited cities that are directly accessible. Each of these child nodes leads to a set of disjoint tours. Generating new nodes is referred to as *branching*. If the current node is a leaf node, we evaluate the tour represented by this node with respect to its total cost.

At runtime, the tour whose total cost is known to be minimum at a specific point in time defines an upper bound for the ongoing search procedure. Any intermediate node in the state space tree that evaluates to a higher cost can be proven to lead to a tour with higher total costs and thus has not to be explored any further. On the other hand, lower bounds can be calculated by solving a relaxed version of the problem based on the current state [40]. We calculate the lower bound by adding the weight of a minimum spanning tree (MST) of the not-yet visited cities to the current path [2, 40]. The MST itself is calculated based on Prim's algorithm [35]. We can prune parts of the state space tree if the calculated lower bound of the current node is larger or equal to the current upper bound (because the TSP is a minimization problem). The pruning operation is essential to make branch-and-bound efficient.

Following the branch-and-bound approach, a problem is decomposed into subproblems at runtime. Each of these subproblems captures a part of the state space tree and can be solved in parallel. Technically, these subproblems are described by a set of tasks, which can be distributed across available compute nodes. However, several challenges arise when we map branch-and-bound applications to parallel architectures: Work anomalies are present, which means that the amount of work differs between sequential and parallel processing as well as across parallel application runs. Additionally, branch-and-bound applications are highly irregular, i.e., task sizes are not known a priori and unpredictable by nature. Consequently, solving the TSP requires the runtime system to cope with dynamic problem decomposition and load balancing to avoid idling processing units. Every task that captures a specific subproblem can produce new child tasks (cf. Fig. 3). Thus, termination detection is another strong requirement to detect if a computation has been completed. Additionally, updates on the upper bound have to be distributed fast to enable efficient pruning for subproblems processed simultaneously in the distributed system.

5.2 Design and Use of the Development Framework

In the following, we describe a development framework for elastic branch-and-bound on top of TASKWORK. We employ the TSP as an example application to show how to use the framework. Elastic parallel applications can be implemented with this framework without considering low-level, technical details.

TASKWORK provides a generic task abstraction that can be used to build new development frameworks and programming models. In the context of branch-and-bound, we define a task as the traversal of the subtrees rooted at all unvisited input nodes. Additionally, each task has access to the graph structure describing the cities as vertices and the paths as edges. This graph structure guides the exploratory construction of the state space tree. All visited cities are marked in the graph. This representation allows to split the currently traversed state space tree to generate new tasks.

New tasks have to be created at runtime to keep idling processing units and newly added ones busy. Therefore, the branch-and-bound task definition

```
1  public void search() {
2    while(!openNodes.isEmpty()){
3      if(migrate()) return;
4
5      Node currentNode = openNodes.getNext();
6
7      getUpperBound();
8
9      Node[] children = currentNode.branch();
10     for(Node child : children) {
11       if(child.isLeafNode()) {
12         if(child.getCost() < current_best_cost){
13           current_best_cost = child.getCost();
14           current_best_tour = child.getPath();
15           setUpperBound();
16         }
17       }else if(child.getLowerBound() < current_best_cost){
18         openNodes.add(child);
19       }
20     }
21
22     potentialSplit();
23   }
24 }
```

Fig. 4. The elastic branch-and-bound development framework allows developers to implement parallel search procedures without considering low-level details such as concurrency, load balancing, synchronization, and task migration [28].

allows the specification of an application-specific `split` operation. This operation branches the state space tree by splitting off a new task from a currently executed task. This split-off task can be processed by another worker thread running on another compute node. To limit the amount of tasks generated, we make use of TASKWORK's potential splits, i.e, the `split` operation is only triggered, when new tasks are actually required. As depicted in Fig. 4, here, the `potentialSplit` operation is executed after a node has been evaluated. TASKWORK decides if a split is required. If so, it executes the application-specific `split` operation that takes nodes from the `openNodes` list to create a new (disjoint) task. Otherwise it proceeds regularly, i.e., it evaluates the next node. In the following, we describe how to implement task migration, bound synchronization, and termination detection based on TASKWORK.

Task Migration. To enable task migration, developers check if migration is required (cf. Fig. 4). In this case, a task simply stops its execution. The migration process itself is handled by TASKWORK. This means that a compute node that has been selected for decommissioning automatically stops all running worker threads, pushes the affected tasks to the local task pool, and starts the migration of these tasks to other compute nodes (cf. Sect. 4.5).

Bound Synchronization. Pruning is based on a global upper bound. In case of the TSP, the total cost of the best tour currently known is used as the global upper bound. The distribution of the current upper bound is essential to avoid excess computation (due to an outdated value). By employing the synchroniza-tion component (cf. Sect. 4.7), we initiate an update of the global upper bound whenever the local upper bound is better then the current global upper bound observed. Technically, we specify an update rule that compares the total costs of two tours. If a better upper bound has been detected, TASKWORK ensures that the new upper bound is propagated through the hierarchy levels of the parallel system. At the programming level, `getUpperBound` and `setUpperBound` (cf. Fig. 4) are implemented based on the `getVar` and `setVar` operations (cf. Sect. 4.7).

Termination Detection. Activating termination detection enables parallel applications to register for a termination event, which can be also used to retrieve the final result. In this case, the final result is a tour whose total cost is minimum and thus solves the TSP.

6 Experimental Evaluation

In this section, we present and discuss several experiments to evaluate TASK-WORK. First, we describe our experimental setup. Second, we introduce the benchmark applications for parallel tree search that are used for the evalua-tion. Third, we report on the parallel performance and scalability by measuring speedups and efficiencies for both the TSP application implemented with the elastic branch-and-bound development framework and the described benchmark applications. Finally, we measure the effects of elastic scaling on the speedup of an application to assess the inherent overheads of dynamically adapting the number of compute nodes at runtime.

6.1 Experimental Setup

Compute nodes are operated on CentOS 7 virtual machines (VM) with 1 vCPU clocked at 2.6 GHz, 2 GB RAM, and 40 GB disk. All VMs are deployed in our OpenStack-based private cloud environment. The underlying hardware consists of identical servers, each equipped with two Intel Xeon E5-2650v2 CPUs and 128 GB RAM. The virtual network connecting tenant VMs is operated on a 10 GBit/s physical ethernet network. Each compute node runs a single worker thread to process tasks and is connected to one of three ZooKeeper servers (forming a ZooKeeper cluster). Our experiments were performed during regular multi-tenant operation.

6.2 Benchmark Applications

Because work anomalies occur in the context of our branch-and-bound applica-tion, we additionally use two benchmarks for parallel tree search to rigorously evaluate TASKWORK. Work anomalies result from the search procedure being executed in parallel by different compute nodes on different subtrees of the search tree. As a result, the amount of work significantly differs between sequential and parallel processing as well as across parallel application runs. We describe the benchmark applications in the following.

Unbalanced Tree Search (UTS). Unbalanced Tree Search [32] is a benchmark designed to evaluate task pool architectures for parallel tree search. UTS enables us to generate synthetic irregular workloads that are not affected by work anomalies and thus support a systematic experimental evaluation. Different tree shapes and sizes as well as imbalances can be constructed by means of a small set of parameters, where each tree node is represented by a 20-byte descriptor. This descriptor is used as a random variable based on which the number of children is determined at runtime. A child node's descriptor is generated by an SHA-1 hash function based on the parent descriptor and the child's index. As a result, the generation process is reproducible due to the determinism of the underlying hash function.

We generate UTS problem instances of the geometric tree type, which mimics iterative deepening depth-first search, a commonly applied technique to deal with intractable search spaces, and has also been extensively used in related work [9,32,34]. The 20-byte descriptor of the root node is initialized with a random seed r. The geometric tree type's branching factor follows a geometric distribution with an expected value b. An additional parameter d specifies the maximum depth, beyond which the tree is not expanded further. The problem instances employed for our measurements are UTS_1 ($r = 19$, $b = 4$, $d = 16$) and UTS_2 ($r = 19$, $b = 4$, $d = 17$).

WaitBenchmark. This benchmark was taken from [38], where it has been used in the context of parallel satisfiability (SAT) solving to systematically evaluate task pool architectures. The irregular nature of these applications is modeled by the benchmark as follows. To simulate the execution of a task, a processing unit has to wait T seconds. The computation is initialized with a single root task with a wait time T_{init}. At runtime, tasks can be dynamically generated by splitting an existing task. Splitting a task $Task_{parent}$ is done by subtracting a random fraction T_{child} of the remaining wait time T_R and generating a new task $Task_{child}$ with T_{child} as input:

$$Task_{parent}\{T_R\} \rightarrow (Task_{parent'}\{T_R - T_{child}\}, Task_{child}\{T_{child}\}). \quad (1)$$

6.3 Basic Parallel Performance

We report on the basic parallel performance of TASKWORK by measuring speedups and efficiencies for the TSP application implemented with the elastic branch-and-bound development framework. To evaluate the parallel performance, we solved 5 randomly generated instances of the 35 city symmetric TSP. Speedups and efficiencies are based on the execution time T_{seq} of a sequential implementation executed by a single thread on the same VM type. Table 1 shows the results of our measurements with three parallel program runs per TSP instance. As we can see, the measured performance is highly problem-specific.

Table 1. Performance measurements of TSP instances [28].

Problem instance	T_{seq} [s] (1 VM)	T_{par} [s] (60 VMs)	Speedup S [#] (60 VMs)	Efficiency E [%] (60 VMs)
TSP35$_1$	1195	32.9 ± 2.0	36.3	60.48
TSP35$_2$	1231	55.7 ± 4.0	22.1	36.87
TSP35$_3$	2483	103.5 ± 2.1	24.0	39.99
TSP35$_4$	3349	115.5 ± 6.3	29.0	48.31
TSP35$_5$	10286	167.4 ± 12.4	59.5	99.20

6.4 Scalability

To evaluate the scalability of a parallel system, one has to measure the standard metrics in parallel computing, i.e., the parallel execution time T_{par}, the speedup S, and the parallel efficiency E, for different numbers of processing units. $T_{par}(I,p)$ is the parallel execution time for a given input I measured with p processing units and $T_{seq}(I)$ is the sequential execution time for a given input I. The problem size $W(I)$ is defined as the number of (basic) computational steps in the best sequential algorithm to solve a problem described by I [14]. Under the assumption that it takes unit time to perform a single computational step, the problem size is equivalent to the sequential execution time $T_{seq}(I)$. To evaluate the scalability of TASKWORK, we report on two different measurement approaches: First, we measured the speedup with the UTS benchmark and the WaitBenchmark for a fixed problem size. Second, we measured the so-called *scaled speedup* with the WaitBenchmark. The scaled speedup of a parallel system is obtained by increasing the problem size linearly with the number of processing units [14]. We discuss the results in the following.

First, we report on the scalability of TASKWORK with a fixed problem size, which is thus independent of the number of processing units contributing to the computation. Figure 5 depicts the results of our measurements for three different problem instances: Two problem instances of the UTS benchmark UTS_1 ($r=19$, $b=4$, $d=16$) and UTS_2 ($r=19$, $b=4$, $d=17$) and a problem instance of the WaitBenchmark with a fixed initial wait time of the root task of $T_{init} = 600$ [s].

Second, we report on the scalability of TASKWORK with a problem size that is increased linearly with the number of processing units. In the case of the WaitBenchmark, the input is defined as the initial wait time of the root task T_{init}. The problem size can be defined as $W(T_{init}) = T_{init}$. Moreover, the sequential execution time $T_{seq}(T_{init})$ required by the best sequential algorithm to solve a problem described by T_{init} is $T_{seq}(T_{init}) = T_{init}$. This makes it easy to create a fixed problem size per processing unit, which requires us to increase the problem size W with the number of processing units p employed by the parallel system. For our measurements, we defined an initial wait time of the root task of $T_{init}(p) = p \cdot 60$ [s]. The speedups and efficiencies obtained are depicted in Fig. 6. The results of our measurement show close to linear speedups. A parallel

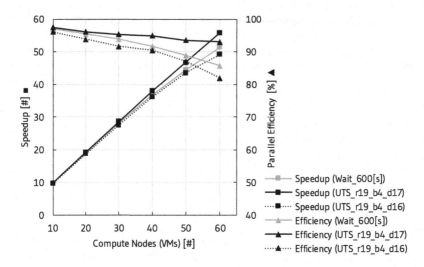

Fig. 5. The problem instances shown are UTS_1 ($r = 19$, $b = 4$, $d = 16$), UTS_2 ($r = 19$, $b = 4$, $d = 17$), and the WaitBenchmark with an initial wait time of the root task of $T_{init} = 600$ [s]. Speedups and efficiencies given are arithmetic means based on 3 parallel program runs for 6 setups leading to 54 measurements in total.

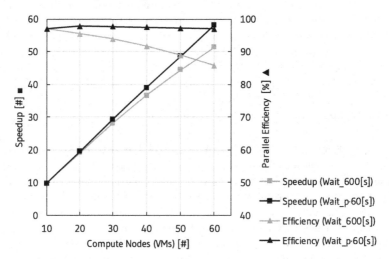

Fig. 6. The problem instances shown are the WaitBenchmark with an initial wait time of the root task of $T_{init}(p) = p \cdot 60$ [s] and the WaitBenchmark with an initial wait time of the root task of $T_{init} = 600$ [s]. Speedups and efficiencies given are arithmetic means based on 3 parallel program runs.

system is considered to be scalable when the scaled speedup curve is close to linear [14]. As expected, the (scaled) speedup curve is much better compared to the one obtained by our scalability measurements with $T_{init} = 600$ [s], which are also depicted in Fig. 6.

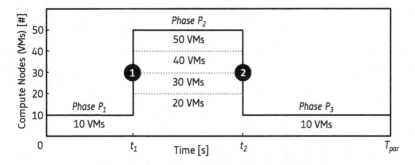

Fig. 7. We adapt the number of compute nodes (physical parallelism) at times t_1 and t_2 and measure the effects on the elastic speedup $S_{elastic}$ [28].

6.5 Elastic Scaling

In the cloud, compute resources can be provisioned or decommissioned at runtime by means of an elasticity controller. To make use of newly provisioned compute resources, the runtime system has to adapt to this change (cf. Sect. 3). A fundamental question that arises in this context is: *How fast* can resources be effectively employed by the application? This is a fundamentally new perspective on parallel system architectures that also has to be considered for evaluation purposes.

We propose a novel experimental method that shows the capability of a parallel system to dynamically adapt to a changing number of compute resources. Because parallel systems are designed with the ultimate goal to maximize parallel performance, our method evaluates the effects of dynamic resource adaptation on performance in terms of the speedup metric. Our experiment is described in Fig. 7 and comprises three phases. We start our application with 10 compute nodes (VMs) in Phase P_1. At time t_1, we scale out by adding more VMs to the computation. To evaluate the elastic behavior without platform-specific VM startup times, we employ VMs that are already running. At time t_2, we decommission the VMs added at t_1. At phase transition ❶, TASKWORK ensures task generation and efficient load balancing to exploit newly added compute nodes. At phase transition ❷, the task migration component ensures graceful decommissioning of compute nodes (cf. Sect. 4.5). We can easily see if newly added compute resources contribute to the computation by comparing the measured elastic speedup $S_{elastic}$ (speedup with elastic scaling) with the *baseline speedup* $S_{baseline}$ that we measured for a static setting with 10 VMs. To see how effectively new compute resources are employed by TASKWORK, we tested several durations for Phase P_2 as well as different numbers of VMs added (cf. Fig. 7) and calculated the percentage change in speedup S_{change} as follows:

$$S_{change} = \frac{(S_{elastic} - S_{baseline})}{S_{baseline}} \cdot 100 \qquad (2)$$

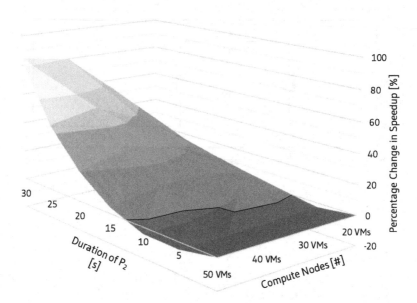

Fig. 8. The percentage change in speedup is calculated based on different durations of Phase P_2 and different numbers of compute nodes (VMs) added to the parallel computation at runtime. The number of VMs shown is the total number of VMs employed in Phase P_2.

S_{change} allows us to quantify the relative speedup improvements based on elastic scaling. Both $S_{elastic}$ and $S_{baseline}$ are arithmetic means calculated based on three program runs.

For our measurements, we employ the TSP application implemented based on the elastic branch-and-bound development framework. To avoid work anomalies, we disabled pruning to evaluate elastic scaling. All measurements are based on a TSP instance with 14 cities. The results of our measurements are depicted in Fig. 8, which shows the percentage change in speedup achieved for different durations of Phase P_2 and different numbers of compute nodes (VMs) added to the computation at runtime. 40 VMs added (leading to 50 VMs in total in Phase P_2) can be effectively employed in 15 s. Higher speedup improvements can be achieved by increasing the duration of Phase P_2. We also see that for a duration of only 10 s, adding 40 VMs even leads to a decrease in speedup whereas adding 20 VMs leads to an increase in speedup (for the same duration). This effect results from the higher overhead (in form of task generation, load balancing, and task migration) related to adding a higher number of VMs. On the other hand, as expected, for higher durations of Phase P_2, employing a higher number of VMs leads to better speedups. Note that the percentage of time spent in Phase P_2 (with respect to the total execution time) affects the actual percentage change in speedup, but not the effects that we have described.

7 Conclusion

In the presented work, we tackle the challenge of developing and operating elastic parallel tree search applications. We discuss related system-level challenges and show how to enable elastic parallel computations as well as cloud-aware coordination of distributed compute resources for the application class considered. Based on our findings, we present a novel runtime system that manages the low-level complexities related to elastic parallel applications to ease their development. Elastic parallel computations are enabled by means of load balancing, task migration, and application-specific task generation, which requires only minor effort at the programming level. Whereas the described development framework is specifically designed for elastic parallel branch-and-bound applications, other application classes that generate tasks at runtime (e.g., n-body simulations [18]) might also benefit from the design principles presented.

Many challenges are left on the path towards elastic parallel applications. Our long-term goal is to understand how to design, develop, and manage elastic parallel applications and systems. Therefore, we investigate design-level, programming-level, and system-level aspects [25,28] as well as delivery and deployment automation [22,23,26,29]. In this context, we are confident that TASKWORK provides a solid foundation for future research activities.

Acknowledgements. This research was partially funded by the Ministry of Science of Baden-Württemberg, Germany, for the Doctoral Program *Services Computing*.

References

1. Anstreicher, K., Brixius, N., Goux, J.-P., Linderoth, J.: Solving large quadratic assignment problems on computational grids. Math. Program. **91**(3), 563–588 (2001). https://doi.org/10.1007/s101070100255
2. Archibald, B., Maier, P., McCreesh, C., Stewart, R., Trinder, P.: Replicable parallel branch and bound search. J. Parallel Distrib. Comput. **113**, 92–114 (2018)
3. Asanovic, K., et al.: A view of the parallel computing landscape. Commun. ACM **52**(10), 56–67 (2009)
4. Blochinger, W., Dangelmayr, C., Schulz, S.: Aspect-oriented parallel discrete optimization on the cohesion desktop grid platform. In: Sixth IEEE International Symposium on Cluster Computing and the Grid, 2006, CCGRID 2006, vol. 1, pp. 49–56, May 2006
5. Blochinger, W., Küchlin, W., Ludwig, C., Weber, A.: An object-oriented platform for distributed high-performance symbolic computation. Math. Comput. Simul. **49**, 161–178 (1999)
6. Blochinger, W., Michlin, W., Weber, A.: The distributed object-oriented threads system DOTS. In: Ferreira, A., Rolim, J., Simon, H., Teng, S.-H. (eds.) IRREGULAR 1998. LNCS, vol. 1457, pp. 206–217. Springer, Heidelberg (1998). https://doi.org/10.1007/BFb0018540
7. Blumofe, R.D., Joerg, C.F., Kuszmaul, B.C., Leiserson, C.E., Randall, K.H., Zhou, Y.: Cilk: an efficient multithreaded runtime system. J. Parallel Distrib. Comput. **37**(1), 55–69 (1996)

8. Blumofe, R.D., Leiserson, C.E.: Scheduling multithreaded computations by work stealing. J. ACM **46**(5), 720–748 (1999)
9. Bungart, M., Fohry, C.: A malleable and fault-tolerant task pool framework for x10. In: 2017 IEEE International Conference on Cluster Computing (CLUSTER), pp. 749–757. IEEE (2017)
10. Cormen, T., Leiserson, C., Rivest, R., Stein, C.: Introduction to Algorithms, 3rd edn. (2009)
11. Da Rosa Righi, R., Rodrigues, V.F., Da Costa, C.A., Galante, G., De Bona, L.C.E., Ferreto, T., et al.: AutoElastic: automatic resource elasticity for high performance applications in the cloud. IEEE Trans. Cloud Comput. **4**(1), 6–19 (2016)
12. Galante, G., De Bona, L.C.E., Mury, A.R., Schulze, B., Da Rosa Righi, R., et al.: An analysis of public clouds elasticity in the execution of scientific applications: a survey. J. Grid Comput. **14**(2), 193–216 (2016)
13. Gendron, B., Crainic, T.G.: Parallel branch-and-branch algorithms: survey and synthesis. Oper. Res. **42**(6), 1042–1066 (1994)
14. Grama, A., Gupta, A., Karypis, G., Kumar, V.: Introduction to Parallel Computing, 2nd edn. Pearson Education, London (2003)
15. Gupta, A., et al.: Evaluating and improving the performance and scheduling of HPC applications in cloud. IEEE Trans. Cloud Comput. **4**(3), 307–321 (2016)
16. Gupta, A., et al.: The who, what, why, and how of high performance computing in the cloud. In: IEEE 5th International Conference on Cloud Computing Technology and Science, vol. 1, pp. 306–314, December 2013
17. Gupta, A., Sarood, O., Kale, L.V., Milojicic, D.: Improving HPC application performance in cloud through dynamic load balancing. In: 13th IEEE/ACM International Symposium on Cluster, Cloud, and Grid Computing, pp. 402–409, May 2013
18. Hannak, H., Blochinger, W., Trieflinger, S.: A desktop grid enabled parallel Barnes-Hut algorithm. In: 2012 IEEE 31st International Performance Computing and Communications Conference, pp. 120–129 (2012)
19. Haussmann, J., Blochinger, W., Kuechlin, W.: Cost-efficient parallel processing of irregularly structured problems in cloud computing environments. Cluster Comput. **22**(3), 887–909 (2018). https://doi.org/10.1007/s10586-018-2879-3
20. Hunt, P., Konar, M., Junqueira, F.P., Reed, B.: ZooKeeper: wait-free coordination for internet-scale systems. In: Proceedings of the 2010 USENIX Conference on USENIX Annual Technical Conference, USENIXATC 2010, p. 11, Berkeley (2010)
21. Junqueira, F., Reed, B.: ZooKeeper: Distributed Process Coordination. O'Reilly Media, Inc., Sebastopol (2013)
22. Kehrer, S., Blochinger, W.: AUTOGENIC: automated generation of self-configuring microservices. In: Proceedings of the 8th International Conference on Cloud Computing and Services Science (CLOSER), pp. 35–46. SciTePress (2018)
23. Kehrer, S., Blochinger, W.: TOSCA-based container orchestration on Mesos. Comput. Sci. Res. and Dev. **33**(3), 305–316 (2018)
24. Kehrer, S., Blochinger, W.: Elastic parallel systems for high performance cloud computing: state-of-the-art and future directions. Parallel Process. Lett. **29**(02), 1950006 (2019)
25. Kehrer, S., Blochinger, W.: Migrating parallel applications to the cloud: assessing cloud readiness based on parallel design decisions. SICS Softw. Intensive Cyber-Phys. Syst. **34**(2), 73–84 (2019)

26. Kehrer, S., Blochinger, W.: Model-based generation of self-adaptive cloud services. In: Muñoz, V.M., Ferguson, D., Helfert, M., Pahl, C. (eds.) CLOSER 2018. CCIS, vol. 1073, pp. 40–63. Springer, Cham (2019). https://doi.org/10.1007/978-3-030-29193-8_3

27. Kehrer, S., Blochinger, W.: A survey on cloud migration strategies for high performance computing. In: Proceedings of the 13th Advanced Summer School on Service-Oriented Computing. IBM Research Division (2019)

28. Kehrer, S., Blochinger, W.: TASKWORK: a cloud-aware runtime system for elastic task-parallel HPC applications. In: Proceedings of the 9th International Conference on Cloud Computing and Services Science (CLOSER), pp. 198–209. SciTePress (2019)

29. Kehrer, S., Riebandt, F., Blochinger, W.: Container-based module isolation for cloud services. In: 2019 IEEE International Conference on Service-Oriented System Engineering (SOSE), pp. 177–186 (2019)

30. Mauch, V., Kunze, M., Hillenbrand, M.: High performance cloud computing. Future Gener. Comput. Syst. **29**(6), 1408–1416 (2013)

31. Netto, M.A.S., Calheiros, R.N., Rodrigues, E.R., Cunha, R.L.F., Buyya, R.: HPC cloud for scientific and business applications: taxonomy, vision, and research challenges. ACM Comput. Surv. (CSUR) **51**(1), 8:1–8:29 (2018)

32. Olivier, S., et al.: UTS: an unbalanced tree search benchmark. In: Almási, G., Caşcaval, C., Wu, P. (eds.) LCPC 2006. LNCS, vol. 4382, pp. 235–250. Springer, Heidelberg (2007). https://doi.org/10.1007/978-3-540-72521-3_18

33. Poldner, M., Kuchen, H.: Algorithmic skeletons for branch and bound. In: Filipe, J., Shishkov, B., Helfert, M. (eds.) ICSOFT 2006. CCIS, vol. 10, pp. 204–219. Springer, Heidelberg (2008). https://doi.org/10.1007/978-3-540-70621-2_17

34. Posner, J., Fohry, C.: Hybrid work stealing of locality-flexible and cancelable tasks for the APGAS library. J. Supercomput. **74**(4), 1435–1448 (2018)

35. Prim, R.C.: Shortest connection networks and some generalizations. Bell Syst. Tech. J. **36**(6), 1389–1401 (1957)

36. Rajan, D., Thain, D.: Designing self-tuning split-map-merge applications for high cost-efficiency in the cloud. IEEE Trans. Cloud Comput. **5**(2), 303–316 (2017)

37. Rajan, D., Canino, A., Izaguirre, J.A., Thain, D.: Converting a high performance application to an elastic cloud application. In: IEEE Third International Conference on Cloud Computing Technology and Science (CloudCom), pp. 383–390 (2011)

38. Schulz, S., Blochinger, W.: Parallel sat solving on peer-to-peer desktop grids. J. Grid Comput. **8**(3), 443–471 (2010)

39. Schulz, S., Blochinger, W., Held, M., Dangelmayr, C.: COHESION - a microkernel based desktop grid platform for irregular task-parallel applications. Future Gener. Comput. Syst. **24**(5), 354–370 (2008)

40. Sedgewick, R.: Algorithms. Addison-Wesley Publishing Co., Inc, Boston (1984)

Rule-Based Security Monitoring of Containerized Environments

Holger Gantikow[1], Christoph Reich[2(✉)], Martin Knahl[3], and Nathan Clarke[4]

[1] science + computing AG, Atos, Tübingen, Germany
gantikow@gmail.com
[2] Institute for Cloud Computing and IT Security, Furtwangen University,
Furtwangen, Germany
christoph.reich@hs-furtwangen.de
[3] Faculty of Business Information Systems, Furtwangen University, Furtwangen,
Germany
martin.knahl@hs-furtwangen.de
[4] Center for Security, Communications and Network Research, Plymouth University,
Plymouth, UK
N.Clarke@plymouth.ac.uk

Abstract. Containers have to be secured in a multi-tenant environment. To secure the use of containerized environments, the effectiveness of a rule-based security monitoring approach have been investigated.

The approach of this paper can be used to detect a wide range of potentially malicious behaviour of workloads in containerized environments. Additionally is able to monitor the actual container runtime for misuse and misconfiguration. In order to evaluate the detection capabilities of the open-source tools utilized in a container, various scenarios of undesired behaviour are closely examined. In addition, the performance overhead and functional limitations associated with workload monitoring are discussed. The proposed approach is effective in many of the scenarios examined and its performance overhead is adequate, if appropriate event filtering is applied.

Keywords: Container virtualization · Docker · Security · Monitoring · Anomalous behaviour · System call tracing

1 Introduction

Virtualization at the operating system level using containers has gained popularity over the past few years, mainly driven by the success of Docker. As all containers share the same kernel of the underlying Linux host system, a lower resource overhead compared to virtual machines can be achieved with this lightweight virtualization type [10]. This is particularly important when deploying an application and its dependencies independently of the underlying host system is at the center of interest, as it is important with micro-service architectures, for example. Containers are often used to provide basic components,

© Springer Nature Switzerland AG 2020
D. Ferguson et al. (Eds.): CLOSER 2019, CCIS 1218, pp. 66–86, 2020.
https://doi.org/10.1007/978-3-030-49432-2_4

such as web servers, databases, service discovery services or message brokers. In addition, containers offer the advantage that they can be easily integrated into suitable *Continuous Integration, Delivery and Deployment* (CI/CD) tools and pipelines and can be distributed to be run on different runtimes with the help of several standards as specified by the *Open Container Initiative* (OCI) [27,28]. Containers have also made their way into the domain of *High Performance Computing* (HPC). Containerized HPC environment have the benefits of deploying user-provided code, improving collaboration through simplified distribution, allow simple reproducibility, and have nevertheless a low performance overhead. For containers used in HPC, a number of solutions were developed, which differ significantly in terms of isolation mechanisms, that are the focus of this paper. These HPC specific solutions include *Shifter* [16], *Charliecloud* [31], and above all *Singularity* [21].

Recent surveys [34] show, that Docker deployments are still most widespread, with a share of 83% of the investigated systems. For this reason, the authors of this paper focus on the Docker container runtime, although, many aspects can be applied to other solutions as well. However the development of general purpose container runtimes is ongoing and alternatives to Docker are appearing, such as Podman [7]. Approaches that focus strongly on security, but are characterized by a much smaller deployment rate, are for example SCONE [3] and gVisor [39]. Besides of the great efforts of increasing the security of the technology, in particular Docker [6], is sometimes viewed critically. Most frequently it is listed as one of the major challenges [30], when deploying container technology in production. It should be noted that the situation has improved significantly in recent years with the addition of complementary security options. However, these are often disabled by default or being deactivated to ensure smooth operation in terms of compatibility with a wide range of applications. However a current survey indicates that 94% of the participants still have container security concerns and fear a rise of container security incidents [37].

To further increase the security level of containerized environments, this paper propose applying rule-based security monitoring to containerized environments. This paper[1] explores the suitability of the approach for detecting a) various types of undesired behaviour that might indicate misuse and attacks of workloads running *inside a container*, and b) misconfigurations and attempts to extend privileges and reduce isolation mechanisms in place at the *container runtime level*.

The rest of this paper is organized as follows: *Sect.* 2 provides a brief introduction to security mechanisms that can be applied to containerized environments. *Section* 3 describes the special monitoring characteristics regarding containerized workloads. *Section* 4 discusses related work concerning container virtualization.

---

[1] **Note:** This paper is both a revised and extended version of a previous publication [14]. The present version is characterized by an extension of the security monitoring approach beyond the containerized workloads to the container runtime itself, in order to recognize misconfigurations and attempts to weaken isolation settings or extend privileges there.

Section 5 introduces the rule-based security monitoring approach evaluated in *Sect.* 6. *Section* 7 discusses limitations of the proposed approach and future work. The paper concludes in *Sect.* 8.

2   Containers and Security

The Linux Kernel features *Control Groups* (cgroups) and *Namespaces* are used to provide resource limiting (CPU, memory, IO) and process isolation and represent the basic components of containers. These mechanisms are used to protect the host and other containers from resource starvation by one container and to provide containerized processes a confined instance of the underlying global system resources. Linux currently provides the seven namespaces *cgroups, IPC, Network, Mount, PID, User, UTS.*

Meanwhile, most container runtimes provide support for already established Linux security mechanisms that complement the essential mechanisms *cgroups* and *namespaces*. To provide *Mandatory Access Control* (MAC) *AppArmor* and *SELinux* can be utilized, which use the *Linux Security Module* (LSM) framework. These technologies provide means to limit the privileges of a process and thus mitigate harmful effects in the event of an attack.

Another Linux Kernel feature to decrease risks arising from undesired behaviour is the *Secure Computing Mode* (seccomp), which makes it possible to implement a very basic sandbox in which only a reduced number of system calls are available. In that way, individual unneeded system calls can be specifically denied. However, this requires a high degree of knowledge of the system calls required in a specific containerized workload and must therefore be adapted on a per-container basis. The default seccomp profile provided with Docker only disables 44 of over 300 system calls [8] to maintain wide application compatibility while providing a somewhat higher level of protection. This includes sane defaults that can be applied to all containers, such as blocking the *reboot* system call, which denies that a reboot of the host system can be triggered from inside a container.

There exist further *preventive security measures* to secure containerized environments, described in greater detail in an overview paper [13],

These includes at the Linux Kernel level the possibility to remap the container root user inside a container to a non-privileged user outside the container (*User Namespaces*) or to use the *Linux capabilities*, which divide the privileges of the superuser into distinct units, and can be activated or deactivated individually. However, capabilities are inferior to seccomp in terms of granularity. For example, the capability *SYS_ADMIN* bundles a very large set of functionalities, which could be used to deactivate further security measures [38].

Another important role play tools that perform static analysis for vulnerabilities on container images (*CVE scanner*), since they can be used to prevent images with vulnerable code from being available or launched in the containerized environment in the first place.

In general, the isolation provided by containers is still to considered to be weaker than that of hypervisor-based approaches. While for instance *Denial of*

Service (DoS) protection provided by cgroups is to be considered effective as long as appropriate limits are defined, better protection against *Information Leakage* is still in development.

Currently not all Linux subsystems are namespace-aware and in many locations more information about the host system can be collected than it would be possible in a virtual machine. Above all the */proc* file system should be mentioned here, because it offers many possibilities for information leakage [15], which can provide information for a tailor-made attack.

The risk of *privilege escalation*, allowing the modification of files on the host system or a container breakout with full privileges on the host system, pose a serious problem as well. This is often caused by misconfiguration, for example when containers are started with elevated privileges or reduced isolation. For example, starting a container with the *–privileged* flag causes the container to behave like a process with elevated rights outside of a container as all capabilities are granted to the container. This flag is required for special use cases, such as running Docker inside Docker and should never be used in a regular scenario [33].

Therefore a complementing preventive security measures is proposed adopting a *rule-based security monitoring*, with the aim to detect misuse and common attacks in containerized workloads, as well as misconfigurations and attempts to weaken isolation or escalate privileges at the runtime level.

For the scope of this paper, we consider some widespread attack scenarios and take advantage of containerization specific characteristics for monitoring. Use cases at the containerized workload level include unauthorized file access as it can precede information leakage, unexpected network connections and application startup, and attempted privilege escalation. Use cases monitored at the runtime level include exposure of the Docker REST API, various container lifecycle events and modifications to security and performance isolation settings.

3   Containers and Monitoring

The monitoring of containerized workloads requires a new approach, since traditional agent-based approaches cannot be applied directly. Docker Containers in particular follow the concept of application containers, which are made up of exactly one process per container. This is in contrast to the operating system containers used by LXC, which, while using the shared host kernel for all containers, start them as almost full-fledged Linux systems that behave almost like a VM and allow for several services. Adding a monitoring agent to a container would break the *single process per container* model and moreover require a modification of the container image. The need for image modification can be an unacceptable condition in environments where users demand the integrity of the images they provide. Therefore, adding a process to a container that performs the monitoring functionality *from within a container* is usually not advisable.

Also less suitable is the approach of using *sidecar containers*, which are started additionally and take over the monitoring function in a dedicated way. These would have to be started with elevated privileges and would result in increased resource consumption if a dedicated sidecar container were started for each container.

Therefore, this approach rely on one monitoring agent per host. Thus no image adjustment has to be performed, the one process per container model can be maintained and no additional overhead is caused by sidecar containers. In addition, a feature of container virtualization is beneficial: containerized workloads are transparent to the host system as regular processes. This means that a much more accurate view of the virtualized workload can be collected by the host system with containers than would be possible with VMs. Also, the collected state information can be directly assigned to the corresponding workload since there are no concurrent activities in a container that could distort the picture, as likely caused by the guest system in a VM.

As a data source, our approach relies on the system calls that are issued by the monitored containers. These get enriched with further context by the tools presented in Sect. 5. System calls have the advantage that they map exactly what a process is currently performing. In principle, further traditional performance metrics such as CPU load, memory usage, I/O throughput could be included in the system described for additional insights, but is not implemented as of now.

4   Related Work

There are several projects available to increase the security in containerized environments, that build up on top of the basic container security technologies briefly introduced in Sect. 2. The use of the complementing Linux Kernel security features Capabilities, Seccomp and MAC is being recommended by a measurement study on Container Security [23]. According to the authors, these mechanisms provide more effective measures in preventing privilege escalation than the basic isolation mechanisms (i.e. Namespaces and Cgroups) that build the foundation of containers.

The projects relying on the complementing Linux Kernel security features include policy generators such as *LicShield* [25], which generates container-specific AppArmor profiles based on a learning phase - or *SPEAKER* [22], which divides the time a container is running into different phases and assigns optimized custom seccomp profiles to them. This benefits from the fact that a service usually requires significantly fewer unique system calls after the start and initialization phase.

The exclusive use of performance metrics collected at the hypervisor level for security monitoring is discussed in approaches like [26]. His effort to detect malicious behaviour in hypervisor-based environments can be transferred to containerized environments, but does not provide the accuracy system calls can provide. Furthermore, an approach based on performance data only offers the possibility to determine *what* is happening, but not *why*, unless additional data sources can be analyzed.

The usage of system calls for detecting malicious behaviour dates back to the seminal work of Forrest. She proposed the usage of system call sequences to distinguish between normal and anomalous behaviour [12]. Concurrent processes such as background processes did however affect the detection accuracy. This situation is improved by the use of containerized workloads, since the one application per container approach significantly reduces concurrency that leads to distortion of results.

Abed [1] investigates an approach where traces collected by *strace* are used for anomaly detection without prior knowledge of the containerized application. However, mimicry attacks [17] can be used to circumvent the utilized Bag of System Calls approach.

Borhani [2] provides a paper that reports on the real-world feasibility of Falco, but focuses less on its limitations but on the *Incidence Response* aspect.

The combination of system calls to detect anomalies with different approaches from the field of Machine Learning has been investigated by a number of authors. Among them Maggi [24], who used Markov models for system calls and their arguments and [20] who extended them with system call specific context information and domain knowledge. An approach with neural networks based on convolutional and recurrent network layers is offered by Kolosnjaji [18]. His approach increased the detection rate of malware. Focus on distributed data collection and processing of large amounts of data is put by Dymshits [9], who uses an LSTM-based architecture and sequences of system call count vectors.

To the best of our knowledge, we are not aware of literature that addresses security monitoring of the container runtime interfaces.

5 Overview of Proposed System

Our approach is based on the Open Source tools *Sysdig* [36] and *Falco* [35], which will be introduced in the following briefly. They differ from other options, such as *strace* and *eBPF* [11], by native support for several container engines, including Docker, LXC and rkt. This support enables filtering of collected data based on individual containers, specific system calls, file name patterns, or network connection endpoints. The ability to use filters also significantly reduces collection and processing effort.

5.1 Sysdig

Sysdig uses two core components to implement its functionality. A kernel module (*sysdig_probe*) that uses the Linux Kernel facility *tracepoints* serves as a collection component to capture all system calls of a process (or containerized process) as *events*. These traces are then passed to a daemon that serves as the processing component.

Sysdig combines the functionality of a number of well-known analysis tools, including *strace, tcpdump* and *lsof* and combines them with transaction tracing. The combination of the individual functionality offers a considerably deeper view of the system and individual processes than would be possible with a single tool. Therefore, Sysdig is also well suited for error analysis on a system. As already mentioned, Sysdig offers various possibilities for filtering to reduce the amount of data collected. In the context we utilized it, filtering for individual system calls, arguments passed to them, such as file names, source of an event, like the container or process name, were beneficial.

5.2 Falco

Falco is best described as a *behavioural activity monitor* that complements Sysdig's system call capture functionality with the ability to detect anomalous activities based on rules. To do so it relies on the same *sysdig_probe* kernel module for system call capturing.

At the core of the applicable rules are Sysdig filter options, which are referred to as *conditions*. If a condition is evaluated as *true*, meaning that an event matched the given requirements, the event is flagged as anomalous behaviour. This presupposes, however, that exact knowledge of the desired behaviour of a container is available to be able to define the conditions that specify a violation. An anomalous activity could include starting an unauthorized process, accessing unusual paths in file systems, outgoing network connections, or attempts to modify system binaries and configuration files.

However, Falco can only detect point anomalies, i.e. single events where the described conditions are met, such as the usage of an undesired system call. The rule set currently does not provide means to allow the detection of collective anomalies or contextual anomalies where multiple conditions or additional preconditions have to be met. This limits the detection capabilities to a certain extent, as the critical examination in the evaluation will show. In addition, Falco only *detects* behavioural anomalies. A subsequent mitigation beyond logging and notification derived therefrom is currently not provided.

5.3 Architecture

The architecture (see Fig. 1) is based on the corresponding figure from [14], but has been adapted to reflect the extension of the rule-based monitoring approach to the container runtime.

As already touched, both Sysdig and Falco use the same (*sysdig_probe*) kernel module for capturing system calls. System calls are the means by which user-level processes interact with the operating system when they request services provided by it, such as opening a file or initiating a network connection. As system calls are the only entry point into the kernel to request such functionality, they are of high value when it comes to capturing the behaviour of a process. The Sysdig kernel module not only captures the identifiers of the system calls, but also the call parameters used and the return values received, which provides further possibilities for evaluation.

Sysdig is responsible for the display and processing of the recorded events. It was primarily used to create and test the Sysdig filters to be used as Falco conditions for classifying an event as anomalous behaviour. The actual classification is carried out by Falco. Falco uses rules to be created in advance (Fig. 1, *Rules*)

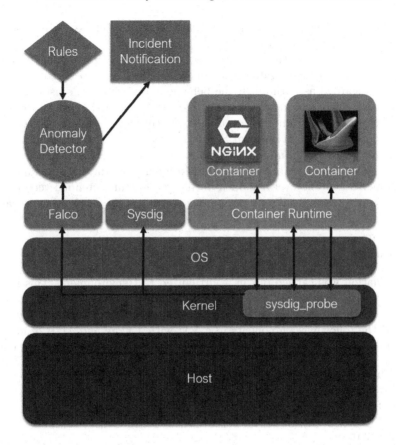

Fig. 1. Proposed rule-based security monitoring architecture, based on [14].

to decide on deviant behaviour and can perform a basic notification (Fig. 1, *Incident Notification*) using logging frameworks, plain e-mail or messengers after a rule matches.

We are currently investigating how the current *Incident Notification* can be extended to *Incident Mitigation* based on the severity of an event. One feasible and minimalistic approach would be to pause the workload, which is characterized by undesired behaviour, retrieve the full state for further analysis and to restore it after analysis if appropriate.

6   Evaluation

In order to examine the applicability of the rule-based approach, security monitoring was applied to two relevant layers in a containerized environment: a) *Container Execution Level* (Sect. 6.2), which concerns misuse and attacks occurring inside of containerized workloads, and b) *Container Runtime Level* (Sect. 6.3), takes misconfigurations and attempts to weaken isolation or extend privileges at the container runtime interface itself into consideration.

The investigation on the two layers is each divided into two phases. In the initial phase it was investigated if and how Sysdig can be used to detect the behaviour regarded as harmful. If the behaviour was detectable using a Sysdig filter, a Falco rule was derived from this filter. In the second phase, the rule was then tested for its suitability for automated detection of undesired behaviour.

We would like to point out that Sects. 6.1 *Test Environment* and 6.2 *Studied Misuse and Attacks at Container Execution Level* were incorporated unmodified from the paper [14], since both the test environment and the evaluated use cases at container execution level remained unchanged for this extended version. The same applies to Sect. 7.1 *Performance Evaluation*, as the section has remained unmodified as well.

6.1   Test Environment

The evaluation was carried out in a virtualized test environment. This means, referring to Fig. 1, that the host system is actually a virtual machine in our case. However, this has no influence on the functionality of the described approach. We used the following components in a VM with 1 Core and 4 GB of memory and did not impose additional container resource limits, unless otherwise noted:

OS: Debian GNU/Linux 9.5 (stretch)
Kernel: 4.9.0-8-amd64
Docker: Docker version 18.06.1-ce, build e68fc7a
Sysdig: 0.24.1
Falco: 0.13.0

Unless otherwise specified Debian GNU/Linux 9.5 (stretch) as container image has been used.

6.2   Studied Misuse and Attacks at Container Execution Level

In order to examine the rule-based security monitoring approach for its suitability to detect common misuses and attacks as they may occur in containerized workloads, a series of scenarios was defined and evaluated for their detectability. In the following section, these scenarios are briefly presented and the creation of the Sysdig filter and the Falco rule are presented on an exemplary basis.

Unauthorized File Access. For the test setup of the *Unauthorized File Access* we used the deliberately insecure web application *WebGoat* [29]. We used the already-available *webgoat* image on Dockerhub and evaluated the detectability of the task *Bypass a Path Based Access Control Scheme*. This represents a *directory traversal* attack where the successful attacker can access files outside the root directory of the web server. Such an attack is often used to gain access to configuration files with passwords.

The following code represents the Sysdig *condition*, which also serves as the basis for a Falco rule set.

```
container.name=webgoat
and evt.type=open
and evt.dir="<"
and fd.type=file
and not (fd.directory contains "/webapp")
```

The condition is true if the container name[2] is *webgoat* and the system call *open* accesses a file outside a path containing the string */webapp*.

The example shows that it can be easily generalized and can be used, in addition to restricting a service to its corresponding root directory, to monitor activity to *access to non-namespaced resources* or other resources that could lead to information leakage. An attempted write access, for example to directories containing system binaries, can also be detected in this way. Furthermore, the condition itself can be extended by further event parameters that have to be fulfilled, so that it is possible to detect when a process not approved for this purpose tries to access a specific device.

Start of Unauthorized Application

A similarly well generalizable test case is the detection of the *Start of Unauthorized Applications* inside a container.

```
list: authorized_processes
 items: [ps, hostname]
condition:
 container.name=debian-test
and evt.type=execve
and evt.dir="<"
and not (proc.name in (authorized_processes))
```

The condition thus recognizes the execution of programs that are not *ps* or *hostname*. This can be used to allow a container to start only its corresponding service and to log, for example, if a crypto miner or a (remote) shell is started, as might be the case in a successful remote attack. The list *authorized_processes* serves as a white list here.

Container Breakout (Using *nsenter*)

Another test case examined was the detection of certain processes that are related to specific threats, i.e. are maintained on a black list if necessary. In this example the command *nsenter* was used to run a process within the name spaces of another process, which is detectable by filtering for the system call *setns*. Although this mechanism is typically blocked from within a container by other measures, there is still a risk of misconfiguration. In addition, it can be useful to be able to log the access from the host into a container by this procedure by adapting the container identifier to *container.id = host*.

---

[2] The *container name* refers to the name of the running container instance as returned by *docker ps* and not to the image name in general. The respective container ID (*container.id*) could also be used as an alternative to the name.

Unexpected Network Connection

In order to detect if a container establishes undesired connections to the internet, for example to download malicious code for an exploit or to open a remote shell, the detectability of *Unexpected Network Connections* was also examined. This can be implemented by creating a white list with approved targets or limiting it to specific TCP ports.

Loading of Kernel Module

Although it is not possible in the default configuration to load kernel modules on the host from the container, the recent breakout from a Docker evaluation environment *Play with Docker* [33] inspired us to consider this case. As described in the referenced case, this can lead to a privilege escalation with full administrative privileges on the host and thus control over additional containers.

Denial of Service (DoS)

Even though (if applied) cgroups can prevent a resource starvation of the host and other containers in terms of CPU shares and memory, there is the possibility, depending on the configuration, to fill up shared file systems, which is why this test case had to be investigated.

Buffer Overflow

The last test case examined was whether it is in principle possible to detect buffer overflows using our rule-based approach. Abusing a buffer overflow is a common security exploit, so that memory areas with executable code are overwritten with malicious code, which can be the basis for an attack.

6.3   Security Monitoring at Container Runtime Level

Inspired by attacks made possible by misconfigurations that expose the Docker REST API to the Internet [5], the previous work of monitoring container-ized workloads was extended to also monitor the container runtime/engine for unwanted behaviour. This approach is also in line with the recommendations of NIST, which recommends to examine the container runtime more closely for risks [32]. The advantage of monitoring on this layer is that these activities are independent of the workload in the containers, i.e. no prior knowledge is required. Thus the rules can be activated directly on a large number of hosts in a containerized environment.

We chose three areas of priority for the monitoring of the container runtime: a) Monitoring the access to the *Docker REST API*, with the focus of detect-ing misconfigurations that expose the API over network. Monitoring the Docker *command-line interface* (CLI) (*docker ** commands) for b) *container lifecycle events* and c) the modification of *container security settings*. Scenarios b) and c) are particularly relevant for environments in which users, e.g. members of the docker group, have direct access to the *docker* CLI without *role-based access control* (RBAC) mechanisms or restrictive wrappers around the CLI being in place. In particular, c) can be misused in various ways to extend privileges on the host to a level similar to *root* access and reduce security and performance isolation. We have identified a number of misuse scenarios that are briefly presented below.

Docker REST API

Since Docker 0.5.2 the REST API endpoint, which is used by the Docker CLI to interact with the Docker Engine, switched from a (locally bound) TCP socket to a UNIX socket, where access is controlled by the traditional UNIX permissions. The configuration option to globally expose the REST API over HTTP(S) can still be enabled. As this may lead to an attacker taking over the Docker Host, the hosts that are able to connect should be restricted to trusted hosts only and the API endpoints should be secured with HTTPS and certificates. We identified the following undesired events:

Exposure of API. Since exposure of the Docker REST API endpoint over the network can have high security implications, monitoring for such misconfigurations should be performed. The indicator used herefore is a process binding to port TCP/2375 (HTTP) or TCP/2376 (HTTPS).

Connection to API. In addition to monitoring for exposure, it should also be monitored whether connections are established to these ports. This is important, if the monitoring was started after the exposure of the API endpoints.

Container Lifecycle Events

The Container Lifecycle Events offer a variety of options that are well-suited to be monitored. We have grouped the commands according to their functionality and their potential for misuse, which we will describe briefly below.

Typical Lifecycle Events. Commands in this group represent typical lifecycle commands (*pull, run, exec, pause, unpause, start, stop, kill*), which for instance are used to download images or start a container. These commands usually have no security-critical context, but should be logged for auditing reasons. Especially if *exec* is used to execute commands inside an already running container, as this indicates administrative intervention.

Circumvention of Registries. On a production system, it is unlikely if an image is not downloaded from an image registry that might contain curated images, but is loaded locally from the file system. In such a situation, this could mean that an attacker is trying to launch an image that he has previously manually downloaded.

Publication of Images. The same level of unlikelihood applies to saving, exporting or uploading an image. Such events appear out of place on a production system and could indicate that an attacker tries to export container images and extract them.

Exposure of Services. In an environment where containers provide network accessible services, publishing a service from the container is a valid intent. In environments where this is not the case, the event when container ports are exposed to the host could indicate misuse, such as to provide access for third parties.

Container Security Settings

Unrestricted access to the Docker CLI provides a variety of controls that may allow a user to run a container with privileges very close to an administrative account on the host system. Alternatively, restrictions can be modified to weaken the default isolation of a container. We have identified a number of attack scenarios that should be monitored accordingly.

Usage of Additional Host Resources. It is possible to pass host resources into the container. These can be local file system directories, complete devices, including GPUs. While there are use cases where this can be a practical approach, such an event can have far-reaching security implications, as this can provide privileged access to the resource for the user starting a container this way.

Weakening of DoS Protection. When starting a container, a large number of performance limits can be imposed, such as limits for CPU and memory consumption. There are also additional settings that may be used to protect against fork bombs (PID limit) or the *Out of Memory* (OOM) killer. According to [4], the activation of these limits is a suitable mean to ward off the effects of an attempted DoS through a container. Consequently, modifications to these settings must be viewed critically. In the default setting, no resource limits are active. However, in production operation such limits should be applied.

Modification of Namespaces. An adjustment of the namespace isolation can lead to reduction of the default isolation, thus reduced security. Especially if a namespace is set to =*host*, as this results in a sharing of the corresponding host namespace with the container. Rare occasions where this would be acceptable include monitoring containers that require an unrestricted system view.

Extension of Privileges. The strongest possibility to extend the privileges through a container is the option of starting a container in *privileged* mode. This results in the container receiving the full set of capabilities and also cgroups-based limitations not being applied. This results in a containerized process that has at least the same privileges as if run directly on host. As the security implications are severe (see [33]) this behaviour is only justified in very rare cases, such as requiring *Docker in Docker* or as a *temporary* workaround.

Modification of Security Options. The –*security-opt* setting is one of the most powerful controls as it allows to carry out adjustments on a variety of security tools that were integrated later, This flag is used to modify SELinux settings, specify the AppArmor profile to be applied, grant the gaining of new privileges and also specify which seccomp profile to use or disable seccomp protection altogether. Modifications made here should therefore be examined with particular caution.

Modification of Performance Restrictions. In addition to the DoS protection settings, there are other settings to distribute the host's capacity between multiple containers. These include measures to limit the IO throughput of devices. Manual adjustments should be examined critically.

6.4   Results

Table 1 summarizes the detectability of the scenarios presented in Sect. 6.2 regarding *Misuse and Attacks at Container Execution Level*. For each scenario it is shown whether a filter for general detection can be created with Sysdig, whether a automated detection can be implemented with Falco, and what can be used as an indicator of the undesired behaviour.

Table 1. Summary of the detectability of various misuse and attack scenarios using Sysdig and Falco, based on [14].

Scenario	Sysdig	Falco	Indicator
Unauthorized File Access	Yes	Yes	Violation of white list with authorized files and directories
Start of Unauthorized Applications	Yes	Yes	Violation of white list with authorized application names
Container Breakout	Yes	Yes	Black list - *nsenter* called - or violation of white list
Unexpected Network Connection	Yes	Yes	Violation of white list with authorized communication partners
Loading of Kernel Module	Yes	Yes	Black list - *insmod* called - or violation of white list
Denial of Service	Yes	No	Frequency of occurrences
Buffer Overflow	No	No	Not applicable

As the table shows, it is possible to create a rule for Falco in almost all of the cases investigated, if the event can be detected by a Sysdig filter. Many of the examined cases can be restricted in terms of examined objects through the use of a white list or black list based approach. This is possible for example with the detection of non-authorized file access, the start of a non-authorized application - or similar, easily derivable scenarios. However, this requires an exact knowledge of the workload to be examined and an adjustment of the lists on a per image basis.

Since Falco does not currently provide support for the occurrence frequency of an event, it is currently not possible to use Falco for the detection of DoS attacks. One-time access to a service itself can be captured by Sysdig - and thus also converted into a Falco condition. However, the frequency of events cannot be taken into account.

The recognition of a buffer overflow is also not feasible as intended, since it can normally also not be recognized by static analysis. The execution of a particular exploit that can trigger a buffer overflow could in principle be detected by relying on the system calls and their respective order. However, Falco can only detect anomalies based on a single system call, not on their sequence in a particular order. In addition, the approach would not be generalizable and remain tied to a specific exploit. Blocking the execution of an exploit using the process identifier or binary name is not worth the effort, as this can be circumvented by renaming it. The exclusive operation of approved applications and the detection of unapproved network lines is more effective here.

Tables 2, 3, 4 present the results of the evaluation of *Security Monitoring at container runtime level*, broken down into the three areas, as of Sect. 6.3. The tables list in each case the title of the scenario, the feasibility of detection with Sysdig and Falco, as well as the respective indicators for the occurrence of the threat.

The results show a distinct picture. In all three areas it is possible to detect the corresponding events through Sysdig filters with very little effort and to convert them into corresponding Falco rules, which allow for an automated monitoring. In most cases it is sufficient to filter the call of the Docker CLI for the corresponding sub command or command line parameters. The search terms used are specified in the column of the respective scenario as *indicator*.

Table 2. Summary of the detectability of exposure of and connections to the *Docker REST API* using Sysdig and Falco.

Scenario	Sysdig	Falco	Indicator
Exposure of API	Yes	Yes	**bind()** to TCP/2375 or TCP/2376
Connection to API	Yes	Yes	Connection to TCP/2375 or TCP/2376

Table 3. Summary of the detectability of various *Docker Lifecycle Events* using Sysdig and Falco.

Scenario	Sysdig	Falco	Indicator
Typical Lifecycle Events	Yes	Yes	`pull, run, exec, pause, unpause, start, stop, kill`
Circumvention of Registries	Yes	Yes	`import, load`
Publication of Images	Yes	Yes	`export, save, push`
Exposure of Services	Yes	Yes	`--publish , -p, --publish-all , -P`

Table 4. Summary of the detectability of modifications to *Docker Security Settings* using Sysdig and Falco.

Scenario	Sysdig	Falco	Indicator
Usage of Additional Host Resources	Yes	Yes	`--mount, -v, --volume, --device, --gpu`
Weakening of DoS Protection	Yes	Yes	`-m, --memory, -c, --cpu, --blkio-, --device-, --pids-limit, --ulimit --oom-kill-disable`
Modification of Namespaces	Yes	Yes	`--ipc, --network, --pid, --userns, --uts`
Extension of Privileges	Yes	Yes	`--privileged mode, --cap-add`
Modification of Security Options	Yes	Yes	`--security-opt`
Modification of Performance Restrictions	Yes	Yes	`*iops, *bps`

The proposed approach for monitoring on the container runtime layer offers the possibility to capture a wide range of potentially malicious behaviour with limited effort. Even if the lifecycle commands are rather logged for audit purposes, the method is useful to get an overview of events in the environment, especially if users are granted interactive access to the Docker CLI. As mentioned before, it is possible to roll out identical rule sets to monitor the runtime layer to a large number of container hosts in a containerized environment without having to know about the workloads running inside the containers. However, one should think about how to classify the severity of each event[3], since pausing a container is considered much less critical than starting a privileged container.

7 Discussion

Our research has shown that there are a number of limitations in the tools used that should not go unmentioned. For example, Falco does not support DoS detection because the rules used do not support the frequency of occurrence of an event. Here one would wish for a threshold value to be adjustable in the rules, so that notifications take place only if an event occurred n times during a specific time interval.

Falco's rules also do not allow the integration of load sensors, so that for example a notification could be given when certain load thresholds have been reached, or these could be used as a decision-making assistance for alleged false positives.

---

[3] Currently Falco provides the priority categories *emergency, alert, critical, error, warning, notice, informational, debug.*

It has been shown that profound knowledge about the properties and requirements of a containerized application is almost mandatory for the creation of rules. Although there are certainly generalizable rules, the example of the web application (see Sect. 6.2) shows that applications regularly have a different locations where they keep their data. Other individual properties include the name of the service to be run in the container, so that all other applications can be blocked, or which network connections are necessary. Depending on the environment, this may not be a concern, for example, if an environment consists of a large number of containers, all of which are started from the same image. In this case, the appropriate rule set can be applied to all of the running containers and be maintained on based on the shared image. In more individual environments, or environments in which users may use containers for interactive work, the configuration effort is significantly higher.

The white/black list approach also has limitations, i.e. when an attacker knows the content of the lists and can prepare himself accordingly. Especially file name-based approaches can be bypassed by renaming files easily.

However, the tools used are characterized by the fact that they can also be applied to other container runtimes. Although we have only tested the use with Docker, rules for monitoring containers can be applied to containers started with other runtimes. For the monitoring of the Runtime CLI a higher adaptation effort is necessary, as the rules utilized where Docker CLI specific.

Table 5. Sysdig overhead for various statistics of sysbench-fileio benchmark in comparison to baseline run without Sysdig.

Sysbench-fileio statistic	Sysdig with full capture	Sysdig with filter
Operations performed (total)	1,81%	0,00%
Requests/sec executed	4,72%	2,97%
Total number of events	4,72%	2,97%
Total time taken by event execution	5,48%	0,67%
Per-request statistics: "avg" in ms	10,53%	3,51%
Average Overhead	5,45%	2,02%

7.1 Performance Evaluation

To determine the performance overhead caused by security monitoring, we made use of a traditional benchmark tool: *Sysbench* [19], of which we created a containerized version. To exclude buffering effects when using the filesystem-level benchmark *fileio* included with Sysbench, we used it with a test file four times the amount of the available memory. During each 5 min run of the benchmark a corresponding capture file was created with Sysdig and afterwards several performance indicators of the *sysbench-fileio* run were evaluated.

In order to be able to rate how high the benefit of using filters is a) a *full capture* and b) a capture with an active *filter* was created, which limited the recording to the *open()* system call, as one would use if one only wanted to log file accesses of a container. As baseline served measurements of the *sysbench-fileio* without activated Sysdig capturing and all benchmark runs (deactivated Sysdig, Sysdig with full capture, Sysdig with filter) were averaged over three runs each. All runs were performed in the same virtual test environment described in Sect. 6.1.

It was observed that over several measurements the average overhead in case a) (full capture) was 5,45%, whereas the use of the filter reduced the overhead in case b) to 2,02%. The use of the filter also affected the size of the capture file. In b) only 270 events needed to be recorded, resulting in a 1,2 MB trace file, whereas the unfiltered case a) logged 3.270.522 events in a 270 MB file on average. This implies, that if possible, filters should be activated for data and overhead reduction. The overhead, broken down by individual *sysbench-fileio statistic*, is shown in Table 5.

8   Conclusions

The investigated approach has shown the general applicability of a rule-based approach for monitoring containerized environments. The focus was on the monitoring of workloads running in containers and of the interfaces of the Docker Container Runtime. It has been shown that the approach can detect a variety of undesired behaviour with a low performance overhead. In addition, the creation of an appropriate set of rules, especially for the monitoring of commands sent via the CLI, can be done with moderate effort.

However, when monitoring containerized workloads, automated rule creation should be performed, since the requirements typically differ from workload to workload, i.e. in most cases they can only be generalized on a per-image basis. In cases where it is not possible to create a corresponding set of rules, one should consider the use of a behaviour monitor that compares the current behaviour against a stored reference model. However, this approach would also require a certain amount of time for the creation of a behaviour model, so that this approach cannot be applied directly as well.

Scenarios that are not yet covered should also be considered, e.g. if commands such as *nsenter* or the associated system call *setns)* can be used to execute commands within a running container by bypassing *docker exec* since its use is monitored.

It is planned that future work will address security monitoring of distributed workloads, where shared workloads strongly interact across host boundaries. Sysdig and Falco already offer corresponding interfaces that cover container schedulers like Kubernetes. We are also interested in further automating rule generation and introducing incident mitigation beyond notification.

References

1. Abed, A.S., Clancy, T.C., Levy, D.S.: Applying bag of system calls for anomalous behavior detection of applications in linux containers. In: 2015 IEEE Globecom Workshops, GC Workshops 2015 - Proceedings (2015). https://doi.org/10.1109/GLOCOMW.2015.7414047
2. Borhani, A.: Anomaly detection, alerting, and incident response for containers. SANS Institute InfoSec Reading Room (GIAC GCIH Gold Certification) (2017)
3. Arnautov, S., et al.: SCONE: secure linux containers with intel SGX. In: Osdi, pp. 689–704 (2016). https://doi.org/10.5281/ZENODO.163059
4. Chelladhurai, J., Chelliah, P.R., Kumar, S.A.: Securing docker containers from Denial of Service (DoS) attacks. In: Proceedings - 2016 IEEE International Conference on Services Computing, SCC 2016, pp. 856–859 (2016). https://doi.org/10.1109/SCC.2016.123
5. Chikvashvili, Y.: Cryptocurrency miners abusing containers: anatomy of an (Attempted) attack (2019). https://blog.aquasec.com/cryptocurrency-miners-abusing-containers-anatomy-of-an-attempted-attack. Accessed 31 July 2019
6. Combe, T., Martin, A., Di Pietro, R.: To docker or not to docker: a security perspective. IEEE Cloud Comput. 3(5), 54–62 (2016). https://doi.org/10.1109/MCC.2016.100
7. Containers Organization: Podman (2019).https://podman.io/. Accessed 31 July 2019
8. Docker Inc.: Seccomp security profiles for Docker (2019). https://docs.docker.com/engine/security/seccomp/. Accessed 31 July 2019
9. Dymshits, M., Myara, B., Tolpin, D.: Process monitoring on sequences of system call count vectors. In: Proceedings - International Carnahan Conference on Security Technology 2017-October, pp. 1–5 (2017). https://doi.org/10.1109/CCST.2017.8167792
10. Felter, W., Ferreira, A., Rajamony, R., Rubio, J.: An updated performance comparison of virtual machines and linux containers. In: 2015 IEEE International Symposium on Performance Analysis of Systems and Software (ISPASS), pp. 171–172, March 2015. https://doi.org/10.1109/ISPASS.2015.7095802
11. Fleming, M.: A thorough introduction to EBPF (2017). https://lwn.net/Articles/740157/. Accessed 14 Jan 2019
12. Forrest, S., Hofmeyr, S., Somayaji, A., Longstaff, T.: A sense of self for Unix processes. In: Proceedings 1996 IEEE Symposium on Security and Privacy, pp. 120–128 (1996). https://doi.org/10.1109/SECPRI.1996.502675. http://ieeexplore.ieee.org/document/502675/
13. Gantikow, H., Reich, C., Knahl, M., Clarke, N.: Providing security in container-based HPC runtime environments. In: Taufer, M., Mohr, B., Kunkel, J.M. (eds.) ISC High Performance 2016. LNCS, vol. 9945, pp. 685–695. Springer, Cham (2016). https://doi.org/10.1007/978-3-319-46079-6_48
14. Gantikow, H., Reich, C., Knahl, M., Clarke, N.: Rule-based security monitoring of containerized workloads. In: Proceedings of the 9th International Conference on Cloud Computing and Services Science, Heraklion, Crete - Greece, pp. 543–550 (2019). https://doi.org/10.5220/0007770005430550
15. Gao, X., Gu, Z., Kayaalp, M., Pendarakis, D., Wang, H.: ContainerLeaks: emerging security threats of information leakages in container clouds. In: Proceedings - 47th Annual IEEE/IFIP International Conference on Dependable Systems and Networks, DSN 2017, pp. 237–248 (2017). https://doi.org/10.1109/DSN.2017.49

16. Jacobsen, D.M., Canon, R.S.: Contain this, unleashing docker for HPC. Cray User Group 2015, p. 14 (2015). https://www.nersc.gov/assets/Uploads/cug2015udi.pdf
17. Kang, D.K., Fuller, D., Honavar, V.: Learning classifiers for misuse detection using a bag of system calls representation. In: Proceedings of the 2005 IEEE Workshop on Information Assurance and Security United States Military Academy, West Point, NY, pp. 511–516 (2005)
18. Kolosnjaji, B., Zarras, A., Webster, G., Eckert, C.: Deep learning for classification of malware system call sequences. In: Kang, B.H., Bai, Q. (eds.) AI 2016. LNCS (LNAI), vol. 9992, pp. 137–149. Springer, Cham (2016). https://doi.org/10.1007/978-3-319-50127-7_11
19. Kopytov, A.: Sysbench: scriptable database and system performance benchmark (2019). https://github.com/akopytov/sysbench. Accessed 14 Jan 2019
20. Koucham, O., Rachidi, T., Assem, N.: Host intrusion detection using system call argument-based clustering combined with Bayesian classification. In: IntelliSys 2015 - Proceedings of 2015 SAI Intelligent Systems Conference, pp. 1010–1016 (2015). https://doi.org/10.1109/IntelliSys.2015.7361267
21. Kurtzer, G.M., Sochat, V., Bauer, M.W., Favre, T., Capota, M., Chakravarty, M.: Singularity: scientific containers for mobility of compute. Plos One **12**(5), e0177459 (2017). https://doi.org/10.1371/journal.pone.0177459
22. Lei, L., et al.: SPEAKER: split-phase execution of application containers. In: Polychronakis, M., Meier, M. (eds.) DIMVA 2017. LNCS, vol. 10327, pp. 230–251. Springer, Cham (2017). https://doi.org/10.1007/978-3-319-60876-1_11
23. Lin, X., Lei, L., Wang, Y., Jing, J., Sun, K., Zhou, Q.: A measurement study on linux container security. In: 2018 Annual Computer Security Applications Conference (ACSAC 2018), pp. 418–429. ACM, New York (2018). https://doi.org/10.1145/3274694.3274720
24. Maggi, F., Matteucci, M., Zanero, S.: Detecting intrusions through system call sequence and argument analysis. IEEE Trans. Dependable Secure Comput. **7**(4), 381–395 (2010). https://doi.org/10.1109/TDSC.2008.69
25. Mattetti, M., Shulman-Peleg, A., Allouche, Y., Corradi, A., Dolev, S., Foschini, L.: Securing the infrastructure and the workloads of linux containers. In: 2015 IEEE Conference on Communications and Network Security, CNS 2015 (Spc), pp. 559–567 (2015). https://doi.org/10.1109/CNS.2015.7346869
26. Nikolai, J.: Hypervisor-based cloud intrusion detection system. In: 2014 International Conference on Computing, Networking and Communications (ICNC) (2014). https://doi.org/10.1109/ICCNC.2014.6785472
27. Open Container Initiative: OCI Image Format Specification vol 1.0.0. Technical report (2017). https://github.com/opencontainers/image-spec/releases/tag/v1.0.0
28. Open Container Initiative: OCI Runtime Specification vol 1.0.0. Technical report (2017). https://github.com/opencontainers/runtime-spec/releases/tag/v1.0.0
29. OWASP: Owasp webgoat project (2018). https://www.owasp.org/index.php/Category:OWASP_WebGoat_Project. Accessed 14 Jan 2019
30. Portworx: 2018 container adoption survey. Technical report, December 2018. https://portworx.com/wp-content/uploads/2018/12/Portworx-Container-Adoption-Survey-Report-2018.pdf
31. Priedhorsky, R., Randles, T.C., Randles, T.: Charliecloud: unprivileged containers for user-defined software stacks in HPC. In: SC17: International Conference for High Performance Computing, Networking, Storage and Analysis, vol. 17, pp. 1–10 (2017). https://doi.org/10.1145/3126908.3126925. http://permalink.lanl.gov/object/tr?what=info:lanl-repo/lareport/LA-UR-16-22370

32. Souppaya, M., Morello, J., Scarfone, K.: Application container security guide. NIST Special Publication 800-190 (2017). https://doi.org/10.6028/NIST.SP.800-190. https://nvlpubs.nist.gov/nistpubs/SpecialPublications/NIST.SP.800-190.pdf
33. Stoler, N.: How i hacked play-with-docker and remotely ran code on the host (2019). https://www.cyberark.com/threat-research-blog/how-i-hacked-play-with-docker-and-remotely-ran-code-on-the-host/. Accessed 14 Jan 2019
34. Sysdig: Docker usage report 2018 - An inside look at shifting container usage trends (2018). https://sysdig.com/blog/2018-docker-usage-report/
35. Sysdig: Sysdig falco: behavioral activity monitoring with container support (2019). https://github.com/draios/oss-falco. Accessed 14 Jan 2019
36. Sysdig: Linux system exploration and troubleshooting tool with first class support for containers (2019). https://github.com/draios/sysdig. Accessed 14 Jan 2019
37. Tripwire: State of container security report. Technical report, January 2019. https://www.tripwire.com/solutions/devops/tripwire-dimensional-research-state-of-container-security-report-register/
38. Walsh, D.: Container tidbits: adding capabilities to a container (2016). https://rhelblog.redhat.com/2016/11/30/container-tidbits-adding-capabilities-to-a-container/. Accessed 10 Jan 2019
39. Young, E.G., Zhu, P., Caraza-Harter, T., Arpaci-Dusseau, A.C., Arpaci-Dusseau, R.H.: The true cost of containing: a gVisor case study. In: Proceedings of the 11th USENIX Conference on Hot Topics in Cloud Computing, HotCloud 2019, p. 16. USENIX Association, Berkeley (2019). http://dl.acm.org/citation.cfm?id=3357034.3357054

A Feasibility Study of an Agile and Data-Centric Method for Prototyping Services Based on Open Transport Data

Nicolas Ferry[(✉)], Aida Omerovic, and Marit Kjøsnes Natvig

SINTEF, Trondheim, Norway
{nicolas.ferry,aida.omerovic,Marit.K.Natvig}@sintef.no

Abstract. Data under open licenses and in reusable formats, often referred to as "open data", is increasingly being made accessible by both public and private actors. Government institutions, municipalities, private companies and entrepreneurs are among the stakeholders either having visions of new open data-based services, or just looking for new ideas on potential innovations based on open data. It is, however, in both cases, often unclear to the service developers how the open data actually can be utilized. A main reason is that the data needs to be retrieved from multiple sources, understood, quality checked and processed. While gaining insights on possible services that can be created on the top of open data, a service developer has to undergo an iterative "trying and failing" exercise of service prototyping. In order to be practically feasible, such a process needs to be agile and efficient. Open data from the transport sector is in this study particularly focused on and used as a case. The open transport data are characterized by many challenges common for open data in general, but also a few specific ones. One of those challenges is the need for combining (often real-time) data from rather many sources in order to create a new service. This paper is an extension of our earlier research, which introduced a novel data-centric and agile approach to early service prototyping based on open transport data. In particular, we present a refinement of the initial approach and its evaluation in a significantly extended trial and discussion about the lessons learned from it.

Keywords: Service prototyping · Open transport data · DevOps

1 Introduction

During the past several years, increasingly many private and public actors all over the world have been actively releasing data under open licenses and often in reusable formats [2]. The goal is to foster creation of new and innovative digital services. The innovation and economic potential is becoming more and more visible, as documented by a European study [4], thus attracting governments, municipalities, companies and entrepreneurs to take part in the ecosystem of the data provision and creation of innovations on the top of open data. Once the data are released and announced through a public catalogue, a developer needs to understand its format and content, evaluate its quality and then (at least partially) create a new service through several iterations. This

© Springer Nature Switzerland AG 2020
D. Ferguson et al. (Eds.): CLOSER 2019, CCIS 1218, pp. 87–100, 2020.
https://doi.org/10.1007/978-3-030-49432-2_5

process is necessary in order to try out the ideas and evaluate feasibility of the envisioned service. Such a creative process of "trying and failing" to develop new services needs to be highly agile and efficient. The process is however slowed down since the data openly available online frequently consist of rather unstructured information [10], which makes service prototyping difficult and expensive [16]. It is also a challenge that the quality of the dataset descriptions and the meta data announced might not be good enough to give the developer with the information needed [3,12].

This paper is an extension of our earlier research [6], which introduced a novel data-centric and agile approach to early service prototyping based on open transport data. In particular, we present a refinement of the initial approach and its evaluation in a significantly extended trial and discussion about the lessons learned from it

The approach is novel in the sense that it is data-centric and focuses on how to develop an idea into a prototype rather than how to implement a solution. The approach is motivated by the identified challenges as well as experiences gained from the "Open Transport Data"[1] (OTD) research and innovation project, as well as from applying the data which has been harvested into an open catalogue by the project. We exemplify our approach on an open transport data service and discuss the lessons learned so far. We also outline a roadmap for the forthcoming research towards a comprehensive approach for agile prototyping of open transport data-based services.

Section 2 discusses the challenges related to the use of open data. Section 3 gives an overview of the approach. Section 4 reports on trial of the approach conducted by prototyping a service based on real-life open transport data, and Sect. 5 summarizes the related works, the lessons learned in this trial, and discusses the threats to validity of the results. We also propose the priorities for future work which aims to provide a comprehensive approach for agile prototyping of open transport data-based services.

The work builds upon and is an extension of our earlier research [6]. Parts of this paper are therefore re-used from the publication of the previous research, in order to ensure completeness and readability of this publication. Main extensions of this paper include: (i) a description of how we identified the main challenges that a method for service prototyping based on open data should address (Sect. 2), (ii) an extension of the state of the art (see Sect. 5), (iii) a refinement of the initial approach (see Sect. 3), (iv) a significant extension of the trial (see Sect. 4), and (v) a detailed elaboration of the experiences and lessons learned from the trial (see Sect. 5).

2   Challenges

We have through the above mentioned OTD project, which gathers some of the major public and private actors from the transport sector in Norway, addressed service prototyping in the context of open data from the transport domain. The project has conducted several use cases, and the insights from those were used to design a survey and semi-structured interviews, in order to identify the main challenges that a method for service prototyping should address. The survey was distributed through several channels, the main of which were the network members of "Intelligent Transport Systems"

---

[1] https://www.sintef.no/en/open-transport-data/.

(ITS) Norway (gathering organisations and companies in the transport sector); a meetup group on open data in Oslo region in Norway; participants at hackathons; and the networks of governmental organisations providing open data, among others the Norwegian Public Road Administration and the Norwegian Mapping Authority. Google forms were used for all channels except in interaction with the participants at hackathons. During the hackatons, the respondents received a paper version of the survey.

To get more in-depth details on the use of open data and related challenges, the overall questions asked that triggered the responses were:

1. What is your background with respect to education?
2. What is your experience with use of open data?
3. Which data have you used?
4. Which data have you searched for, but not been able to find?
5. What are the most important problems you have experienced regarding use of open data?
6. How has the use of open data influenced product and functionality ideas?

In addition, the researchers also carried out semi structured interviews with participants at the hackathons to enable the respondents to provide additional information. During the interviews, one researcher asked the questions while another one observed, recorded the interview and addressed missing issues. Some of the interviews were also carried out via telephone upon agreements at the hackathons.

The following list includes the main challenges that have been identified, *i.e.*, the challenges that a developer faces when prototyping services on the top of open data:

- Discovery of relevant datasets through metadata search and visualisation of datasets to better understand the data content. Public catalogues and data portals are still not comprehensive and metadata for describing the contents are only to a limited degree standardized and available.
- Understanding and using varying application programming interfaces (APIs) for data retrieval. Even though API description standards exist (*e.g.*, OpenAPI), they are not commonly used, and APIs are not documented in a standardised way.
- Combining multiple sources of open data, in order to create value added services. Travel planners will for example need information on addresses, stop points, route plans and position data from several transport service operators, maps, etc.
- Accessing real-time data from IoT and sensors. The amount of such data will increase, and new services will use real-time data streams on, for example, the conditions at locations and the movement of people, vehicles and goods.
- Handling of large volumes of data, which is possibly unstructured.
- Handling proprietary data formats. For example, standards exist for data on public transport, but for other transport types (*e.g.*, car sharing, city bikes, ride sharing) there are no standards, and proprietary data formats are used.
- Understanding the data. In many cases, domain knowledge is required in order to sufficiently understand the data contents. This is a challenge due to lack of documentation and metadata, as described above.

Clearly, these characteristics impose requirements to the approach followed for prototyping the services based on open transport data. Our goal is that a service developer (*e.g.*, an entrepreneur with limited programming background) can incrementally explore the possibilities and ideas while creating a service prototype. To that end, the approach has to be highly iterative, comprehensible to non-expert developers and cost-efficient. To the best of our knowledge regarding state of the art (summarized in Sect. 3), there is currently no approach which sufficiently meets the above mentioned needs and challenges. In particular, the existing approaches fail to be sufficiently agile, scalable and comprehensible in order to fit for gradual prototyping through consolidation of many data sources through multiple iterations.

3   Overview of the Approach

In this section we introduce our approach for the iterative prototyping of services based on open data. We propose a seven-step prototyping process for the development of services based on open transport data, as depicted in Fig. 1.

Fig. 1. Data oriented early prototyping process [6].

In the following we describe the details of each of the steps depicted in Figure 1. Some of the steps have been extended with additional information compared to [6].

1. **Search Data:** The developer needs to identify the data sources and datasets which the forthcoming prototyping iteration will be based upon. Catalogue, data repositories, and search engines can help finding the relevant datasets. When datasets are found, the developer wants to quickly judge the relevance of the dataset. However, this task can be tedious as datasets typically lack proper description and meta-data

and since open data is typically released with terminologies and structures dependent on the domain they originate from. Due to its open nature, the data is not prepared for a specific application and can be used in many different contexts which were not necessarily anticipated at release time. In addition, as stated in [13]: "*it can be difficult to determine not only the source of the dataset that has the information that you are looking for, but also the veracity or provenance of that information*".

2. **Access and Understand Data:** Once found, the data needs to be accessed and understood by the developers. For this, they typically need to manipulate and test the data. Indeed, in many cases, only looking at the documentation of the data (when available) is not enough, as documentation typically fails to represent aspects such as the missing data, data accuracy, etc. This process consists first in understanding how the identified datasets or data streams can be accessed, second in actually accessing the data, and finally in looking at different samples of the data in order to properly understand its contents, structure, etc. These activities are often done in an ad-hoc manner as the APIs to retrieve data are typically not following API description standards.

3. **Identify Added Value:** From this stage, the developer can identify the potential usage area for the data that will enable the creation of new added value services. This step requires looking into the details of the data in order to understand its contents and to identify which parts of it are relevant for our service. It is important at this stage to evaluate several samples of data in order to establish the overall quality of the data - *e.g.*, data accuracy and the missing data.

4. **Specify Capabilities:** At this stage, the developer can start specifying the features that will be offered by the prototype. This activity will be affected by the availability of data and its identified added value.

5. **Prepare Data:** Once the capabilities of the service are identified, and before its implementation, the developers need to manage and prepare the data for further analysis and processing as part of the service business logic. This includes the following activities: data characterization, data organization, data filtering, restructuring and compression. At the end of this stage, the data should be ready to be consumed by the business logic of the service. In addition, it should fit its needs and requirements.

6. **Prototype Service:** This stage consists in the actual development, delivery and deployment of a prototype that implements the business logic of the service specified at step 4.

7. **Identify Missing Data:** At the end of a prototyping iteration, once a new set of features have been added, the developer identifies which features should be added to the prototype in the forthcoming iteration, as well as which data are required.

In case additional data is required to deliver the service with the desired capabilities, developers can enter a new iteration of the prototyping process. If not, the prototype can then be used in other stages of the product life cycle such as code and deployment stages, for instance when part of its implementation needs to be re-developed to meet the production requirements (*e.g.*, specific framework needs to be used), or to the testing stage.

4 Trial of the Approach

We tried out our approach in the context of the OTD project, where we developed a service aiming at *(i)* supporting user (the citizens) in planning public transport trips in Oslo, as well as *(ii)* counting all the ongoing deviations within the public transport (*e.g.,* tram delays, problems with a bus). More precisely, this service first loads a map of Oslo and displays all the stops in the city. A user can then plan a travel by clicking on two of these stops. A route, including details about the stops, is then proposed to the user as a path on the map (see Fig. 2). In addition, the service displays statistics about the number of deviations in the city. The scope of the trial were open data available for the public transportation within the city of Oslo, Norway.

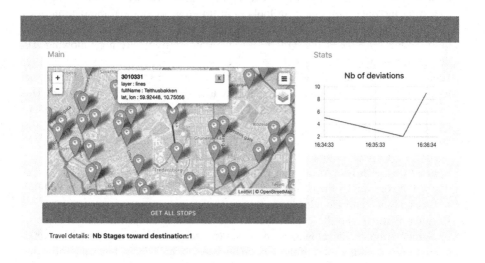

Fig. 2. A Simple Travel Planner as a trial of the approach.

During the trial we instantiated all the steps of the approach presented in Sect. 3. In the following, as described in [6], we recall the activities we performed in each of the steps.

Search Data. We first searched for data in the Open Transport Data CKAN catalogue[2] (see Fig. 3) using "transport" and "Oslo" as keywords but we could not find relevant data. By contrast, when using the "Ruter" keyword (Ruter is the public transport authority for Oslo), we found the API of a "route planning" service.

Access and Understand Data. We first selected the Ruter Sirisx API[3] which allowed us to retrieve, for one stop (*i.e.,* buses, tram, and subway stops), the list of ongoing

---

[2] http://78.91.98.234:5000/.

[3] https://sirisx.ruter.no.

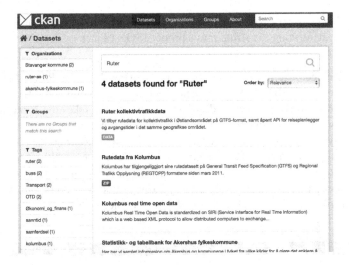

Fig. 3. Open Transport Data CKAN [6].

deviations in all the lines using this stop. It is exposed as a REST API and can be accessed using classical tools such as "curl" or a "REST console". However, the API is little documented and we identified that we could not use exactly this service as it requires a JSON object containing the identifier of the stop of interest, as input. We thus searched again in the catalogue for another API providing such information, and we selected the Ruter Reise API[4] as it provides details about all the public transportation stops in Oslo, regardless of the transportation mode. We verified that the information between the two services was matching semantically - *i.e.*, we stored identifiers of a few stops from the Ruter Reise API service and thereafter we called the Sirisx API using these identifiers.

Identify Added Value and Specify Capabilities. We analyzed the data from both the Ruter Reise and the Sirisx APIs. We could easily find the relevant information and in general the data was accurate even though the textual description of a deviation was sometimes incomplete or missing. Using these APIs we could retrieve and provide users with live information about the deviations associated to one or several stops. We also decided to retrieve and store this information on a regular basis to compute the average number of deviations over a week in the whole city.

Prepare Data. We prepared the data in two ways. First, by filtering it to only manipulate the part relevant for our service. Second, we prepared the data for further analysis. The data from the Reise API describing the stops was obtained in the form of a JSON object stringified. Unfortunately, the JSON obtained was not properly formatted as it used single quotes instead of doubles. In addition, some Norwegian language

---

[4] https://reisapi.ruter.no/help.

characters where not properly encoded. We thus implemented a mechanism to fix this issue before transforming the string into a proper JSON object.

Prototype Service. We implemented our service using the Node-RED platform[5], an open source project by IBM that uses a visual dataflow programming model for building applications and services. Using Node-RED, an application takes the form of a set of *nodes* (*i.e.*, software components) wired with *links* that are encapsulated in a *flow*. A flow can easily be exposed as a service using specific Node-RED nodes. Thanks to the large community behind Node-RED, a large set of nodes are available off-the-shelf and for free, making it rather easy to implement new applications and services. We had to implement specific nodes for accessing the two APIs and for computing the average number of deviation over a week[6]. The final flow is depicted in Fig. 4.

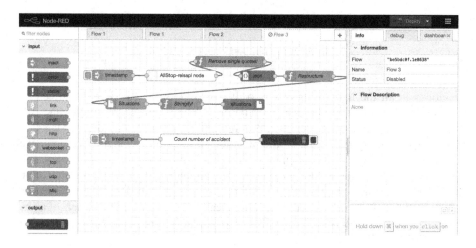

Fig. 4. Data preparation using Node-RED [6].

Identify Missing Data. We did not find it necessary to implement this step in the trial, as the prototype already covered the intended functionality.

5   Discussion and Related Work

This section briefly puts our work in the context of most essential related work in general, namely Agile Software Development. This is followed by a detailed discussion of the lessons learned from the trial, including how the specific steps relate to the related work which is particularly relevant to them. Finally, an elaboration on threats to validity and reliability, is provided.

---

[5] https://nodered.org.
[6] https://github.com/SINTEF-9012/OTD-components.

5.1 Related Work in General

The principle of iterative and incremental software development has already been advocated for many years by the Agile Software Development (ASD) manifesto and its principles. The ASD cycle [5] relies on the following six stages: plan, design, develop, test, review and release. Our approach is inspired by the ASD methodology and aims to be integrated as a part of the ASD process. It focuses on prototyping and aims to be used in the plan stage where a prototype would be used to prove feasibility of the service and to discuss future development activities. It could also be used in the design stage in order to understand and discuss the features to be offered, as well as in the development stage of the ASD process.

More recently, the DevOps principles are being widely adopted by the software industry. DevOps advocates a set of software engineering best practices and tools, to ensure Quality of Service whilst continuously evolving complex systems and foster agility, rapid innovation cycles, and ease of use [8]. In particular, DevOps put a lot of emphasis on automation and collaboration between development and operation activities with continuous feedback between Dev and Ops. The DevOps infinite loop consists of the following stages: plan, code, test, deploy, operate, and monitor[7]. As for the Agile methodology, our approach could take place as part of a DevOps process either in the planning or coding stages.

In 2018, Gartner introduced DataOps in the Hype Cycle for Data Management[8]. At the moment, DataOps, which is inspired by the DevOps movement, is still in its infancy. It strives to speed the design, implementation, and production of data processing and analytics applications. Similar to our approach, data is a first class concern in DataOps. However, it is mainly focusing on big data applications.

5.2 Lessons Learned from the Trial

This section summarizes the challenges we faced during the trial and the lessons learned with respect to each step of the approach.

Search Data. During our trial, we first observed that many catalogues of datasets (and data sources) are available on the web through data portals, but it was difficult to make sure that we were using the best candidate. Data portals leverage data catalogue systems to store, publish and discover datasets. CKAN, DKAN, and Socrata are amongst the most famous data catalogue systems used by data portals. CKAN[9] is an open-source data catalogue system that supports the publication, sharing, search and management of datasets in a domain-independent way. CKAN exposes a powerful RESTful JSON API to manage data catalogues. DKAN[10] offers similar features but it is based on Drupal whilst Socrata[11] is a commercial platform. In the context of our Open Transport Data

---

[7] Please note that the terminology and the number of stages change from one source to another.

[8] https://www.gartner.com/en/newsroom/press-releases/2018-09-11-gartner-hype-cycle-for-data-management-positions-three-technologies-in-the-innovation-trigger-phase-in-2018.

[9] http://ckan.org.

[10] https://getdkan.org.

[11] http://socrata.com.

project, CKAN has been adopted, as it is the solution powering major data portals such as the European data portal[12]. In terms of tooling, we observed that there may be a need for a cross-catalogue search engine (*i.e.*, an engine enabling searching on multiple catalogues).

In addition, as already presented in Sect. 3, searching the most relevant datasets or data sources for building a specific service is challenging due to the lack of metadata about *(i)* the datasets (or data sources) and *(ii)* the semantic overlaps between different datasets (or data sources). For example, it would be interesting to link datasets by means of automatic annotations with keywords that would form a domain specific ontology [9].

Similarly, once we selected our datasets or data sources, it was impossible to assess if these were the best candidates. However, in this case, it is worth noting that our agile approach, where we can start over again after trying to use the dataset, helps assessing the quality and value of different data sources.

Understand Data and Identify Value. Identifying the value of the datasets is also challenging as it can be difficult to evaluate the quality of the data. For instance, when dealing with large datasets or data streams, it is difficult to identify if some data is missing. As an example, in a large dataset with data recorded every second for a few months, it might be difficult to check if a few days or hours of recordings are missing. More generally, information about the reliability of a data source is typically not provided.

Prepare Data. The preparation of the data does not necessarily involve complicated tasks. Some tools and methods facilitating manipulation of open data do exist. For instance, the Linked Data Stack [1] is a software stack consisting of a number of loosely coupled tools, each capable of performing certain sets of operations on linked data, such as data extraction, storage, querying, linking, classification, and search. The LinDA project [7] developed a set of tools for linked data publishing, packaged into the LinDA Workbench. In the cases of both Linked Data Stack and LinDA, the complexity of provisioning resources and managing the web application rests on the service developer who must install the tools and maintain the infrastructure. The COMSODE project [14] provided a set of software tools and methodology for open data processing and publishing. COSMODE is not available as an online service, but rather as a set of tools that need to be individually managed, which implies additional burden on the developer. Datalift [17] is a software framework for linked data publishing. It is considered as an "expert tool" [17]. For example, it comes with no GUI to support data publishers in the data publication process. The Linked Data AppStore [15] is a Software-as-a-Service platform prototype for data integration on the web. Common for the mentioned tools and approaches is that they either only partially cover the prototyping process, or that they are too extensive and therefore unfit for a DevOps-driven agile approach. After a few steps of manipulation, it can be difficult to actually understand the status of the data being manipulated (*i.e.*, structure, format, or even the actual content of the data). In such a case, tools providing a means to visualize the data after each manipulation, would be highly beneficial. This applies not only to datasets but also to data streams.

---

[12] https://www.europeandataportal.eu.

Prototype Service. Our approach is meant to be used during the prototyping phase of the overall life-cycle management of a service. However, it appears that this prototyping phase, by itself, would benefit from using classical tools for the continuous and agile development and operation of services. For instance, once a prototype has been implemented, it typically has to be deployed and tested in an sandbox environment. Similarly, more advanced prototypes could undergo a canary testing - *i.e.*, routing a subset of users or requests to the prototype. A deep analysis of how our approach fits within the main Agile and DevOps processes, is required.

Moreover, the migration from a prototype to a service in production is challenging. In particular, the service will most likely need to be re-implemented using tools, languages, and frameworks adapted for production. For instance, a service that consumes data streams will rely on a stream processing framework. Such frameworks are typically designed for continuously processing data in real-time. The most prominent stream processing frameworks such as Apache Storm[13], Apache Flink[14], Heron [11] and Apache Spark[15], usually rely on the concepts of: data sources (*i.e.*, the entity producing the data), events (*i.e.*, the abstractions that encapsulate the data from the data source), data streams (*i.e.*, sequences of events), processing components (*i.e.*, the entities responsible for actually performing operations on the data streams), and data flows (*i.e.*, orchestrations/topologies of data streams and processing components). Even though prototyping platforms such as Node-RED, to some extent, share common concepts with these frameworks, the migration from one to another is not straightforward. To the best of our knowledge, there are no tools supporting such migration. This applies not only to the implementation of the service itself but also to the deployment, installation and configuration of the framework. For instance, in order to parallelize and distribute the processing activity, processing components and data streams are often executed on a cluster of machines managed by a coordination platform such as Zookeeper[16] or YARN[17]. This also applies for classical batch processing frameworks such as Hadoop[18].

5.3   Threats to Validity and Reliability

The validity of the results depends to a large extent on how well the threats to validity and reliability have been handled. This section discusses the essential aspects of such threats in our context. In the original study [6], we argued that several threats to validity and reliability were present. Majority of those threats also apply to this research, although the evaluation has been more comprehensive. In fact, the refinement of the approach and the extended evaluation have brought additional arguments regarding the presence of the validity threats. However, our recent results and extensions of the previous research have also partially addressed some of the weaknesses which were identified during the original study.

---

[13] http://storm.apache.org.

[14] https://flink.apache.org.

[15] https://spark.apache.org.

[16] https://zookeeper.apache.org.

[17] https://hadoop.apache.org/docs/current/hadoop-yarn/hadoop-yarn-site/YARN.html.

[18] https://hadoop.apache.org.

In terms of validity, our trial is only to a limited degree representative for the contexts intended to be within the scope of our approach. The service prototyped has a specific, rather limited, functionality based on few data sets and involving only fictitious end-users. In a realistic setting, the functionality may have been far more comprehensive, relying on several larger, more different and distributed data sets. The quality of the data sets may also be at widely different levels. In addition, the number of the end users and the frequency of their requests may be far higher then what was the case in our trial – this may have impacted scalability and performance of the solution. None of these properties of the context were present in our trial, hence they have not been tested. A realistic setting would also involve prototyping and even integration of several services, thus introducing additional complexity that we did not cover in our evaluation.

The trial has, however, given strong indications of feasibility of the approach. No particular customizations of the approach (once the refined version was proposed and ready for evaluation) were needed for the trial. Thus, we have reason to believe that it should be possible to reapply our approach on new services.

Reliability is concerned with demonstrating that the empirical research can be repeated with the same results. Of course, a trial like the one we have conducted can not give solid repeatable evidence. There are several contextual factors influencing what happens, particularly the choices made by the researchers during the service development. As our main goal has been to propose a refined version of the approach and test its feasibility through the trial, performance evaluation of the approach itself was not addressed. Ideally, we should have exposes the method to several teams aiming to prototype both the same service as well as other services, under comparable and controlled conditions. Such a setting would provide more relevant evidence for reliability of the results.

It is, in terms of evaluation with respect to reliability, also a weakness that the researchers who tried out the approach also participated in design of the approach. As such, it is also a threat to reliability of the evaluation results, as we cannot know to what degree another service developer would have obtained the same results.

Hence, we do need to further evaluate the approach in more realistic settings. There is also a need for a baseline for comparing this approach with the alternative ones, in order to assess its characteristics such as usability, usefulness and cost-effectiveness. It should be a part of the future work. Further empirical evaluation is also needed for assessing scalability of our approach with respect to complexity and size of the services to be developed.

Overall, we have drawn useful experiences from developing and instantiating the approach in the example. Although the mentioned threats to validity and reliability are present in the study, we argue that the results indicate feasibility and suggest strengths and weaknesses of the approach.

6   Conclusions

This paper is an extension of our previous research [6] where an initial approach to early and continuous service prototyping based on open data, was proposed. The approach has been based on a the needs identified throughout the "Open Transport Data" research and innovation project, and in particular the challenges identified through a survey and interviews. We have tried out feasibility of the approach on an open transport data service, and elaborated in detail on the results and the experiences. Main contributions of this paper include: refinement of the initial approach and refinement of the state of the art. Moreover, the trial has been significantly extended and presented in detail. We also provide a detailed elaboration of the experiences and lessons learned from the trial. In this paper we present an agile and data-centric approach for the early prototyping of services. The results of our feasibility study indicate the benefits and drawbacks of the approach. In particular, as main benefit, we argue that it fosters a "try and fail" development process where developers implementing services on top of open data can play, test, and understand the data while implementing a service. In future stage we will investigate how the approach could be seamlessly integrated in the overall development and operation process of a service.

Acknowledgement. This work has been funded by the Open Transport Data Project under Norwegian Research Council grant no. 257153, as well as by the H2020 programme under grant agreement no 780351 (ENACT).

References

1. Auer, S., et al.: Managing the life-cycle of linked data with the LOD2 stack. In: Cudré-Mauroux, P., et al. (eds.) ISWC 2012. LNCS, vol. 7650, pp. 1–16. Springer, Heidelberg (2012). https://doi.org/10.1007/978-3-642-35173-0_1
2. Barometer, O.D.: Open data barometer global report. WWW Foundation (2015)
3. Beno, M., Figl, K., Umbrich, J., Polleres, A.: Open data hopes and fears: determining the barriers of open data. In: 2017 Conference for E-Democracy and Open Government (CeDEM), pp. 69–81. IEEE (2017)
4. Carrara, W., Chan, W., Fische, S., Steenbergen, E.V.: Creating value through open data: study on the impact of re-use of public data resources. European Commission (2015)
5. Cockburn, A.: Agile Software Development: The Cooperative Game. Pearson Education, London (2006)
6. Ferry, N., Omerovic, A., Natvig, M.K.: Towards early prototyping of services based on open transport data: a feasibility study. In: Proceedings of the 9th International Conference on Cloud Computing and Services Science, CLOSER 2019, Heraklion, Crete, Greece, 2–4 May 2019, pp. 257–262 (2019). https://doi.org/10.5220/0007675402570262
7. Hasapis, P., et al.: Business value creation from linked data analytics: the LinDA approach. In: 2014 Conference on eChallenges e-2014, pp. 1–10. IEEE (2014)
8. Humble, J., Farley, D.: Continuous Delivery: Reliable Software Releases through Build, Test, and Deployment Automation. Addison-Wesley Professional, Boston (2010)
9. Jiang, S., Hagelien, T.F., Natvig, M., Li, J.: Ontology-based semantic search for open government data. In: The proceedings of the IEEE 13th International Conference on Semantic Computing (ICSC), pp. 7–15. IEEE (2019)
10. Kim, G.H., Trimi, S., Chung, J.H.: Big-data applications in the government sector. Commun. ACM **57**(3), 78–85 (2014)
11. Kulkarni, S., et al.: Twitter heron: Stream processing at scale. In: Proceedings of the 2015 ACM SIGMOD International Conference on Management of Data, pp. 239–250. ACM (2015)

12. Martin, S., Foulonneau, M., Turki, S., Ihadjadene, M.: Open data: barriers, risks and opportunities. In: Proceedings of the 13th European Conference on eGovernment (ECEG 2013), pp. 301–309. Academic Conferences and Publishing International Limited, Reading (2013)
13. Noy, N., Brickley, D.: Facilitating the discovery of public datasets (2017). https://ai.googleblog.com/2017/01/facilitating-discovery-of-public.html
14. Hanečák, P., Krchnavý, S.I.H.: COMSODE publication platform - open data node - final. Technical report, July 2015
15. Roman, D., et al.: The linked data AppStore. In: Prasath, R., O'Reilly, P., Kathirvalavakumar, T. (eds.) MIKE 2014. LNCS (LNAI), vol. 8891, pp. 382–396. Springer, Cham (2014). https://doi.org/10.1007/978-3-319-13817-6_37
16. Rusu, O., et al.: Converting unstructured and semi-structured data into knowledge. In: 2013 11th Roedunet International Conference (RoEduNet), pp. 1–4. IEEE (2013)
17. Scharffe, F., et al.: Enabling linked data publication with the Datalift platform. In: AAAI Workshop on Semantic Cities (2012)

True Service-Oriented Metamodeling Architecture

Michael Sobolewski[1,2(✉)]

[1] Air Force Research Laboratory, WPAFB, Dayton, OH 45433, USA
sobol@sorcersoft.org
[2] Polish Japanese Academy of IT, 02-008 Warsaw, Poland

Abstract. True service-oriented metamodeling architecture provides a set of guidelines and the Service-oriented Mogramming Language (SML) for structuring and expressing of service specifications. SML is an executable language in the SORCER platform based on service abstraction (everything is a service) and three pillars of service-orientation: contexion (context awareness), multifidelity, and multityping. Contexion is related to parametric polymorphism, multifidelity to ad hoc polymorphism, and multityping is a form of net-centric type polymorphism. SML allows for defining complex polymorphic services that can express, reconfigure, and morph service-oriented processes at runtime. In this paper the metaprocess modeling architecture applicable to service-orientation is presented with five types of service-oriented processes. Its runtime environment is introduced with the focus on actualization of emergent service processes expressed in SML with the corresponding Service Virtual Machine (SVM).

Keywords: True service orientation · Contexion · Multifidelities · Multityping · Service Mogramming Language (SML) · Emergent systems · SORCER

1 Introduction

Service-oriented architecture (SOA) emerged as an approach to combat complexity and challenges of large monolithic applications by offering cooperations of replaceable functionalities by remote/local component services with one another at runtime, as long as the semantics of the component service is the same. However, despite many efforts, there is a lack of good consensus on semantics of a service and how to do true SOA well. The true SOA architecture should provide the clear answer to the question: How a service consumer can consume and combine some functionality from service providers, while it doesn't know where those service providers are or even how to communicate with them?

In service-oriented *mogramming* - modeling or programming, or both - three types of services are distinguished: *operation services*, and two types of *request services*. An operation service, in short *opservice*, invokes a service provider operation. An *elementary request service* asks a service provider for output data given input data. A *combined request service* asks cooperation of service providers for output data and

© Springer Nature Switzerland AG 2020
D. Ferguson et al. (Eds.): CLOSER 2019, CCIS 1218, pp. 101–132, 2020.
https://doi.org/10.1007/978-3-030-49432-2_6

utilizes obtained from multiple service providers output data. A *service consumer* utilizes output data of aggregated request services. The end user that creates request services and utilizes the actualized service partnership becomes the coproducer and the consumer of created service cooperation in the network. Software developers develop service provider provisioned in the network and end users develop service partnerships.

A *compute service* is the work performed in which a service provider (one that serves) exerts acquired abilities to execute a computation. The *true compute service* needs the computation and *net-centric* service providers to be expressed and executed under condition that service consumers should never communicate directly to service providers. The combined request service realized by opservices represents the *dynamic partnership* of service providers in the network. In contrast the elementary request service represents the opservice of the selected provider in the network.

Many people think they are doing or talking about SOA, but most of the time they are really doing point-to-point integration projects with APIs, web services, or even just point-to-point XML (REST). The reason why this approach is deficient is because service consumers should never communicate directly to service providers. First, the main concept of SOA is that we want to deal with frequent and unpredictable change by constructing service abstractions and an architecture that loosely-couples the providers of capability from the consumers of capability. It is not possible to have direct reliable communication if variability exists in the network and provided service capabilities evolve over time. Second, if we are relying on black-box middleware and often proprietary technology to manage service communication differences, it simply shifts all the complexity and work from the endpoints to an increasingly more complex, expensive, and brittle middle point. Reworked middleware, what often is done and named as SOA, is not the solution for a dynamic, net-centric communication and architecture.

Multidisciplinary Analysis and Design Optimization (MADO) is a domain of research that studies the application of numerical analysis and optimization techniques for the design of engineering systems-of-systems involving multiple coupled domains and multiple evolving disciplines. The formulation of MADO problems has become increasingly complex as the number of engineering disciplines and design variables included in typical studies has grown from a few dozen to thousands when applying high-fidelity physics-based modeling early in the design process [6]. Therefore, MADO is an appropriate domain for studying real-world service-oriented architectures and systems.

This is achieved by the use of reference architectures and their ability to place information views on multidisciplinary data and integration of heterogeneous tools, applications, and utilities used frequently by distributed engineering teams. There are several trends that are forcing system architectures to evolve due to complexity of engineering problems being solved presently [14]. Users expect a rich, interactive and dynamic user experience on a wide variety of friendly user agents and highly modular and dynamic systems. Systems must be highly scalable, highly available and run locally or in the network, or both. Organizations often want to frequently roll out updates, even multiple times a day. Consequently, it's no longer adequate to develop simple, monolithic applications with statically connected modules. When the dynamic system changes frequently the static user agent cannot catch-up with the backend changes, so it becomes obsolete in evolving and complex highly dynamic MADO systems. In a dynamic system when its backend is morphing constantly to emergent solution [1], the user agent has to support emergent nature of its backend. An emergent system means net-centric to refer to continuously evolving complex community of people, devices, information and services interconnected by a communication network to achieve optimal benefit of resources and better synchronization of flowback events and their consequences to the users. An emergent system means also service oriented (SO) and scalable with multiple computational fidelities of underlying services so the communication network of services can be scaled up and down dynamically, from a single computer to a large number of computers with relevant computational fidelities [15, 16].

Top-down and bottom-up problem solving describes two different methods of reasoning: working at the top is considered strategic and declarative, while working at the bottom is tactical and imperative. How a given situation is actually perceived and processed will vary with the person, experience, process expression and actualization chosen. However, the approach is to do whatever is best for managing complexity of the solution by a combination of programming paradigms in designing processes. There is no universal programming paradigm that works well for all situations. Different paradigms are more applicable to different classes of problems and solutions. One should always carefully choose the right paradigm to match the particular sub-problem, or component service at hand. Programming paradigms are not language-specific; therefore, basic paradigms should be available in a service-oriented language as well.

An algorithm is a process expression for solving a problem in the form of a self-contained step-by-step set of statements to be performed with an explicit control flow defined. Statements often refer to a subroutine as a sequence of instructions designed to perform a frequently used task within an algorithm. The emphasis on an explicit control flow distinguishes an imperative programming language [9] from a declarative programming language.

In declarative programming a process is expressed by the logic of computation without describing its control flow. In particular, the logic of computation in functional programming is defined by a function composition. The result of execution of a function composition depends only on inputs and the function composition. There is no a shared state that the execution of function composition depends on. A functional program is stateless but imperative programs usually take advantages of a shared state in an executing algorithm.

Object-oriented programming is a convenience and ability to reason about implemented object operations as subroutines, called methods, with a shared state represented by instance and class variables encapsulated in objects. Being able to hide details of subroutines and their data structures can help reason about the logic of object cooperation such that each object in cooperation manages its own state by own implementation of its subroutines (methods).

Service semantics can be declarative, imperative, or object-oriented depending how multi-machine subroutines, corresponding to executable codes, can be combined into service providers in the network. Therefore, a blend of declarative, imperative, and object-oriented programming should be supported by SO programming languages intended for solving complex problems and building heterogeneous distributed SO systems.

Each programming paradigm introduces distinguishing principles of its programming model but also depends on its lower level paradigm. The pillars of SO programming introduced in this paper are layered on pillars of object-orientated, procedural, and functional programming as illustrated in Fig. 1. The pillars of SO programming are focused on context awareness of services, management of service multifidelities, and multitype management of services for registering, looking up, and referencing both a single service provider and cooperation of service providers. Each paradigm abstraction based on: functions, procedures, objects, and services is the foundation of corresponding pillars. The ceilings: FP, PP, OOP, and SOM correspond to functional, procedural, object-oriented programming, and service-oriented mogramming, respectively. SO mogramming is not a replacement for any programming paradigm, it just inherits programming styles from the layers below and complements them with higher-level service abstractions.

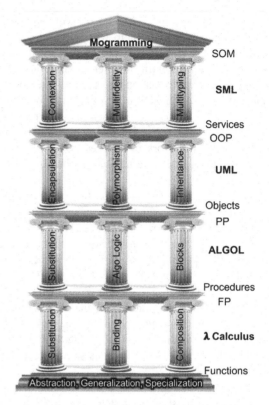

Fig. 1. The service mogramming gate.

Mogramming [4] that combines multiple programming paradigms uniformly [12]. A *service mogram* is an expression of cooperation of routines and models as component services that in turn comprise of operation services, all represented in the Service Mogramming Language (SML). Mogram exhibit hierarchically organized net-centric executable codes represented by its operation services, a of the *net-centric service processor*.

The Service-ORiented Computing EnviRonment (SORCER) [14, 19]) adheres to the true SO architecture based on formalized service abstractions and the three pillars of SO programming presented in Sect. 2. Evolution of the presented approach started with the FIPER project [10] funded by NIST ($21.5 million) at the beginning of this millennium then continued at the SORCER/TTU Laboratory [19], and maturing for real world aerospace applications at the Multidisciplinary Science and Technology Center, AFRL/WPAFB [2, 4–7, 13].

The remainder of this paper is organized as follows: Sect. 2 relates to a service-oriented conceptual framework called Meta-Service Facility (MSF); Sect. 3 describes service semantics in SORCER; Sect. 4 gives introduction to SML; Sect. 5 illustrates introduced concepts of SML with an example of multifidelity model; Sect. 6 describes briefly the object-oriented platform of SORCER; then we conclude with the final remarks and comments.

2   Meta-Service Facility (MSF)

The Meta-Object Facility (MOF) is the Object Management Group (OMG) standard for object-oriented model-driven engineering [18]. Its purpose is to provide a type system for entities in the CORBA (Common Object Request Broker Architecture) architecture and a set of interfaces through which those types can be created and manipulated. Similarly, the Meta-Service Facility (MSF) is a reference service-oriented methodology that focuses on creating and exploiting service models, which are conceptual models of all the topics related to specific structures of request services in SML. Hence, it highlights and aims at abstract representations of the knowledge and activities that govern a particular domain service, rather than the computing concepts in that domain. Its purpose is to provide a type system and semantics for entities in the SORCER (Service-Oriented Environment) architecture. MSF is a metamodel defined by the Multifidelity Service System (MSS, defined in Sect. 2.1, 12) that specifies how the SML model should conform to the conceptual MSF framework.

A *computing service* is the work performed in which a service provider (one that serves) exerts acquired abilities to execute a computation. A *service provider* corresponds to actualization of a *request service*. A single service provider actualizes *elementary request service*, but a *combined request service* is actualized by a cooperation of service providers. Therefore, a *request service* may represent a process expression realized by cooperation of service providers. In this Section, we assume that a mathematical function represents a request service to be actualized by a corresponding actualization, executable code or a combination of executable codes. An elementary request service is actualized by an executable code, but a combined request service (function composition) is actualized by a combination of executable codes.

2.1   Multifidelity Function Systems

A function is a prescription that assigns to every entity of one set X an entity of another (or the same) set Y what is declared by stating its domain X and codomain Y as follows:

$$f : X \rightarrow Y \tag{1}$$

such that exists a relation $R \subseteq X \times Y$ and each pair $<x, f(x)> \in R$. A relation R is called a realization of a function f. So, a function f is like a process $f = (X, Y, R)$. Each input x that is in the set X of inputs is paired with one output y in the set Y of outputs:

$$y = f(x) \tag{2}$$

A function of two or more variables is considered to have a domain consisting of ordered pairs or tuples of argument values. The arity of a relation R is the dimension of the domain in the corresponding Cartesian product. A function of arity n thus has arity $n+1$ considered as a relation.

A set F of interrelated multivariable functions is called a functional system FS

$$FS = <X, Y, F> \tag{3}$$

with domain X and codomain Y, such that for each function $f_i \in F$, there exist a realization $R_i \subseteq X^n \times Y$ where X^n is the Cartesian power of a set X.

A multifidelity function f

$$f = <X, Y, R_f, mFi_f> \tag{4}$$

is a mapping with multiple realizations $mFi_f = \{R_i\}, i = 1, 2, \ldots, m$ with a selected realization $R_f \in mFi_f$. A selected realization R_f is said to be a fidelity of function f.

Let's denote a fidelity of a function f as $fi(f)$, then each input tuple x of X is paired with one output tuple y of the set Y according to its fidelity $fi(f)$ where n is the arity of function f, provided $(x, f(x)) \in fi(f)$

$$y = f(x, fi(f)) \tag{5}$$

A *multifidelity function* f is a dynamic process $f = (X, Y, fi(f), mFi_f)$, with a substitutable fidelity $fi(f) \in mFi_f$.

A fidelity substitution fp, called a projection in FS, is a mapping:

$$fp : F \to FR \tag{6}$$

where F is a set of multifidelity functions, FR is a set of all realizations of functions F in FS, such that for each function $f \in F, fp(f) \in mFi_f$ and $fp(f) = fi(f))$, for $mFi_f \subseteq FR \subseteq P(X \times Y)$.

A *fidelity morpher fm* is a mapping that defines fidelities of functions in association with the inputs and outputs of functions, as follows:

$$fm : F \times X \times Y \to FR \tag{7}$$

where for each $f \in F$, and $x \in X$ and $y \in Y$, $fm(f, x, f(x)) \in mFi_f$ and $mFi_f \subseteq FR$.

A multifidelity function system is a triplet:

$$MFS = <F, FP, FM> \tag{8}$$

where F is a set of interrelated functions with a related set of fidelity projections FP and a set a fidelity morphers FM. Realizations of functions F under fidelity management defined by FP and FM are called functional multifidelities. Note that a single projection $fp \in FP$ defines a realization of multifidelity functions F in MFS while a set of multiple fidelity projections for the same F is a metasystem – a system of projected systems. A set FP of projections allows for a reconfiguration of MFS. A set of morphers FM defines self-morphing of MFS based on runtime inputs and outputs interpreted by morphers applying accordingly fidelity projections FP.

Multifidelity functions are polymorphic functions. Multifidelity is a kind of ad hoc polymorphism in which a polymorphic function can denote a number of distinct and potentially heterogeneous realization (implementations) depending on the type of arguments to which it is applied. The term ad hoc in this context refers to the fact that this type of polymorphism is not a fundamental feature of the type system.

A *total fidelity* R_0 of a multifidelity function f is a fidelity such that $R_0 \in mFi_f$ and for each $R_i \in mFi_f, R_i \cap R_0 \subset R_0$. If $R_i \cap R_0 \subset R_j \cap R_0$ for $R_i \in mFi_f$ and $R_j \in mFi_f$, then R_i is said to be lower fidelity than R_j or R_j is higher fidelity than R_i. A total fidelity of function f can be considered as a realization of a total function f and any lower fidelity as a realization of a partial function of function f. Lower fidelities of a function $f \in F$ are often used when the exact domains of its realizations in mFi_f, are not known or they are proper subsets of the domain R_0.

Note that a fidelity of a multifidelity function is not related directly to a fuzzy concept (like in fuzzy sets or rough sets) of which the membership boundaries of a set $R_i \in mFi_f$ can vary considerably according to current context or conditions. Here boundaries of all sets R_i are fixed once and for all fidelities. It means we are not concerned with a vague or imprecise definition of function; we might have a precise (analytic) realization as well. We can consider lower fidelities as good approximations of R_0 under some conditions. In such situation, a lower fidelity can be more beneficial, "cheaper" to compute than a higher fidelity, while a higher fidelity is also available but considered not preferred all the time due to, for example, time-consuming realization.

Let's specialize a multifidelity process f in MFS defined by a realization R_f (4) as a multifidelity functionality or subroutine $fi(f) = R_f$ (function, procedure, method, service). Let's also specialize both a domain and a codomain to a set C of all tuples of elements from sets X and Y. A tuple in C is called a *tuple context* of the set C of all tuple contexts. If $<x, f(x)> \in R, x \in X, f(x) \in Y$ and $X \subseteq C$ and $Y \subseteq C$ then the function f such that:

$$f : C \to C \tag{9}$$

is called *context aware* or *contextion function* (in short, *contextion*). Later we consider all request services as contextions, unless otherwise stated.

Depending on the programming semantics of function $f \in F$, defined by a programming subroutine, the multifidelity function system MFS with the applied pillars of programming (see Fig. 1) can be specialized as functional, procedural, object-oriented, service-oriented, or a programming system with any combination of programming paradigms needed. Despite many efforts, there is a lack of good consensus on what is the proper semantic of true service and how to do true SOA well. In the following Subsection a conceptual multifidelity service-oriented system is proposed with multifidelities and context awareness as two pillars of service orientation. All pillars are revisited later with the third one, multityping, defined in Sect. 3.

2.2   Multifidelity Service Systems

Service-oriented architecture (SOA) is an architectural approach in which applications make use of services available in the network. It emerged as the approach to combat complexity and challenges of large monolithic applications by offering cooperation of replaceable local/remote component services with one another at runtime, as long as the semantics of the component service is the same. A service network is a structure that brings together local/remote *service providers* to deliver service cooperation represented by the net-centric *request services* – expressions of the hierarchically organized cooperations of service providers. The net-centricity of request services and replaceability of local/remote service providers is defined in SML using multitypes of *provider services* also called *operation services*, in short *opservices*, as explained in Sect. 3. In a conceptual multifidelity service system MSS, the semantics of local/remote service providers (delivering executable codes) is generalized to replaceable multifidelity realizations of *service functions* – *service contextions*. Semantically request services are like cooperation activities but opservices like service provider actions.

In a multifidelity function system *MFS* system defined in (8) both a domain and a codomain of functions are abstracted to a set C of tuple contexts. However, in *MSS* data used by request services is embedded in *service contexts* – collections of hierarchically organized attributed tuples, a kind of service taxonomy or ontology. Combined request services use an evolving shared context while executing cooperative problem solving and return the result service context that contains outputs of all participating services. The design principle for aggregating data into service contexts and processing shared contexts by all cooperating services working in unison is called *service context awareness*. Service context awareness, also called service *contextion*, is a form of parametric polymorphism. In particular, a service contextion is a mapping from input service context to output service context. Using contextion, a function or a data type can be expressed generically so that it can handle inputs and outputs identically without depending on their type. Request services (multifidelity service contextion) and service context types (data types) are *generic services* and *generic datatypes* and form the basis of *generic service-oriented programming*.

A *service context* is a collection of related *named entries* such that each name is uniquely associated with a constant, calculated, or undefined value. Names of entries create a namespace of the context in terms of domain attributes. A sequence of attributes associated with a context value is called a *path*. Attributed paths of context entries specify the semantics of context data. Note that a tuple context is an ordered collection of input/output data while a service context is unordered semantic map (ontology) that associates values with context paths shared in the network for cooperating service providers.

Given the set *ES* of all entries, the set of all service contexts *CS* is equal to P(*ES*), the powerset of *ES*. Contexts with constant values are called *data contexts* or *data models* and denoted by *DC*. Contexts that contain evaluated entries are called *context models* and denoted by *CM*. Therefore, the set of contexts *CS* is the union

$$CS = DC \cup CM \tag{10}$$

A *request service*, called a *contextion function* or simply *contextion,* is a mapping

$$c : DC \rightarrow DC \tag{11}$$

such that $c(dc_{in}) = dc_{out}$ for $dc_{in} \in DC$ and $dc_{out} \in DC$. A context dc_{out} is an output context of the service request $c \in RS$ for an input context dc_{in}.

A multifidelity function system *MFS* defined in (8) with a set F of functions replaced by the set RS of multifidelity request services with the set CS of service contexts is called a *multifidelity service system* defined as follows:

$$MSS = <CS, RS, SP, SM> \tag{12}$$

where SP is a set of service projections, SM is a set a service morphers. Realizations of service requests RS under fidelity management defined by SP and SM are called service multifidelities.

A multifidelity from the computing perspective refers to a computing environment with multiple implementations for a given computing process, meaning there are different computing processes to choose from [15–17]. When selecting fidelities for a complex computing process, it is important to appropriately balance the fundamental tradeoff between cost and computability of total versus partial service realizations at runtime. Such tradeoff in complex systems can be part of the computational process itself with fidelity management based on analysis of intermediate input and output service contexts at runtime with *morph-fidelities,* fidelities associated with service morphers from SM. Morphers based on contextion inputs and outputs reconfigure fidelities of contextions RS in MSS by applying corresponding projections from SP [15].

In SML various types of request services are distinguished with two main categories: elementary and combined request services along with five types of contextions described in Sect. 3. On the one hand, a multifidelity function system *MFS*, as defined in (7), is a conceptual framework for multifidelities in SML. On the other hand, a multifidelity service system *MSS* defines context awareness as parametric polymorphism for input/outputs of service contextions in *MSS*.

2.3 Multitypes of Provider Services

A *service provider* is a multifidelity realization of an *elementary request service* in the multifidelity service system *MSS* (12). In contrast, an *operation service,* in short, an *opservice,* is an expression of a direct service provider in SML, then request services use opservices directly. This allows to distinguish service operations for service *actualization* from various combinations of request services for service *cooperation.*

A *service type* is an attribute of service provider which tells the request service how its service consumer intends to use a required service provider. An association $<op, tp>$ of a service type tp and its operation op that represents a contextion is called a *service signature.* A service provider may implement multiple service types each with multiple operations. Therefore, a signature type can be generalized to a *multitype* that serves as a classifier of service providers in the network. A multitype signature $< op, tp_1, tp_2, \ldots, tp_n >$ is an association of a service operation *op* and a multitype in the form of the list of service types $tp_1, tp_2, \ldots, tp_n$ implemented by a service provider. The service type of a multitype associated with an operation is called a *primary service type*, usually the first service type in the list of service types of the signature. If all service types of a signature are of interface type, then such signature is called *remote*. If a primary type of a signature is a class type, then a signature is called *local*.

An instance of a service provider actualized by a signature is called a *providlet*. Note that binding to a service provider in the network is dynamic, so the identity of a service provider instance is undetermined in a request service. Service signatures in request services are free variables to be bound to providlets - redundant service provider instances available or provisionable in the network.

Multityping is a form of subtype polymorphism in which a service provider multitype (subtype) is related to another multitype (supertype) by dynamic binding the service multitype to local/remote service provider instances, meaning that service signatures of request services can also operate on subtypes of service providers. Net-centric multityping leads to *multitype management* - coordination of the service activities: registration, discovery, provisioning, and lookup - all based on a service multitype implemented by service providers. However, *multi-multitype management* is the organization and coordination of provisioning and binding a combined request service with multiple service signatures, using its *multi-multitypes*, to a group of service providlets. A multi-multitype of a combined request service is the classifier of a service providlet group in the network as the instruction set of the dynamic *service processor* for the request service. Net-centric multi-multitype grouping for combined service requests is oblivious of implementation, location, and invocation protocols of participating self-contained service providlets.

Multityping defines the inheritance hierarchy of service providers in the network. A multitype N is assignable from a multitype M, if N and M are the same, or each service type of N is assignable from a service type of multitype M. If N is assignable from M, then N is said to be a *supermultitype* of M. If M is a *submultitype* of N, then multityping relation is defined, as N is assignable from M, to mean that any signature of type M can be safely used in a context where a signature of type N is expected. Therefore, if a providlet of multitype N is required while in the network exists a providlet of type M and N is assignable from M, then the signature of multitype N can be bound to the providlet of multitype M. The same applies to multi-multitypes that define the inheritance of service providlet groups in the network.

3   Service Semantics in SORCER

Service semantics can be either declarative, imperative, OO, SO, or a blend of them. A blend of relevant combinations of request services should be supported by SO languages intended for solving complex problems and building distributed heterogeneous SO systems. Therefore, elementary and combined services should be expressed in a programming language with adequate semantics and syntax. Each programming paradigm introduces distinguishing principles of its programming model but also depends on its lower level-supporting paradigm. Therefore, the pillars of SO programming introduced in this paper are layered on pillars of OO, procedural, and functional programming (see Fig. 1). The pillars of true SO programming: contexting, multifidelity, and multityping describe the basic traits of request services as described in Sect. 2. The presented metafidelity service system *MSS* (12), is a metamodel for the SML service semantics described in this Section, the SML syntax (Sect. 4) and the reference SORCER architecture (Sect. 6). The term semantics reflects the need to not only model something in the real world, but to model the meaning that this something has for the purpose of the metamodel – service-oriented computing. SML expressions are executed with a Service Virtual Machine (SVM) presented in Sect. 6.

A *service consumer* is a combination of request services, but a *service provider* delivers executable codes (as executable applications, tools, or utilities) to be actualized via *operation services* (of Signature and Evaluator types, called *exec-opservices*) used by *elementary request services* (of Task and Entry types), see Fig. 2. SML *request services* say what to do, but *service providers* run executable codes that are expressed by opservices. *Combined request services* represent SO processes by hierarchically organized elementary and other request services that in turn run cooperations of executable codes expressed by opservices. In other words, in SML exec-opservices are *provider services* – service specifications or contracts, but service providers are implementations of them. A set of opservices of a combined request service binds at runtimes to the collection of service providers called the *service provider partnership*. The executable codes of the partnership form the instruction set of the dynamic *net-centric service processor*.

A *pipeline service* is a set of opservices connected in series, where the output of one opservice is the input of the next one. The opservices of a pipeline can be executed sequentially or in parallel. A pipeline is a combined opservice of Evaluator type that can be used with looping and branching evaluators to form structured algorithms. Exec-opservices can be concatenated with cxt-opservices that preprocess/postprocess service contexts used by exec-opservices and request services.

A *domain service,* in programming dialect called a *mogram* [4], is either a routine (imperative domain) or model (declarative domain), or both. It provides for declarative/imperative transitions within a model across both component models and routines (*transmodel*) and for transitions within a routine across both component routines and models (*transroutine*). The *Transroutine* and *Transdomain* types are subtypes of the *Transdomain* type along with the *Collaboration* type as shown in Fig. 2.

A *domain service* is either *declarative* – a model, or *imperative* – a routine. Models are collections of functional compositions of entries, but routines are either *structured blocks* of routines or *workflow jobs* comprised of component routines and elementary routines called *tasks*. In principle, a model is a hierarchically composed domain of entries, but a routine is a domain of a hierarchically structured tasks.

Subordinated domain of a transroutine or a transmodel contribute directly to its transdomain responses - the output context of the transdomain. However, a service *collaboration* is the transdomain focused on cooperation of subordinated domains toward collaboration driven by an explorer/optimizer. It means that direct results of component domains are used by the exploration/optimization process returning an indirect result.

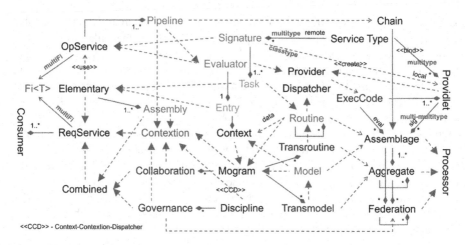

Fig. 2. The service relationships in SML for process expression and actualization. By the same color of Domain its subtypes Routine and Model are indicated. The same coloring convention applies to color of Transdomain and its subtypes Collaboration, Transroutine, and Transmodel.

The *Domain* type is the direct supertype of *Context* and the subtype of *Contextion*. Subtypes relationships of the Domain type are shown in Fig. 2 by the same color with its subtypes: *Routine* and *Model* and direct generalizations as well. The coloring convention applies to the color of *Transdomain* and its subtypes (*Collaboration*, *Transmodel*, *Transroutine*) as well.

A *discipline service* is a triplet: a *<context, contextion, dispatcher>* (CCD), such that a context is the input data, a contextion is the process expression (request service), and a dispatcher is the controller (routine service) of the discipline. A dispatcher configures and dispatches its contextion to be executed in the network then returns the proper result. CCD is the architectural service pattern for developing and deploying disciplinary services as self-contained services with multifidelity components (contexts, contextions, and dispatchers) for constructing runtime triplets to be used in federated service with centralized governance. Therefore, any contextion can be used to create a discipline fidelity of multifidelity disciplines. Next, multiple heterogeneous local/remote disciplines can be combined into a multidisciplinary service under control of the shared central governance.

A *governance service* is a specification of transdisciplinary supervised cooperation of federated disciplines. Federated disciplines can be seen as a cooperation of heterogeneous contexts (states) unified under common governance to be realized by a supervisor (governor).

Service provider partnerships are runtime collections of service providers that realize service cooperations expressed by request services. From the service actualization point of view, a *pipeline* depends on the Chain of service providers bound to the concatenation of opservices, but a combined request service depends hierarchically on actualization of component elementary request services, which in turn depend on actualization of opservices executing corresponding executable codes of corresponding service providers. Partnerships represent dynamic cooperations of Chain, Assemblage,

Aggregate, and Federation type – see Fig. 2. An assemblage refers to grouping providers of elementary request services used in domains as routines or models. An aggregate refers to grouping assemblages for transdomains as transroutines, transmodels, and collaborations. Finally, the federation refers to governing of discipline services, that in turn federate partnerships of discipline contextions specified by the governance service as shown in Fig. 2.

To illustrate the structure of service federalism with five types of combined request services, let us consider governance service A depicted in Fig. 3. It is the functional cooperation A(B(E, F(I, J)), C, D(G(K), H)) of three disciplines (two with collaborations B and D and one with a pipeline C), two additional collaborations (F and G), and five assemblies (E, I, J, K, H). The governance A binds hierarchically to service federation FS of three disciplines at runtime with 23 service providers by 21 elementary services and 2 opservices.

SO federalism is a model of net-centric governance – a federal (central) contextion with federated contextions of disciplines (like states), and an opservices corresponding to providlets (citizens). The rules of governance are realized by the service operating system (SOS – a kind of federal government). SOS coordinates execution of federated disciplines downstream from the governance via request services to opservices. It does so by hierarchically executing service providers referenced by multitypes of opservices at runtime. The main purpose of SOS is to satisfy interests of service consumers and to fulfill their needs using capabilities of hierarchical service partnerships for request services - from federations, aggregates, assemblages, chains, and opservices down to service providers of executable codes.

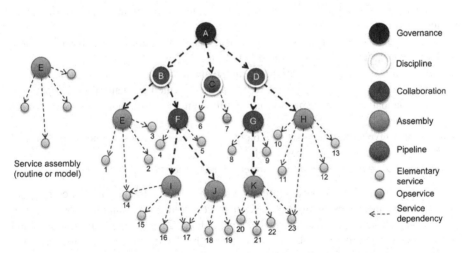

SF = {{{1,14,2,3}, {4,5, {14,15,16,17}, {17,18,19}}, {6, 7}, {{{8,9,} {20,21,22,23}}, {10,11,23,12,13}}}

Fig. 3. Governance service – multidisciplinary service as a cooperation of seven types of services.

Entries and tasks depend on operation services: evaluators and signatures, respectively. Entries use various types of multifidelity evaluators, to invoke executable codes. A signature is a multitype provider service (a net-centric handle) to be bound at runtime to the remote/local service providlet to execute a signature operation. The unique signature-based architecture allows for configuration and execution of distributed dependencies of combined request services by uniform handling of local and remote service providers at various levels of granularity and fidelity. When dealing with net-centric complexities, you have a case to distribute services, otherwise create a modular monolith with locally executable services. Later, when complexity of the system becomes unmanageable you can deploy almost instantly the existing local providers as network providers on as-needed basis, and then run updated services of the original monolith in the network. In SORCER it is done by changing the primary service type of signatures from the class type to the interface type, or just selecting the remote service fidelity. When using the signature-based approach, service providers never communicate directly with each other. The signature with the primary service type as an *interface type* is called a *remote signature* and with a *class type* is called an *local signature*. When executing a combined request service, SOS creates the hierarchical service partnership with the relevant network connectivity at runtime and executes the exec codes of the partnering providers.

Governance request services allow for creating large scale multidisciplinary federated systems. However, most discipline processes (contextions) are expressed by mograms required for constructing effective heterogenous discipline service to be federated. A *domain* is a contextion composition expressing a service combination by one of the five design patterns:

1. *entry model* – is a declarative expression of interrelated higher-order entries (contentions) in a context model.
2. *service block* – is an expression of concatenated subroutines with branching and looping tasks as a block-structured subroutine.
3. *service job* – is an object-oriented composite (workflow) of subroutines with a control strategy for each component job to be executed sequentially or in parallel, synchronously or asynchronously, with context pipes between component subroutines.
4. *service transroutine* – is a service block or service job (transroutine) comprised of both subroutines and service models
5. *service transmodel* – is context model comprised of both models and subroutines.

The presented above mogramming abstractions reduce representational complexity of typical SO processes, so it makes easer to comprehend a computing paradigm of each service design pattern: functional (1), procedural (2), and object composite (3 and 4). Therefore, each mogram abstraction exposes the details which really matter to the domain-specific users from the perspective of preferred programming paradigm and hide the other details (service types, exec codes of evaluators, providlets implementing multitypes) regarding development and deployment of service providers implemented with lower level programming abstractions and languages used by software developers. The above four service design patterns reflect corresponding programming styles shown in Fig. 1. The mogram design patterns allow to blend multiple programming styles within a single combined requested service.

The presented service semantics of request service in SORCER allows to summarize the three SO pillars (see Fig. 1) as follows:

1. *Contextion* allows for a mogram to be specified generically, so it can handle context data uniformly with required data types of context entries to be consistent with ontologies of service providers. Contextion as the form of parametric polymorphism is a way to make a SO language more expressive with one generic type for inputs and outputs of all request services.

2. Morphing a request service is affected by the initial fidelities selected by the user and morphers of morph-fidelities. Morphers associated with morph-fidelities use heuristics provided by the end user that dependent on the input service contexts, and subsequent intermediate results obtained from service providers. *Multifidelity management* is a dispatch mechanism, a kind of ad hoc polymorphism, in which fidelities of request services are reconfigured or morphed with fidelity projection at runtime.

3. Service multityping as applied to service signatures and providers is a form of subtype polymorphism with the goal to find a remote instance (providlet) of the service provider by the range of service types that a service provider implements and registers for lookup. It also allows a multifidelity opservice to call an operation of a primary service type implemented by the service provider as a different service fidelity. With respect to service providers to be provisioned for service signatures of a request service – multi-multityping of the request service specifies which service providers have to be additionally provisioned to complement existing service providers in the network.

4   Introduction to SML

A language can be specified by its metamodel with a great flexibility [4], as shown in Fig. 4. A language can be also specified by a grammar, for example the Java language in EBNF. The primary responsibility of the metamodel layer is to define languages that describe semantic domains to allow users to model a wide variety of different problem domains. The presented approach to true service-oriented metamodeling architecture is based on three abstract service categories: operation services (signatures and evaluators), elementary request services (task and entries) and combined request services (domain, discipline, transdomain, and transdiscipline) used with three pillars of service-orientation: context, multifidelity, and multityping described in Sect. 2.

Therefore, MSF for SML, is like MOF [18] for UML. It is a metamodel defined by the multifidelity service system *MSS* (12) that specifies how the SML model should conform to the conceptual *MSS* system. The SML metamodeling hierarchy along with the UML metamodeling hierarchy is depicted in Fig. 4 to explain the relationship of SML (MSF/M2) to the object-oriented SORCER runtime (MOF/M0). The SORCER operating system manages request services that comprise of hierarchically structured operation services and runs the corresponding net centric service provider partnership (MSF/M0) bound to operation services, that serve as the instruction set (MOF/M1-) of the service processor at MSF/M1-.

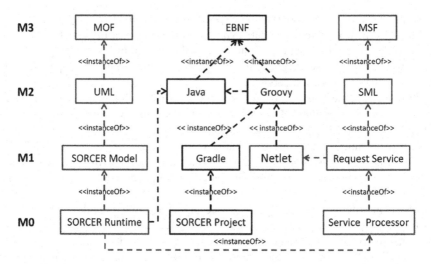

Fig. 4. The UML/SML specific five-layer MOF-MSF metamodel hierarchy.

A request service, called a context model CM in SML conceptually corresponds to a multifidelity service system *MSS* (12) with a collection *RS* of interrelated request services as functional entries in CM used as its domain and codomain. A multifidelity contexton f = (CM, *fi*(f), *mFi_f*) in CM is declared in SML as a service entry as follows:

$$func\ f = ent(\text{``f''}, mFi_f, args(\text{``f}_1\text{''}, \text{``f}_2\text{''}, ..., \text{``f}_k\text{''}))$$

where "f" is a name (a path in CM) of the function *f* declared by the operator *ent*; "f_1", "f_2", ..., "f_k" are argument paths of function f in CM, and *mFi_f* is the multifidelity of function f. By default, a fidelity of function f, *fi*(f) – an *entry evaluator*, is the first realization in the ordered set *mFi_f*. The argument paths "f_1", "f_2", ..., "f_k" in CM bind to values of corresponding entries in CM to create a subcontext of CM as the argument of contexton f.

The *ent* operator defines a generic functional expression declared in a context model CM. Functional entry form higher-order functions – responses of the model. If *ent* declares a constant function, then a model with all such entries is called a *data model* or *data context*.

A *service signature* in SML is an operation service representing either the local or remote operation of a service provider. It declares a service type of provider tp with its operation op, to be invoked in the scope of its service context. A signature association <op, tp> is denoted in SML by sig(op, tp). A functional request service f defined by an operation op to be executed by the service provider implementing a service type tp is declared as follows:

$$func\ f = ent(\text{``f''}, sig(op, tp, inPaths(\text{``}x_1\text{''}, \text{``}x_2\text{''}, ..., \text{``}x_s\text{''}),$$
$$outPaths(\text{``}y_1\text{''}, \text{``}y_2\text{''}, ..., \text{``}y_t\text{''})))$$

or as a multifidelity service entry with multiple signatures:

$$func\ f = ent(\text{``f''}, entFi(sig(op_1, tp_1), ..., sig(op_n, tp_n)))$$

where the operator *entFi* declares a multifidelity of entry f and the operators *inPaths* and *outPaths* specify subcontexts determined by input and output paths in CM as the argument and return values of the operation op.

A service provider may implement multiple service types used to classify its instances in the network by its multitype. In that case a service provider multitype, as a list of implemented service types $tp_1, ..., tp_s$, is the service provider's net-centric identity. Optionally a service provider name with additional attributes can be used as well. Thus, a signature s with a multitype $(tp_1, tp_2, ..., tp_s)$, an operation op_1 of a type tp_1, and an optional service provider name myService takes the following expanded form:

$$sig\ s = sig(op_1, tp_1, tp_2, ..., tp_s, prvName(\text{``myService''}))$$

Note that a signature does not refer to a particular instance of a service provider; its multitype is used for binding to an available instance (providlet) at runtime. Multi-typing is used to manage unpredictability of the unreliable network comprised of replaceable remote service providlets with one another at runtime, as long as the multitype semantics of the service providlets is the same. The local/remote semantics of a service in SML is based on the concept of multityping. If the primary type tp_1 is a class type then the signature works as a service provider constructor – creates an instance at runtime when the service provider needs to be executed, otherwise SOS finds in the network a remote proxy of the service providlet implementing the required multitype.

A *value entry* x (constant function) equal to y, is declared in CM as follows:

$$val\ x = val(\text{``x''}, y),\ for\ value\ y \in Y$$

or a multifidelity variable x

$$val\ x = val(\text{``x''}, entFi(val(\text{``x}_1\text{''}, y_1), ..., val(\text{``x}_k\text{''}, y_k)))$$

A data context dc (of *cxt* type) is an unordered collection of value entries defined as follows:

$$cxt\ dc = context(val(...), ..., val(...))$$

and valuation of the entry x in dc as follows:

$$Object\ y = val(dc, \text{``x''})$$

where "x" is a name of variable (a path) in a data context dc.

A value of an entry x in cxt can be set to v as follows:

$$setValue(dc, \text{``x''}, v)$$

A context model mdl (of mog type) as an unordered collection of value entries and functional entries is declared as follows:

$$mog\ mdl = model(val(...), ..., ent(...), ...)$$

Note that multivariable functional entries of a context model may take other functional entries as arguments to create higher-order functions while function multi-variability is bound to the corresponding subcontext of the underlying model.

Execution of an entry f in a model mdl is declared as follows:

$$Object\ y = exec(mdl, \text{``f''})$$

or

$$Object\ y = exec(mdl, \text{``f''}, c_{in})$$

where $y \in Y$ is an output value and c_{in} is a context used for substitution of entries in mdl.

Evaluation of a model mdl for its responses is declared as follows:

$$cxt\ c_{out} = eval(mdl)$$

or

$$cxt\ c_{out} = eval(mdl, c_{in})$$

where c_{out} is a data context - the result of evaluation of responses for an input context c_{in}. Model evaluations are defined by function compositions of response entries with no explicit strategy for altering the function compositions of the model. However, function compositions can be altered by execution dependencies specified for entries that depend on execution of other entries in the model.

A subset of responses of a model (paths of response entries in the model) can be part of the model declaration by inlining responses "f_1", "f_2", ..., "f_k" as follows:

$$response("f_1", "f_2", ..., "f_k")$$

Alternatively, responses can be updated as required. To increase responses:

$$responseUp(mdl, "f_1", "f_2", ..., "f_k")$$

and to decrease responses:

$$responseDown(mdl, "f_1", "f_2", ..., "f_k")$$

No paths provided for responseDown removes all responses and responseUp may append new responses of the model.

So far, we have defined in SML, an operational service of sig and evaluator types, elementary services of ent and val types, and request services of context and model types. The following statement executes any service sr:

$$Object\ out = exec(sr, arg_1, ..., arg_n)$$

where arg_i is an SML argument of the Arg type. For example, signatures, fidelities, contexts, and models are of Arg type.

The statement executing the operation add of service type Adder takes the form:

$$exec(sig("add", Adder.class),$$
$$context(val("x1", 3.0), val("x2", 1.0), val("x3", 7.0))$$

and returns 11.0 by an instance of a service provider found in the network that implements the service type (interface) Adder. Here, the signature sig("add", Adder.class) binds to an instance of service provider - providlet - implementing the service type Adder. If the class AdderImpl implements the interface Adder, then the execution:

$$exec(sig("add", AdderImpl.class),$$
$$context(val("x1", 3.0), val("x2", 1.0), val("x3", 7.0))$$

creates an instance of AdderImpl at runtime and calls the method add for a given context on the locally created instance. Therefore, a change of the primary type of signature from interface type to a class type changes a remote call to a local one and vice versa.

A service task is an elementary request service defined by a signature with an input context as follows:

$$mog \; y = task(\text{"y"}, \; sig(op, tp), \; context(...))$$

where "y" is a name of the task y with a given signature and an input context. A multifidelity task is declared in SML as follows:

$$task(\text{"y"}, sigFi(sig(\text{"fi}_1\text{"} , op_1, tp_1),..., sig(\text{"fi}_n\text{"}, op_n, tp_n)), context(...))$$

where the operator *sigFi* declares a multifidelity of task y with the first signature as a default fidelity. A selected fidelity can be preselected or declared as an argument when executing a task or set by the fidelity manager of its containing mogram at runtime.

At its heart, service-orientation is the act of uniform decomposition into self-contained local and/or remote executable codes, represented by exec-operations services, interconnected and replaceable at runtime. In SML interconnections of functional entries and service tasks (see Fig. 2) are declared by a combined request service (models and subroutines) that binds operation services (evaluators and signatures) to remote/local executable codes at runtime.

In SML a service subroutine is a request for a procedural (block) or workflow (job) service type. A service task is an elementary subroutine used in combined subroutine. A combined subroutine is a collection of subroutines and/or mograms grouped together within the scope of SML operators, either block or job. A *subroutine block* is a concatenation of component mograms along with flow-control tasks: conditional (opt, alt) and loop (loop) tasks. The SML semantics of opt, alt, and loop is the same as the corresponding UML operators used with interaction frames (combined fragments) in sequence diagrams. A *subroutine job* (service workflow) is an object-oriented composite of component subroutines and/or mograms, optionally with an explicit control strategy and service pipes for interprocess communication between components of the workflow.

Subroutines can be used as evaluators of entries in context models, but responses of evaluated context models can be used as data contexts in subroutines. That way, either a subroutine blended with models, or a model blended with subroutines, creates a service combination of models and/or subroutines – a service mogram. The SML *ent* operator, in most obvious cases, declares a service entry of the type according to its evaluator type. However, specialized SML entry operators, for example: *val, prc, lmb, snr,* and *srv* correspond to entry subtypes: value, procedure, lambda, service neuron, and service, respectively; can be used to indicate directly requested entry subtypes.

A mogram m_{in} to be executed by exerting cooperating service providers is declared as follows:

$$mog \; m_{out} = exert(m_{in})$$

An exerted mogram m_{out} contains the result of execution and all net-centric information regarding providlets and execution of their tasks. The result operator returns the output context of the exerted mogram mog_{out} as follows:

$$cxt\, c_{out} = result(m_{out})$$

The value y of variable x in c_{out} is specified by the *value* operator as follows:

$$Object\; y = value(c_{out} , \text{``x''})$$

or from the exerted mogram directly:

$$Object\; y = exec(mog_{out}, \text{``x''})$$

An evaluation result c_{out} of a mogram m_{in} is a data context declared as follows:

$$cxt\, c_{out} = eval(m_{in})$$

Note, that the eval operator returns an output context c_{out} but the exert operator an executed mogram m_{out}.

A mogram is a collection of interacting request services (entries, tasks, models, and subroutines) that bind at runtime to a cooperation of service providers via mogram opservices. Multifidelity mograms can morph during execution under control of the fidelity mangers and related morphers with the goal to return the emerged result of the evolving net-centric cooperation of service providers - a morphing system of systems. A mogram, is also called an *exertion* [11] due to *exert* operator applied to mograms.

To illustrate SML in action we refer the reader to the examples, in the open source SORCER project [20], in the module *examples*, in particular multifidelity test cases: at sml/src/test/main/java/mograms/ModelMultiFidelities.

5   An Example of a Multifidelity Model in SML

To illustrate the introductory SML syntax presented above in action, a simple context model is declared in SML with four multifidelity entries (mFi1, mFi2, mFi3 and mFi4), four metafidelities (sysFi2, sysFi3. sysFi4, sysFi5), four morphers (morpher1, morpher2, morpher3, morpher4) as lambda expressions, and five provider services used in entries and tasks of the model mdl below. Signatures in entries are remote and in tasks local.

```
// multifidelity model with four morph-fidelities
// (mphFi) and corresponding morphers
mog mdl = model(inVal("arg/x1", 90.0),
    inVal("arg/x2", 10.0), inVal("morpher3", 100.0),
    ent("mFi1", mphFi(morpher1, add, multiply)),
    ent("mFi2", mphFi(entFi(ent("ph2", morpher2),
      ent("ph4", morpher4)), average, divide, subtract)),
    ent("mFi3", mphFi(average, divide, multiply)),
    ent("mFi4", mphFi(morpher3, t5, t4)),
    fi2, fi3, fi4, fi5,
    response("mFi1", "mFi2", "mFi3", "mFi4", "arg/x1",
      "arg/x2", "morpher3"));

// signatures used in multifidelity entries in mdl above
sig add = sig("add", Adder.class,
    result("y1", inPaths("arg/x1", "arg/x2")));
sig subtract = sig("subtract", Subtractor.class,
    result("y2", inPaths("arg/x1", "arg/x2")));
sig average = sig("average", Averager.class,
    result("y3", inPaths("arg/x1", "arg/x2")));
sig multiply = sig("multiply", Multiplier.class,
    result("y4", inPaths("arg/x1", "arg/x2")));
sig divide = sig("divide", Divider.class,
    result("y5", inPaths("arg/x1", "arg/x2")));

// two service tasks used as fidelities of mFi4 in mdl
mog t4 = task("t4", sig("multiply", MultiplierImpl.class,
          result("result/y",
            inPaths("arg/x1","arg/x2"))));

mog t5 = task("t5", sig("add", AdderImpl.class,
          result("result/y",
            inPaths("arg/x1", "arg/x2"))));

// four morphers used with morph-fidelities
Morpher morpher1 = (mgr, mFi, value) -> {
    Fidelity<Signature> fi = mFi.getFidelity();
    if (fi.getSelectName().equals("add")) {
        if (((Double) value) <= 200.0) {
            mgr.morph("sysFi2");
        } else {
            mgr.morph("sysFi3");
```

```
            }
      } else if (fi.getPath().equals("mFi1")
            && fi.getSelectName().equals("multiply")) {
                  mgr.morph("sysFi3");
      }
};

Morpher morpher2 = (mgr, mFi, value) -> {
      Fidelity<Signature> fi = mFi.getFidelity();
      if (fi.getSelectName().equals("divide")) {
            if (((Double) value) <= 9.0) {
                  mgr.morph("sysFi4");
            } else {
                  mgr.morph("sysFi3");
            }
      }
};

Morpher morpher3 = (mgr, mFi, value) -> {
      Fidelity<Signature> fi = mFi.getFidelity();
      Double val = (Double) value;
      if (fi.getSelectName().equals("t5")) {
            if (val <= 200.0) {
                  ((EntModel)mgr.getMogram())
                    .putValue("morpher3", val + 10.0);
                  mgr.reconfigure(fi("t4", "mFi4"));
            }
      } else if (fi.getSelectName().equals("t4")) {
            // t4 is a mutiply task
            ((EntModel)mgr.getMogram())
                  .putValue("morpher3", val + 20.0);
      }
};

Morpher morpher4 = (mgr, mFi, value) -> {
      Fidelity<Signature> fi = mFi.getFidelity();
      if (fi.getSelectName().equals("divide")) {
            if (((Double) value) <= 9.0) {
                  mgr.morph("sysFi5");
            } else {
                  mgr.morph("sysFi3");
            }
      }
};
```

```
// metafidelities used by morphers
fi fi2 = metaFi("sysFi2", mphFi("ph4", "mFi2"),
  fi("divide", "mFi2"), fi("multiply", "mFi3"));
fi fi3 = metaFi("sysFi3", fi("average", "mFi2"),
  fi("divide", "mFi3"));
fi fi4 = metaFi("sysFi4", fi("average", "mFi3"));
fi fi5 = metaFi("sysFi5", fi("t4", "mFi4"));
```

Let's evaluate mdl subsequently with specified multifidelities and morphers with default fidelities and later with the requested fidelity fi("mFi1", "multiply").

```
// evaluate mdl with default fidelities
cxt out = eval(mdl);
assertTrue(value(out, "mFi1").equals(100.0));
assertTrue(value (out, "mFi2").equals(9.0));
assertTrue(value (out, "mFi3").equals(900.0));
assertTrue(value (out, "mFi4").equals(110.0));

// evaluate mdl the fidelity mFi1
out = eval(mdl, fi("mFi1", "multiply"));
assertTrue(value (out, "mFi1").equals(900.0));
assertTrue(value (out, "mFi2").equals(50.0));
assertTrue(value (out, "mFi3").equals(9.0));
assertTrue(value (out, "mFi4").equals(920.0));
```

Let's restrict morphing of the multifidelity model mdl until the value of entry "morpher3" in mdl is less than 900.0. It is implemented with a service block mdlBlock executing a loop with the condition in the form of lambda expression where cxt is the current context of mdlBlock. The morph fidelity of the entry mFi1 in mdl is selected to multiply when exerting mdlBlock.

```
Block mdlBlock = block(
   loop(condition(cxt ->
        (double) value(cxt, "morpher3") < 900.0),
        mdl));

mdlBlock = exert(mdlBlock, fi("multiply", "mFi1"));
assertTrue(value(context(mdlBlock),
        "morpher3").equals(920.0));
```

The above examples can be found in the SORCER-multiFi project [20] in the module examples at sml/src/test/java/sorcer/sml/mograms/ModelMultiFidelities, test cases morphingFidelities and morphingFidelitiesLoop.

6 The SORCER Platform

Computing requires a platform (runtime system) to operate. Computing platforms that allow programs to run require a processor, operating system, and programming environment with supporting tools to create and run programs. SORCER is the platform driven by the three pillars of SO: contextion, multifidelity, and multityping. The SORCER programming environment is based on SML and Java APIs with its unique service-oriented operating system (SOS) that manages the net-centric service processor for executing request services. Technically, the service processor comprises of local/remote objects implementing evaluators and service types of signatures. SORCER remote objects (providlets) are deployed with dynamic small-footprint dynamic service containers called service exerters. A service exerter can run concurrently multiple providlets in the network.

The relationship of the basic SORCER types required to implement multifidelity services is depicted in the diagram in Fig. 2 with UML relationships. Services of the Request type are instances of two elementary subtypes: Entry and Task, and the basic request service type Contextion with five subtypes: Pipeline, Domain, Discipline, Collaboration, and Governance. All request services are instances of the common Service type with uniform execution of local and remote services at runtime. Top-level interfaces of the SORCER system that refer to the SO concepts: Fi<T>, Signature, Evaluator, Request, Entry, Task, Contextion, Context, Model, and Provider, all are subtypes of the common Service type.

From the SO point of view creation of user-centric request services – mogramming – is the primary objective assuming that service providers implement multitypes and their operations can be incorporated into net-centric service processor managed by SOS. Note, that multifidelities are used in request services only. A combined request service hierarchically combines elementary requests (entries and tasks) that bind dynamically to executable subroutines of evaluators and service providers, respectively.

Each service provider implements a multitype of service types. Each service type may have multiple implementations in the network. SOS does not know location of service provider instances in the network; it requires only their service types to be implemented in the network. The question is, how to find a required implementation in the network. The answer is, by matching a multitype of the service signature to the multitype of the implementation available in the network. To differentiate from each other, service providers may implement complementary service types, for example, tag interfaces corresponding to implementation details. Complementary types can be registered with primary service types, then both used in signatures when looking up a service provider. Multityping of signatures is the concept of finding providers of the same multitype from redundant instances (providlets) available in the network.

In systems theory emergence is a process whereby larger entities and regularities arise through interactions among smaller or simpler entities that themselves do not exhibit such properties. An emergent SO behavior can appear when a number of simple services operate in an environment, forming more complex behaviors as a service collective (partnership). It can commonly be identified by patterns of accumulating change used by morphers. Emergent behavior is hard to predict since the number of interactions between components of a system increases exponentially with the number of components, thus potentially allowing for many new and subtle types of behavior to emerge. Emergence is often a product of particular patterns of interaction. Negative feedback introduces constraints that serve to fix structures or behaviors. In contrast, positive feedback promotes change, allowing local variations to grow into global patterns. Multifidelity services can be observable and observed. Therefore, the positive or negative feedback received by morphers regarding applied system fidelities from observable multifidelity services can be used to update fidelities, upstream to the metamodel level and downstream for new projected and created instances of the metamodel. The projected and new instances are created by the fidelity management system to form emergent properties of the morphing multifidelity model as illustrated in Fig. 5.

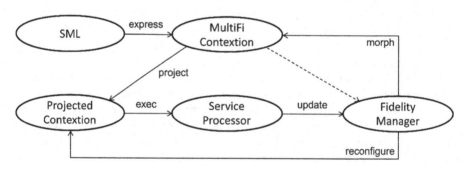

Fig. 5. Morphing and reconfiguring multifidelity service mograms expressed in SML

An emergent modeling platform requires the ability to express a SO system with a given fidelity projection as the instance of the metasystem with multiple fidelity projections. In SML a projected contextion is an instance of a multifidelity contextion – a metasystem. Also, the computing platform requires the ability to execute and morph the evolving system with updated projections managed by the metasystem. SOS enables quick and effective SO communication with net-centric services and allows for evolving updates such that each new instance of the multifidelity system is a new projection of the metasystem.

SML defines two types of multifidelities in contexions: select-fidelities and morph-fidelities. Select-fidelities allow for system reconfiguration, but morph-fidelities allow for self-morphing the structure of the multifidelity request service. Morph-fidelities are observed by a fidelity manager of contexion. Therefore, the positive or negative feedback received from computed fidelities can be used to update fidelities, upstream of already executed services and downstream for new looked up services. The fidelity manager, as the observer of morph-fidelities, updates associated morphers to reconfigure a contexion fidelity projection. Morphers associated with morph-fidelities form emergent properties in the morphing multifidelity system.

A projected contexion, that defines the service cooperation actualized and managed by SOS, is an instance of the metasystem expressed by a multifidelity contexion. To reconfigure or morph a multifidelity contexion its fidelity manager uses projection functions and morphers. Both reconfiguration and morphing allow for adaptivity of system and metasystem respectively, when updates of fidelities and metafidelities are under control of the fidelity manager at runtime. Morphers of morph-fidelities in request services managed by fidelity managers may reconfigure the current contexion or morph to a new projected contexion as shown in Fig. 5.

Adaptive SO systems with morph-fidelities are emergent systems. This type of systems exhibits three types of adaptivities called system-of-system, system, and service agility [15]. Metasystem agility refers to system reinstantiation with metafidelities, system agility refers to updating system fidelity projections, and service agility refers to updating fidelities of elementary request services at runtime.

Virtual machines are based on computer architectures and provide functionality of a physical computer. Service Virtual Machine (SVM) is a network process virtual machine designed to run cooperating executable codes in in the network expressed by combined request services presented in Sect. 3. SVM serves as an abstraction layer for SML in SORCER. Thus, it becomes a multifidelity processor architecture for SML with basic operations corresponding to six categories of opservices: evaluator, signature, getter (filter), setter, appender, and connector. The first two opservices run executable codes locally/remotely (exec-opservices) and the remaining ones (context opservices in short cxt-opservices) preprocess service contexts used as inputs and outputs by request services. With two exec-opservices request services may executed unlimited number of executable codes in the network. Therefore, the network of providlets becomes the native processor for SVM with custom instruction set for request services.

The architecture of SVM with the basic internal components: the thread stack for executing request services, multifidelity projection area, combined request service area, elementary request service area, and opservice area is shown in Fig. 6. The opservice area comprises of two categories of exec-opservices (signatures, evaluators), and four categories of cxt-opservices (setters, getters, connectors, and appenders). Each thread has its own stack that holds a frame for each request service executing on that thread. A new frame is created and added to the top of stack for each component request services to be executed. The frame is removed when the request service returns normally or if an uncaught exception is thrown during the service execution. SVM supports Java methods that call back from JVM into SVM and invoke a request service.

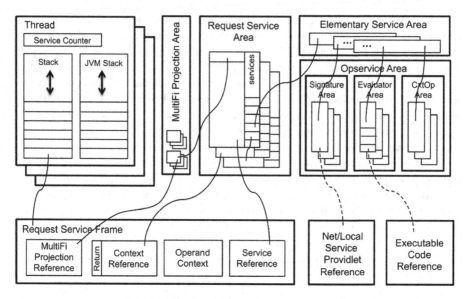

Fig. 6. SML Service virtual machine (SVM).

Each frame contains: multiFi projection, input context with context return, operand context, and a request service reference. The operand context is used during the execution of services in a similar way the general-purpose registers are used in a native CPU. While combined request services comprise of request services, only elementary request services comprise of exec-opservices. Most SVM exec-opservice spends its time manipulating the operand context by operations that produce or consume context values by calling remote/local providlets or executable codes of evaluators.

JVM used by SVM is a kind of native processor for SVM but opservices specify the instruction set of the SVM processor. Remote exec-opservices of SVM may call providlets in the network to execute request service as well. Therefore, via propagation of remote signatures originated from an SVM, the SVM expands itself into the network of cooperating SVMs executing opservices on multiple machines in the network on behave of the originating SVM. Such distributed SVM executing concurrently opservices in the network forms the instruction set of the network multiprocessor. The network multiprocessor becomes a collection of remote and local executable codes bound at runtime to signatures and evaluators executed concurrently by multiple SVNs.

In comparison to an object-oriented virtual machine, for example JVM, SVM request services and opservices correspond to methods and opcodes (bytecodes), respectively. In JVM two types of methods, instance and class methods, are distinguished but in SVM two types of request services, elementary and combined service. Opcodes used by elementary services specify the machine internal operations only, however opservices may execute locally (local signatures) and remotely (remote signatures). The fact that SVM can execute machine instructions in the network at runtime is the primary distinction between SVM and JVM. This essential service-oriented computational feature makes SVM a network-centric virtual machine.

The opservice that is assigned to the runtime data area of the SVM via a request service is executed by the SVM execution engine. The execution engine executes the SVM opcode in the unit of service instruction. It is like a CPU executing the machine command one by one. Each command of the opservice consists of an operand context. The execution engine gets one exec-opservice and execute the executable code, associated either with the evaluator or the providlet, with the operand context, and then executes the next opservice. An SVM request service is written in SML that a human can understand as service-oriented cooperation (pipeline, domain, discipline, collaboration, and governance), rather than in the programming language used to implement the execution engine. The SOS uses the SVM execution engine and manages local and remote service providers for opcodes to be executed and provides common functionalities for handling request and provider services, fidelity management, and context management for SVM.

7 Conclusions

Markov tried to consolidate all work of others on effective computability. He has introduced the term of algorithm in his 1954 book Teoriya Algorifmov [8]. The term was not used by any mathematician before him and reflects a limiting definition of what constitutes a computational process: a mathematical mapping from various initial data to the desired result. The mathematical view of process expression has limited computing science to the class of processes expressed by algorithms. From experience in the past decades it becomes obvious that in computing science the common thread in all computing disciplines is process expression; that is not limited to algorithm or actualization of process expression by a single computer.

A *service* is the work performed in which a service provider (one that serves) exerts acquired abilities to execute a computation. To be the *true service* resulted from the performed computation, both the computation and the service providers have to be expressed then realized under condition that service consumers should never communicate directly to service providers. Asserted cooperations of service providers represented by operation services are called request services. This way, in SML everything is a service. *Request services* represent cooperations of *opservices* bound at runtime to service providers to execute computations. In this paper, service-orientation is proposed as the approach with five types of emergent net-centric multifidelity request service representing the following service request services: pipelines, assemblies, collaborations, disciplines, governances.

The "everything is a service" semantics of SML is introduced for request services to be actualized by dynamic cooperations of service providers in the network. A multifidelity request service is considered as a dynamic representation of a net-centric emergent process defined by the end user. In SORCER, a rectified contexion – a service request embedded into a service provider container, becomes a service providlet – a process expression becomes an executable service provider.

To express emergent processes consistently and flexibly, the actualization of SML by SOS is based on three pillars of services orientation (contexion, multifidelity, and multityping) and on generalization of the pillars of functional, procedural, and object-orient programming (see Fig. 1). Generalization of the existing programming paradigms leads to five types of service combinations (pipeline, domain, discipline, collaboration, and governance). Request services are multifidelity services, but provider services are multitype services. By multitypes of service signatures used in contextions a multi-multitype of service cooperation is determined. Therefore, multitype of a signature and a multi-multitype of contextions are classifiers of instances of service providers (providlets) and cooperations of service providers in the network, respectively. To the best of our knowledge there is no comparable true service-oriented system, programming language based the three pillars of service-orientation and its SVM.

Emergent systems exhibit three types of adaptivities called system-of-systems (metasystem), system, and service agilities. Metasystem agility refers to updating metafidelities (system reinstantiation), system agility refers to updating fidelities of a mogram (system projection), and service agility refers to selecting fidelity of request and opservices [15].

The SORCER architectural approach represents five types of net-centric multifidelity service cooperations expressed by request services created by the end users and executable codes of service providers by software developers. It elevates combination of contextions into the first-class elements of the SO federated process expression. The essence of the approach is that by making specific choices in grouping hierarchically provider services for contextions, we can obtain desirable dynamic properties from the SO systems we create with SML.

Thinking more explicitly about SO languages, as domain specific languages for humans than software languages for computers, may be our best tool for dealing with real world complexity. Understanding the principles that run across process expressions in SML and appreciating which language features and service virtual machines (SVMs) are best suited for which type of processes, bring these process expressions (request services in SML) to useful life. No matter how complex and polished the individual process operations are, it is often the quality of the operating system (SORCER) that determines the power of the computing system. The ability of presented metamodeling architecture with SML and SVM with its execution engine to leverage network resources as services is significant to real-world applications in two ways. First, it supports multi machine executable codes via opservices that may be required by SO applications; second, it enables cooperation of variety of computing resources represented by request services that comprise of opservices actualized by the multi machine network at runtime.

The software as a service (SaaS) approach spreads rapidly because it makes end users more productive. However, lack of service-oriented integration frameworks, forces end users to go back and forth endlessly between the component services (applications) they need and like, is disruptive because it corrodes productivity of complex service-oriented systems. The more services you have, the trickier it gets to move swiftly and meaningfully between them and integrate reliably into large distributed systems.

Embedded service integration in the form of *combined request services* in SML solves a problem for both system developers and end users. Embedded service integration is a transformative development that resolves the stand-off between system developers who need to innovate service integrations and end users who want their services to be productive in their integrated systems, not hold them back. Service integration is key to this, but neither system developers nor end-users want to be distracted by time-consuming integration projects.

The first rule of service-orientation in SORCER: do not morph and do not distribute your system until you have an observable reason to do so. First develop the system with no fidelities and no remote services. Later introduce must-have distribution and multifidelities. Doing so step-by-step you will avoid the complexity of modeling with multifidelities and distribution all at the same time.

The SORCER platform with SML and SVM supports the two-way convergence of modeling (top-down problem solving with context models) and programming (bottom-up problem solving with service pipelines and routines) – mogramming. The platform has been successfully deployed and tested for design space exploration, parametric, and optimization mogramming in multiple projects at the Multidisciplinary Science and Technology Center AFRL/WPAFB [2, 4–7, 13].

Acknowledgments. This effort was sponsored by the Air Force Research Laboratory's Multidisciplinary Science and Technology Center (MSTC), under the Collaborative Research and Development for Innovative Aerospace Leadership (CRDInAL) - Thrust 2 prime contract (FA8650-16-C-2641) to the University of Dayton Research Institute (UDRI). This paper has been approved for public release, case number: 88ABW-2019-4488. The effort is also partially supported by the Polish Japanese Academy of Information Technology.

References

1. Aziz-Alaoui, M., Cyrille Bertelle, C. (eds.): Emergent Properties in Natural and Artificial Dynamical Systems (Understanding Complex Systems). Springer, Heidelberg (2006). https://doi.org/10.1007/3-540-34824-7
2. Burton, S.A., Alyanak, E.J., Kolonay, R.M.: Efficient supersonic air vehicle analysis and optimization implementation using SORCER. In: 12th AIAA Aviation Technology, Integration, and Operations (ATIO) Conference and 14th AIAA/ISSM AIAA 2012-5520 (2012)
3. Kao, J.Y., White, T., Reich, G., Burton, S.: A multidisciplinary approach to the design of a low-cost attritable aircraft. In: 18th AIAA/ISSMO Multidisciplinary Analysis and Optimization Conference, AIAA Aviation Forum 2017, Denver, Colorado (2017)
4. Kleppe A.: Software Language Engineering, Pearson Education (2009). ISBN: 978-0-321-55345-4
5. Kolonay, R.M., Sobolewski M.: Service ORiented Computing EnviRonment (SORCER) for large scale, distributed, dynamic fidelity aeroelastic analysis & optimization. In: International Forum on Aeroelasticity and Structural Dynamics, IFASD 2011, Paris, France, 26–30 June 2011 (2011)
6. Kolonay, R.M.: A physics-based distributed collaborative design process for military aerospace vehicle development and technology assessment. Int. J. Agile Syst. Manag. **7**(3/4), 242–260 (2014)
7. Kolonay, R.M.: MSTC Engineering - A distributed and adaptive collaborative design computational environment for military aerospace vehicle development and technology assessment. In: AIAA 2019-2992, AIAA Aviation Forum 2019, Dallas, Texas (2019)

8. Markov, A.A.: Theory of Algorithms. Keter Press (1971). (trans. by Schorr-Kon, J.J.)
9. O'Hearn, P.W., Tennent, R.D. (eds.): Algol-Like Languages (Progress in Theoretical Computer Science), vol. 1. Birkhäuser (1997). ISBN-10: 0817638806
10. Sobolewski, M.: Federated P2P services in CE environments. In: Advances in Concurrent Engineering, pp. 13–22. A.A. Balkema Publishers (2002)
11. Sobolewski, M.: Object-oriented meta-computing with exertions. In: Gunasekaran, A., Sandhu, M. (eds.), Handbook on Business Information Systems. World Scientific (2010). https://doi.org/10.1142/9789812836069_0035
12. Sobolewski, M., Kolonay, R.: Unified mogramming with var-oriented modeling and exertion-oriented programming languages. Int. J. Commun. Netw. Syst. Sci. 5(9) (2012). http://www.scirp.org/journal/PaperInformation.aspx?paperID=22393(2012). Accessed 28 Oct 2019
13. Sobolewski, M.: Service oriented computing platform: an architectural case study. In: Ramanathan, R., Raja, K. (eds.) Handbook of Research on Architectural Trends in Service-Driven Computing, pp. 220–255. IGI Global, Hershey (2014)
14. Sobolewski, M.: Technology foundations. In: Stjepandić, J., Wognum, N., Verhagen, W.J.C. (eds.) Concurrent Engineering in the 21st Century, pp. 67–99. Springer, Cham (2015). https://doi.org/10.1007/978-3-319-13776-6_4
15. Sobolewski, M.: Amorphous transdisciplinary service systems. Int. J. Agile Syst. Manag. 10 (2), 93–114 (2017)
16. Sobolewski, M.: Service-oriented mogramming with SML and SORCER. In: Proceedings of 9th International Conference on Cloud Computing and Services Science, Greece, 2–4 May, pp. 331–338. SCITEPRESS (2019). ISBN 978-989-758-365-0
17. Stults, I.C.: A multifidelity analysis selection method using a constrained discrete optimization formulation, School of Aerospace Engineering, Georgia Institute of Technology, Dissertation (2009). https://smartech.gatech.edu/handle/1853/31706. Accessed 28 Oct 2019
18. The MetaObject Facility Specification. https://www.omg.org/mof/. Accessed 28 Oct 2019
19. SORCER/TTU Projects. http://sorcersoft.org/theses/index.html. Accessed 28 Oct 2019
20. SORCER Project. https://github.com/mwsobol/SORCER-multiFi. Accessed 28 Oct 2019

A Decomposition and Metric-Based Evaluation Framework for Microservices

Davide Taibi[(✉)] and Kari Systä[(✉)]

TASE - Tampere Software Engineering Research Group,
Tampere University, Tampere, Finland
{davide.taibi,kari.systa}@tuni.fi

Abstract. Migrating from monolithic systems into microservice is a very complex task. Companies are commonly decomposing the monolithic system manually, analyzing dependencies of the monolith and then assessing different decomposition options. The goal of our work is two-folded: 1) we provide a microservice measurement framework to objectively evaluate and compare the quality of microservices-based systems; 2) we propose a decomposition system based on business process mining. The microservice measurement framework can be applied independently from the decomposition process adopted, but is also useful to continuously evaluate the architectural evolution of a system. Results show that the decomposition framework helps companies to easily identify the different decomposition options. The measurement framework can help to decrease the subjectivity of the decision between different decomposition options and to evaluate architectural erosion in existing systems.

Keywords: Microservices · Cloud-native · Microservice slicing · Microservice decomposition · Microservice migration

1 Introduction

Software evolves through its life-time, and often a large part the effort and costs is spent on software maintenance [14]. Furthermore, the incremental development practices in modern software development makes the nature of all the development processes to resemble a maintenance one [18]. A major obstacle to efficient maintenance is the tight coupling between the internal components of the software. In monolithic systems, most changes require modifications to several parts of the systems, and often size and complexity of the modification is hard to estimate in advance.

One approach to tackle the maintenance problem is to decompose the system into small and independent modules [20,25]. Often, at the same time, companies want to utilize benefits of service-oriented architectures and even *microservices*, such as independent development, scaling and deployment [31].

Microservices are an adaptation service-oriented architecture but focuses on of relatively small and independently deployed services, with a single and clearly

© Springer Nature Switzerland AG 2020
D. Ferguson et al. (Eds.): CLOSER 2019, CCIS 1218, pp. 133–149, 2020.
https://doi.org/10.1007/978-3-030-49432-2_7

defined purpose [7]. The independent development and deployment bring several advantages. Different microservices can be developed in different programming languages, they can scale independently from other services, and each microservice can be deployed on the most suitable the hardware. Moreover, small services are easier to maintain and the split to independent responsibilities increases fault-tolerant since a failure of one service will not break the whole system. From the architectural perspective a well-designed microservice encapsulates its data and design choices. Thus, the internal logic of a microservice can be changed without affecting the external interface. This reduces the need for interaction between the teams [29,30].

However, decomposing a monolithic system into a set of independent microservices is a very difficult and complex tasks [31,35]. Decomposition of a system into separately maintained services is difficult as such, but microservice architecture adds further challenges related to performance. Calls inside a microservice are significantly lighter than calls between microservices. Still, the quality of the decomposition – the optimal slicing of the monolith to services – is critical for gaining the assumed benefits of using microservices. The software architects usually perform the decomposition manually but the practitioners have claimed that a tool to support identification different possible slicing solutions [25,31,32] would greatly help the task. Typically, the only helping tools for the software architects have been based on the static analysis of dependencies such as Structure 101[1]. The actual discovery of slicing options has still been done by experienced software architects. In microservices, the dynamic behavior of the system is important too since it affects the performance and maintainability. Since static dependency analysis tools are not able to capture the dynamic behavior we decided to explore slicing based on runtime behavior instead of only considering static dependencies.

In our previous work, we proposed a microservice decomposition framework [36] based on process-mining to ease the identification of splitting candidates for decomposing a monolithic system into separate microservices. The framework is based on logs produced by process mining of the original monolithic system. The decomposition framework has been also validated in our previous study [36] in collaboration with an SME. The results of [36] shows that dynamic call history can be effectively used in the decomposition of microservices. This approach can also identify architectural issues in monolithic systems. The approach can be used by companies to proposed different slicing options to the software architects and to provide additional analysis of the software asset. This would reduce the risk of wrong slicing solutions.

In this paper, we extend the previous decomposition framework [36] proposing a new measurement framework to objectively compare two decomposition options. The measurement framework can be used independently from the decomposition strategy adopted.

The remainder of this paper is structured as follows. Section 2 presents the background on processes for migrating and splitting monolithic systems

---

[1] Structure101 Software Architecture Environment - http://www.structure101.com.

into microservices. Section 3 presents the measurement framework. Section 4 describes our proposed decomposition approach. Section 5 discusses the results. Section 6 presents related works while, finally Sect. 7 draws conclusions.

2 Background and Assumptions

Decomposing a system into independent subsystems is a task that has been performed for years in software engineering. Parnas [20] proposed the first approach for modularizing systems in 1972. After Parnas's proposal, several works proposed different approaches [15]. Recently, the decomposition of systems took on another dimension thanks to cloud-native systems and especially microservices. In microservices, every module is developed as an independent and self-contained service.

2.1 Microservices

Microservices are small and autonomous services deployed independently, with a single and clearly defined purpose [7,19]. In microservices each service can be developed using different languages and frameworks. Each service is deployed to their dedicated environment whatever efficient for them.

The communication between the services can be based on either REST or message queue. So, whenever there is a change in business logic in any of the services, the others are not affected as long as the communication endpoint is not changed. As a result if any of the components of the system fails, the failure will not affect the other components or services, which is a big drawback of monolithic system [7].

As we can see in Fig. 1, components in monolithic systems are tightly coupled with each other so that failure of one component will affect the whole system. Also if there is any architectural changes in a monolithic system it will also affect other components. Due to these advantages, microservice architecture is way more effective and efficient than monolithic systems.

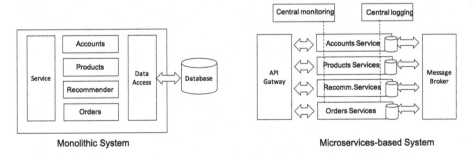

Fig. 1. Architectures of microservices and monolithic systems.

2.2   The Microservice Decomposition Process

Taibi et al. [31] conducted a survey among 21 practitioners who adopted microservices at least two years ago. The aim of the survey was to collect their motivation for, as well as the evolution, benefits, and issues of the adoption of microservices. Based on the results, they proposed a migration process framework composed of two processes for the redevelopment of the whole system from scratch and one process for creating new features with a microservice architecture on top of the existing system. They identified three different processes for migrating from a monolithic system to a microservices-based one. The goal of the first two processes is to support companies that need to migrate an existing monolithic system to microservices by re-implementing the system from scratch. The aim of the third approach is to implement new features only as microservices, to replace external services provided by third parties, or to develop features that need important changes and therefore can be considered as new features, thus gradually eliminating the existing system. All three of the identified processes are based on four common steps but differ in the details.

- *Analysis of the System Structure.* All processes start by analyzing dependencies mainly with the support of tools (Structure101, SchemaSpy[2], or others)
- *Definition of the New System Architecture.* Architectural guidelines or principles, and proposal of a decomposition solution into small microservices are defined. The decomposition is always done manually.
- Prioritization of feature/service development. In this step, all three processes identify and prioritize the next microservices to be implemented. Some processes prioritize microservices based on customer value; others according to components with more bugs; and yet others prioritize the development of new features as microservices, expecting that, in the long run, the new ecosystem of microservices will gradually replace each feature of the existing monolith.
- *Coding and Testing* are then carried out like any other software development project. Developers adopt the testing strategy they prefer. However, in some cases, testing of the different microservices is performed by doing unit testing at the microservices level and black-box testing at the integration level.

In this work, we focus mainly on the first two steps, supporting companies in the analysis of the system structure and in the identification of decomposition alternatives. The architectural guidelines should be defined by the company based on their internal policies.

---

[2] http://schemaspy.sourceforge.net/.

2.3   Architectural Goals

The microservices should be as cohesive and decoupled as possible [7]. The motivation of such architectural characteristics is to keep the maintenance as local as possible. In other words, the changes to the source code should be local to one microservice. Such *decoupled* architecture also supports independent development and deployment of the microservices. Sam Newman [19] describe loose coupling as follows: "a loosely coupled service knows as little as it needs to about the services with which it collaborates".

Cohesion is related to decoupling and measures the degree to which the elements of a certain class belong together. Cohesion measures how weakly the functionalities of different modules are related to each other [6]. High cohesion often relates to low coupling [10, 13]. If the components of the software have high cohesion, the reasoning of the system is easier [13]. Thus, high cohesion supports efficient development and maintenance of the system.

In the design of microservice-based systems the developers target at high cohesion and low coupling by grouping the functionality and components according to the business processes. Then, changes to a functionality should lead changes to one microservice only [19].

Because cohesion and decoupling are key qualities of microservices, the dependency information is needed in the decomposition process. The commonly used dependency analysis tools, such as Structure 101, are based on static analysis of dependencies. They do not know which inter-component calls are really made and they do not recognize the full call paths. Our approach uses the dynamic dependency information that a process mining can provide. The mining provides recommendations, and analysis can then be used for reasoning. At this point, we do not aim at completely automated decomposition. In the next Subsection we report the underlying assumptions of our approach and details of the decomposition process.

2.4   Decomposition Framework Assumptions

The core assumption of our approach is existence of an extended log trace that has been collected at runtime. This means that the whole chain of operations after any external trigger can be traced from the log files. Examples of such external events include any user operations (e.g., clicking on a button) and calls from other applications (e.g., APIs or command line). The log file must include information about all methods and classes involved in serving of the request. The complete execution path must be completely traceable from the entry point to the access to the database (if any) and to the results returned to the client. The log must also include the start and end events. A hypothetical example of the data reported in the log file is shown in Table 1. A trace in Table 1 is identified by a session ID. That ID distinguishes the trace from other sessions.

Table 1. Example of log traces (timestamps are shortened for reasons of space).

Start time	End time	Sess. ID	Class	Method
00:00	00:36	S1	Form.jsp	btnClick()
01:00	01:39	S1	A.java	a()
01:40	01:45	S1	A.java	b()
01:45	01:55	S1	B.java	b()
01:56	02:05	S1	B.java	c()
02:05	02:13	S1	DB.java	query()
02:14	02:21	S1	DB	TABLE A
02:22	03:28	S1	DB	TABLE B
02:29	02:36	S1	B.java	c()
02:36	02:45	S1	B.java	b()
02:46	02:55	S1	A.java	b()
02:56	03:03	S1	A.java	c()
03:04	03:16	S1	Results.jsp	render()

There are several ways to collect the traces. One possible method is to instrument the source code, but using Aspect-Oriented Programming (AOP) can be done too, like in the work done by Suonsyrjä [26]. For some runtime systems it is also possible to instrument the executable file with tools like Elastic APM[3]. For Java programs our current recommendation is to use Elastic APM since the instrumentation with it requires a minimal effort. Depending on the language and on the technology adopted, other tools such as Dynatrace[4] or Datadog[5] could be also used.

3   The Microservice Measurement Framework

In this Section, we propose our microservice measurement framework. The framework has the goal of supporting companies to compare different microservices-based solutions, but also to understand the high-level architectural quality of their current system.

The measurement framework is based on availability of log files from real execution and is composed of four measures: coupling (CBM), number of classes per microservice (CLA), number of duplicated classes (DUP), and frequency of external calls (FEC).

This measurement framework is used on the decomposition framework presented in Sect. 4.

---

[3] The Elastic APM Libraries. https://www.elastic.co/solutions/apm.

[4] Dynatrace https://www.dynatrace.com.

[5] Datadog https://www.datadoghq.com.

3.1   Coupling (CBM)

As reported in Sect. 2.3, in successful decompositions the coupling between microservices should be minimized and cohesion should be maximized. A comprehensive calculation of these measures would require knowledge of information beyond the log traces – for instance knowledge about access to local variables. Thus, we need to rely on approximation. One way to approximate coupling is to estimate it as an inverse to cohesion. Coupling can be considered as inversely proportional to cohesion and therefore, a system with low coupling will have a high likelihood of having high cohesion [10].

In our framework we adopt the metric "Coupling Between Microservice" (CBM) [36], a coupling measure inspired by the well-known Coupling Between Object (CBO) metric proposed by Chidamber and Kemerer [3]. CBO counts the number of classes coupled with a given class. Classes can be coupled through several mechanisms, including method calls, field accesses, inheritance, arguments, return types, and exceptions.

In [36] we calculate the relative CBM for each microservice as follows:

$$\text{CBM}_{MS_j} = \frac{\text{Number of external Links}}{\text{Number of Classes in the Microservice}}$$

In this formula "Number Of External Links" represents the number of call paths to external services. So, external services that are called several times, even by different classes of the microservice, are only counted once. The external services could be other microservices or services external to the whole system. The call frequency of external calls should also be take into account, but we have separate measure presented in Subsect. 3.4 for that.

3.2   Number of Classes per Microservice (CLA)

This measure is an abstraction of the size of the microservice, and allows the developer to discover services that are either two big or too small compared with other microservices. In general, smaller microservices are easier to maintain and thus large microservices should be avoided.

In some cases optimizing for CLA measure leads to compromises to other measurements. For instance, larger number smaller microservices may lead to stronger coupling (CBM) and higher frequency of external calls (FEC).

3.3   Number of Duplicated Classes (DUP)

The execution traces often have common sub-paths, i.e., some classes and methods are common for several execution traces. If traces should be implemented in different microservices, one way to increase independence is to is duplicate part of the code to several microservices. For example, method j of class E (Fig. 4) is used by two execution traces. In that example the decomposition option 1 has one duplicated class, while option 2 requires no classes to be duplicated. Duplicated classes increases size of the system and complicates the maintenance process.

3.4   Frequency of External Calls (FEC)

Calls between microservices are computationally substantially heavier than calls within a microservice. Thus, reducing of the frequency of external calls optimizes the performance and delays. Since our approach is based on log-file analysis, we have the frequency information available.

We use the call frequency presented in Table 3 as an input to a measure relative Frequency of External Calls (FEC):

$$\text{FEC}_{MS_j} = \frac{\text{Number of Call Instances}}{\text{Number of Classes in the Microservice}}$$

As an example consider execution paths and decomposition options in Fig. 4. For the sake of the example we assume that

- Path A.a() → A.b() → B.c() → B.d() is called 200 times
- Path C.e() → C.f() → D.g() → D.h() is called 200 times.
- Path C.e() → C.f() → F.j() → D.g() → D.h() is called 50 times
- Path E.i() → E.j() → F.k() → F.l() is called 100 times.

With the input data we can calculate the number of internal calls, external calls, and FEC per each microservice. In Table 2 we also show the total number of internal in microservices (internal C), total number of calls between microservices (external C) and relative computational load (load). In this example we assume that an external call is 1000 times heavier than an internal call.

Table 2. Example analysis of call frequencies between microservices.

MS split	internal c	external c	load	FEC_{MS1}	FEC_{MS2}	FEC_{MS3}
0: A+B, C+D, E+F	1150	100	101550	0	25	25
1: A+B, C+D+E.j, E+F	1650	0	1650	0	0	0
2: A+B, C+D+E+F	1650	0	1650	0	0	

4   The Decomposition Framework

In this Section, we describe a decomposition framework that uses the data from the execution path analysis to discover the optimal split to micro services. A top-level description of the framework is given Fig. 2.

When the log files are available, the decomposition process defined in (Fig. 2) can be started. The process consists of six steps that are outlined in the following subsections.

Fig. 2. The decomposition process (from [36]).

4.1 Step 1: Execution Path Analysis

As our approach aims to optimize the system for the often used call sequences, the first step of our approach is to identify the most frequently executed call paths from the log files. One way to do that is use of a process-mining tool. In our case, we used DISCO[6] to graphically represent the business processes found in the log files. Other similar tools can be used instead. The outcome of step 1 is a graphical representation of the processes and call graphs. One example of such graphical diagram is presented in Fig. 3. The diagram shows the call paths between classes, methods and data bases with arrows. This figure provides the user with the following information:

- The actually executed call paths in the system. Possible but never executed paths are not shown in this figure.
- Inter-class dependencies in the system. The dependencies are visualized with arrows between methods and classes. The external dependencies to libraries or web-services are also visualized.
- The usage frequency of each path. Process mining tools may present the frequency with thickness of the arrows or in a separate table as in Table 3.
- Branches and circular dependencies. If the system has circular dependencies or branches in the call path, those can easily be found from the visualization.

The call paths, shown with chains of arrows in Fig. 3, form candidates for business processes that are later used in the decomposition to microservices. For example, the path documented in Table 1 is visualized in a business process shown in Fig. 3.

Table 3. Frequency analysis of each execution path (from [36]).

Path	Freq.
A.a(); A.b(), B.b(), C.c(), DB.query, Table A, Table B, ...	1000
A.b(); A.c(), B.a(), C.c(), DB.query, Table A, Table B, ...	150

4.2 Step 2: Frequency Analysis of the Execution Paths

In our approach, the call frequency is a major contributor for the produced recommendations. Thus the frequency should be studied and analyzed. For visual

---

[6] https://fluxicon.com/disco/.

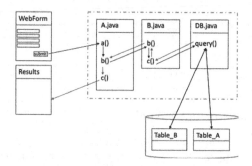

Fig. 3. Simplified process example (from [36]).

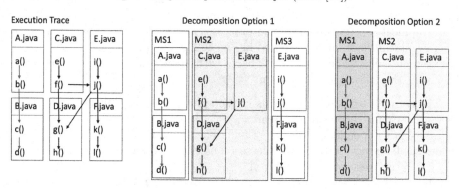

Fig. 4. Microservice decomposition example.

inspection, the process analysis tools can provide help. For instance, in the DISCO tool, the thickness of the arrows reflect the call frequency. In addition to visual inspection, we use concrete numeric data for all execution paths with their usage frequency. So, the output of this step is a table similar to Table 3.

The Frequency Analysis step helps the architect to select the potential decomposition options. The numbers are used to calculate the measures presented in Sect. 3 and used in step 6 (see Subsect. 4.5).

4.3   Step 3: Removal of Circular Dependencies

In this step, we first find circular dependencies by analyzing the execution paths reported in the table generated in the first Step (e.g. Table 3). This can be done with a simple algorithm to discover cycles in the execution paths. In the case of circular dependencies, software architects should discuss with the development team how to break these cycles. One example of the patterns that can be applied to break the cycles is Inversion of Control [17]. However, every cyclic dependency could need a different breaking solution that must be analyzed carefully. The result is a refined version of the execution path table (see Table 3 as example).

Although this step is not part of the decomposition, it is important to consider cyclic dependencies to avoid possible deadlocks, and to better architect the system.

4.4   Step 4: Identification of Decomposition Options

In this step the execution paths from Step 3 are used to identity different decomposition opportunities. Visual inspection of the call graphs like those shown in Fig. 4 is used. We have relied on manual expert-based decomposition, but an algorithm to create different decompositions could be developed.

The execution paths may merge to common sub-paths or split into several branches. This leads to alternative decomposition solutions. This is demonstrated in Fig. 4. If the six source files each providing implementation of a class are assigned to three different microservices as A.java+B.java, C.java+D.java and E.java+F.java, the calls form C.f() to E.j() and E.j() to D.g() are inter-service calls. These calls are heavier operations than local calls and expand the external interfaces of the microservices. If use of external calls is not feasible, there are two other alternatives that can be proposed. The first option is to use three microservices so that class E (or at least function j() of it) is duplicated in two microservices. The other option is to decompose into two microservices as shown in the rightmost part of Fig. 4. Obviously, there is also the alternative to allow external calls and have three microservices with no duplications.

All these options have their advances and disadvantages, and the team should discuss the alternatives is from multiple view points. The consideration could include both functionality of the software – if the paths belong logically together, and development process – what are the consequences of duplication to the development team(s). In addition, the call frequency has to be taken into account. For example in above split and merge case, the team has to consider both the development effort and run-time cost of making the two call external. The metrics discussed Sect. 3 help in analysing the run-time costs.

4.5   Step 5: Metric-Based Ranking of the Decomposition Options

In this step, we apply the measures identified in the Measurement Framework (Sect. 3), to help software architects to assess the quality of the decomposition options.

Sometimes optimization of the measures contradict with each other. Currently, we propose use of judgment of the team, but in the future approaches like Pareto [5] optimization could be used.

4.6   Step 6: Selection of the Decomposition Solution

In final step, the decomposition alternatives identified in Step 4 and the measures collected in Step 5 are used by the software architects to decide which solution to take.

Our approach does not automatically rank the solutions to any order. The software architects should consider the provided recommendations and measurements before selecting the solution. The team should discuss the relevance of the differences in their case.

5   Discussion

In this work we proposed a microservice measurement framework and we applied in our previously proposed decomposition process [36].

The measurement framework is based both on static and dynamic measures collected at runtime. The main benefit of analyzing runtime information is the availability of the data on the usage of each component, together with the dynamic analysis of dependencies. The dynamic measures allow to better understand the behavior of the system, and to analyze the dynamic coupling. Moreover, thanks to the dynamic measures collected, such as the frequency of usage of each method, the software architects can better understood which features is used more, we prioritized the development and the slicing of the monolithic system differently.

Companies could benefit from our lessons learned, by applying our proposed frameworks to decompose their monolithic system, but also to evaluation and monitoring the runtime behaviors or existing microservices to continuously understand possible issues. Moreover, the microservice measurement framework will allow software architects to clearly evaluate different decomposition options, with the usage of repeatable and objective measures.

Despite this approach being very beneficial in our case company, the results could have a different impact on other companies. Researchers can benefit from this approach and extend it further. New optimization metrics could be defined, and in theory, it would be possible to propose an automated decomposition approach that would identify the slices by maximizing the metrics identified. Genetic algorithms could be a possible solution for this idea.

6   Related Work

Fritzsch et al. [8] present a classification for the refactoring approaches. Our approach should be categorized as *Workload-Data aided* in this classification since we use operational data, i.e., dynamic data, in decomposition and analysis.

Bogner et al. have conducted a literature review of maintenance metrics of microservices [1]. The report summarizes several metrics that specialize in service-based systems instead of metrics designed for object-oriented systems. Although that research assume use of static info only, these metrics should be interesting for us in future research.

One case of refactoring a legacy system to a service based system has been reported buy Khadka et al. [12]. Their case has substantial similarities to our approach and case. They also stress the importance and difficulty of finding the right set of services. They also analyze the call paths to find hotspots in the code. However, they do not present a systematic and repeatable process for decomposition. Actually, only a limited set of research works propose systematic approaches for developers in decomposing their systems into an optimal set of microservices.

Chris Richardson [24] put scalability into focus and propose a decomposition approach based on the "scalability cube" where applications can be scaled based on the X, Y or Z axis. The X-axis and Z-axis scaling consists of running multiple copies of an application behind a load balancer. The Y-axis axis scaling is the real microservice decomposition approach, that propose to split the application into multiple, different services. Each service is responsible for one or more closely related functions. The decomposition is then based on two approaches: decomposing based on verbs used into the description of the service or decomposing by noun creating services responsible for all operations related to a particular entity such as customer management. Richardson also recommend to use combination of verb-based and noun-based decomposition when needed.

Richardson [23] also mention this approach in his two decomposition strategies:

- "Decompose by business capability and define services corresponding to business capabilities";
- "Decompose by domain-driven design sub-domain";

In an older version of this page [23] (2017), Richardson proposed other two patterns:

- "Decompose by verb or use 'cases' and define services that are responsible for particular actions";
- "Decompose by nouns or resources by defining a service that is responsible for all operations on entities/resources of a given type".

Kecskemeti et al. [11] proposed a decomposition approach based on container optimization. The goal is to increase the elasticity of large-scale applications and the possibility to obtain more flexible compositions with other services.

Another decomposition possibility is to start from a monolithic system and progressively move towards a microservices-based architecture [39] or delivering separate microservices by splitting a development team into smaller ones responsible for a limited group of microservices.

Vresk et al. [38] defined an IoT concept and platform based on the orchestration of different IoT system components, such as devices, data sources, data processors, and storage. They recommend an approach similar to the one proposed by Richardson's Scalability Cube [24] combining verb-based and noun-based decomposition approaches. The proposed approach hides the complexity stemming from the variation of end-device properties thanks to the application of a uniform approach for modeling both physical and logical IoT devices and services. Moreover, it can foster interoperability and extensibility using diverse communication protocols into proxy microservice components.

Gysel et al. [9] proposed a clustering algorithm approach based on 16 coupling criteria derived from literature analysis and industry experience. This approach is an extensible tool framework for service decomposition as a combination of a criteria-driven methods. It integrates graph clustering algorithms and features priority scoring and nine types of analysis and design specifications. Moreover, this approach introduces the concept of coupling criteria cards using 16 different instances grouped into four categories: Cohesiveness, Compatibility, Constraints, and Communications. The approach was evaluated by integrating two existing graph clustering algorithms, combining actions research and case study investigations, and load tests. The results showed potential benefits to the practitioners, also confirmed by user feedback.

Chen et al. [2] proposed a data-driven microservices-oriented decomposition approach based on data flow diagrams from business logic. Their approach could deliver more rational, objective, and easy-to-understand results thanks to objective operations and data extracted from real-world business logic. Similarly, we adopt process mining to analyze the business processes of a monolithic system.

Alwis et al. [4] proposed a heuristic to slice a monolithic system into microservices based on object subtypes (i.e., the lowest granularity of software based on structural properties) and functional splitting based on common execution fragments across software (i.e., the lowest granularity of software based on behavioral properties). This approach is the closer to our work. However, they analyzed the system by means of static analysis without capturing the dynamic behavior of the system and they did not propose measures to evaluate the quality of the slicing solution proposed.

Taibi et al. [28,33,34], proposed a set of patterns and anti-patterns that should be carefully considered during the microservice decomposition [28,33] recommending to avoid a set of harmful practices such as cyclic dependencies and hard-coded endpoints but also to consider critical anti-patterns and code smells [27] that can be generated into the monolithic system.

7 Conclusions

The decomposition of monolithic systems into microservices is a very complex and error-prone task, commonly performed manually by the software architect.

In this work, we first proposed a new microservice measurement framework based on 4 measures: coupling, number of classes per microservices, number of duplicated classes and frequency of external calls. The goal of our framework is to support software architects to compare different microservice decompositions, by means of a set of objective and repeatable measures.

We instantiated our measurement framework in the context of the previously proposed process-mining decomposition approach [36].

Our goal is not the automated slicing of monolithic systems but to provide extra support to software architect, to help them in identifying different slicing options reducing the subjectivity and to measure and compare the different solutions objectively.

The microservice measurement framework can be adopted independently from the decomposition process used. As example, software architect might manually identify two decomposition options for a monolithic system. The measurement framework will support them in the comparison of their decomposition options.

We recommend companies to apply periodically our measurement framework also in case of existing microservices-based systems. The historical analysis of the evolution of the system might provide useful information on the quality of the system and also be a trigger for future refactorings.

Future works include the validation of the framework, both in the context of manual decompositions and when using process-mining based approaches. Moreover, we want to evaluate the application of our approach in development of a tool to facilitate the identification of the process, the automatic calculation of the metrics, and identification of other measures for evaluating the quality of the decomposition. We already started to develop a tool to automatically identify dependencies between microservices [21] and we published a dataset containing the analysis of 20 projects [22].

We are also planning to further empirically validate this approach with other companies and to include dynamic measures for evaluating the quality of the system at runtime [16,37]. In the future, we are also planning to adopt mining software repositories techniques to identify the areas that changed simultaneously in the past, to help developers to understand pieces of code connected to each other.

Another possible future work is to include identification of partial migration, i.e., migration of a limited set of processes from a monolithic system. Finally, we are also considering to extend this work by proposing not only different decomposition options but also a set of patterns for connecting microservices based on existing common microservices patterns [19,32] and anti-patterns [28, 33,34].

References

1. Bogner, J., Wagner, S., Zimmermann, A.: Automatically measuring the maintainability of service- and microservice-based systems: a literature review. In: Proceedings of the 27th International Workshop on Software Measurement and 12th International Conference on Software Process and Product Measurement, IWSM Mensura 2017, pp. 107–115. ACM, New York (2017). https://doi.org/10.1145/3143434.3143443
2. Chen, R., Li, S., Li, Z.: From monolith to microservices: a dataflow-driven approach. In: 2017 24th Asia-Pacific Software Engineering Conference (APSEC), pp. 466–475, December 2017
3. Chidamber, S.R., Kemerer, C.F.: A metrics suite for object oriented design. IEEE Trans. Softw. Eng. 20(6), 476–493 (1994)
4. De Alwis, A.A.C., Barros, A., Polyvyanyy, A., Fidge, C.: Function-splitting heuristics for discovery of microservices in enterprise systems. In: Pahl, C., Vukovic, M., Yin, J., Yu, Q. (eds.) ICSOC 2018. LNCS, vol. 11236, pp. 37–53. Springer, Cham (2018). https://doi.org/10.1007/978-3-030-03596-9_3

5. Deb, K.: Evolutionary algorithms for multi-criterion optimization in engineering design. In: EUROGEN 1999, pp. 135–161 (1999)
6. Fenton, N., Bieman, J.: Software Metrics: A Rigorous and Practical Approach, 3rd edn. CRC Press, Boca Raton (2014)
7. Fowler, M., Lewis, J.: Microservices (2014). http://martinfowler.com/articles/microservices.html
8. Fritzsch, J., Bogner, J., Zimmermann, A., Wagner, S.: From monolith to microservices: a classification of refactoring approaches. In: Bruel, J.-M., Mazzara, M., Meyer, B. (eds.) DEVOPS 2018. LNCS, vol. 11350, pp. 128–141. Springer, Cham (2019). https://doi.org/10.1007/978-3-030-06019-0_10
9. Gysel, M., Kölbener, L., Giersche, W., Zimmermann, O.: Service cutter: a systematic approach to service decomposition. In: Aiello, M., Johnsen, E.B., Dustdar, S., Georgievski, I. (eds.) ESOCC 2016. LNCS, vol. 9846, pp. 185–200. Springer, Cham (2016). https://doi.org/10.1007/978-3-319-44482-6_12
10. Jabangwe, R., Börstler, J., Šmite, D., Wohlin, C.: Empirical evidence on the link between object-oriented measures and external quality attributes: a systematic literature review. Empir. Softw. Eng. **20**(3), 640–693 (2014). https://doi.org/10.1007/s10664-013-9291-7
11. Kecskemeti, G., Marosi, A.C., Kertesz, A.: The entice approach to decompose monolithic services into microservices. In: 2016 International Conference on High Performance Computing Simulation (HPCS), pp. 591–596, July 2016
12. Khadka, R., Saeidi, A., Jansen, S., Hage, J., Haas, G.P.: Migrating a large scale legacy application to SOA: challenges and lessons learned. In: 2013 20th Working Conference on Reverse Engineering (WCRE), pp. 425–432, October 2013. https://doi.org/10.1109/WCRE.2013.6671318
13. Kramer, S., Kaindl, H.: Coupling and cohesion metrics for knowledge-based systems using frames and rules. ACM Trans. Softw. Eng. Methodol. **13**(3), 332–358 (2004)
14. Lehman, M.M.: On understanding laws, evolution, and conservation in the large-program life cycle. J. Syst. Softw. **1**, 213–221 (1984). https://doi.org/10.1016/0164-1212(79)90022-0
15. Lenarduzzi, V., Sillitti, A., Taibi, D.: Analyzing forty years of software maintenance models. In: 39th International Conference on Software Engineering Companion, ICSE-C 2017, IEEE Press (2017). https://doi.org/10.1109/ICSE-C.2017.122
16. Lenarduzzi, V., Stan, C., Taibi, D., Venters, G.: A dynamical quality model to continuously monitor software maintenance. In: 11th European Conference on Information Systems Management (ECISM) (2017)
17. Martin, R.C.: Agile Software Development: Principles, Patterns, and Practices. Prentice Hall PTR, Upper Saddle River (2003)
18. Mikkonen, T., Systä, K.: Maximizing product value: continuous maintenance. In: Jedlitschka, A., Kuvaja, P., Kuhrmann, M., Männistö, T., Münch, J., Raatikainen, M. (eds.) PROFES 2014. LNCS, vol. 8892, pp. 298–301. Springer, Cham (2014). https://doi.org/10.1007/978-3-319-13835-0_26
19. Newman, S.: Building Microservices, 1st edn. O'Reilly Media Inc., Newton (2015)
20. Parnas, D.L.: On the criteria to be used in decomposing systems into modules. Commun. ACM **15**(12), 1053–1058 (1972)
21. Rahman, M., Taibi, D.: Microservice dependency graph (microdepgraph) (2019). https://github.com/clowee/MicroDepGraph
22. Rahman, M., Taibi, D.: The microservice dependency graph dataset. In: Proceedings of the Joint Summer School on Software Evolution, Software Quality and Bug Prediction with Machine Learning. CEUR-WS, September 2019

23. Richardson, C.: Pattern: Microservice Architecture (2017). http://microservices. io/patterns/microservices.html
24. Richardson, C.: The Scale Cube (2017). https://microservices.io/articles/ scalecube.html
25. Soldani, J., Tamburri, D.A., Heuvel, W.J.V.D.: The pains and gains of microservices: a systematic grey literature review. J. Syst. Softw. **146**, 215–232 (2018)
26. Suonsyrjä, S., Mikkonen, T.: Designing an unobtrusive analytics framework for monitoring Java applications. In: Kobyliński, A., Czarnacka-Chrobot, B., Świerczek, J. (eds.) IWSM/Mensura -2015. LNBIP, vol. 230, pp. 160–175. Springer, Cham (2015). https://doi.org/10.1007/978-3-319-24285-9_11
27. Taibi, D., Janes, A., Lenarduzzi, V.: How developers perceive smells in source code: a replicated study. Inf. Softw. Technol. **92**, 223–235 (2017)
28. Taibi, D., Lenarduzzi, V.: On the definition of microservice bad smells. IEEE Softw. **35**(3), 56–62 (2018)
29. Taibi, D., Lenarduzzi, V., Ahmad, M.O., Liukkunen, K.: Comparing communication effort within the scrum, scrum with Kanban, XP, and Banana development processes. In: Proceedings of the 21st International Conference on Evaluation and Assessment in Software Engineering, EASE 2017, pp. 258–263 (2017)
30. Taibi, D., Lenarduzzi, V., Janes, A., Liukkunen, K., Ahmad, M.O.: ˙Comparing requirements decomposition within the scrum, scrum with Kanban, XP, and Banana development processes. In: Agile Processes in Software Engineering and Extreme Programming, pp. 68–83 (2017)
31. Taibi, D., Lenarduzzi, V., Pahl, C.: Processes, motivations, and issues for migrating to microservices architectures: an empirical investigation. IEEE Cloud Comput. **4**(5), 22–32 (2017)
32. Taibi, D., Lenarduzzi, V., Pahl, C.: Architectural patterns for microservices: a systematic mapping study. In: 8th International Conference on Cloud Computing and Services Science, CLOSER 2018 (2018)
33. Taibi, D., Lenarduzzi, V., Pahl, C.: Microservices anti-patterns: a taxonomy. IWSM/Mensura -2015. LNBIP, vol. 1073, pp. 111–128. Springer, Cham (2020). https://doi.org/10.1007/978-3-030-31646-4_5
34. Taibi, D., Lenarduzzi, V., Pahl, C.: Continuous architecting with microservices and DevOps: a systematic mapping study. In: Muñoz, V.M., Ferguson, D., Helfert, M., Pahl, C. (eds.) CLOSER 2018. CCIS, vol. 1073, pp. 126–151. Springer, Cham (2019). https://doi.org/10.1007/978-3-030-29193-8_7
35. Taibi, D., Lenarduzzi, V., Pahl, C., Janes, A.: Microservices in agile software development: a workshop-based study into issues, advantages, and disadvantages. In: XP Workshops, pp. 23:1–23:5. ACM (2017)
36. Taibi, D., Systa, K.: From monolithic systems to microservices: a decomposition framework based on process mining. In: 9th International Conference on Cloud Computing and Services Science, CLOSER 2019, Heraklion, Greece, 05 2019 (2019)
37. Tosi, D., Lavazza, L., Morasca, S., Taibi, D.: On the definition of dynamic software measures. In: ESEM, pp. 39–48. ACM (2012)
38. Vresk, T., Cavrak, I.: Architecture of an interoperable IoT platform based on microservices. In: MIPRO, pp. 1196–1201. IEEE (2016)
39. Zimmermann, O.: Microservices tenets. Comput. Sci. Res. Dev. **32**(3), 301–310 (2016). https://doi.org/10.1007/s00450-016-0337-0

A Containerized Edge Cloud Architecture for Data Stream Processing

Remo Scolati, Ilenia Fronza, Nabil El Ioini, Areeg Samir,
Hamid Reza Barzegar, and Claus Pahl[✉]

Free University of Bozen-Bolzano, Bolzano, Italy
{remo.scolati,ilenia.fronza,nabil.elioini,areeg.samir,
hamidreza.barzegar,claus.pahl}@unibz.it

Abstract. Internet of Things (IoT) devices produce large volumes of data, which creates challenges for the supporting, often centralised cloud infrastructure that needs to process and store the data. We consider here an alternative, more centralised approach, based on the edge cloud computing model. Here, filtering and processing of data happens locally before transferring it to a central cloud infrastructure. In our work, we use a low-power and low-cost cluster of single board computers (SBC) to apply common models and technologies from the big data domain. The benefit is reducing the volume of data that is transferred.

We implement the system using a cluster of Raspberry Pis and Docker to containerize and deploy an Apache Hadoop and Apache Spark data streaming processing cluster. We evaluate the performance, but of trust support of the system, showing that by using containerization increased fault tolerance and ease of maintenance can be achieved. The analysis of the performance takes into account the resource usage of the proposed solution with regards to the constraints imposed by the devices. Our trust management solution relies on blockchain technologies.

Keywords: Edge cloud · IoT · Container · Cluster architecture · Raspberry Pi · Docker · Big data · Data streaming · Performance · Trust

1 Introduction

Devices that produce data are ubiquitous by now. Connected to the Internet of Things (IoT) a major part of this data is stored or processed in a cloud environment. This data volume is growing exponentially [44].

In order to reduce data volume in transfer, local (pre-)processing of data is a more resource-efficient alternative to the currently used centralised cloud processing model. We present here a lightweight infrastructure following the

© Springer Nature Switzerland AG 2020
D. Ferguson et al. (Eds.): CLOSER 2019, CCIS 1218, pp. 150–176, 2020.
https://doi.org/10.1007/978-3-030-49432-2_8

edge computing model. We specifically aim to provide affordable, low-energy local clusters at the outer edge of the cloud that are partly composed of IoT devices themselves. In more concrete terms, we have build a small low-power, low-cost cluster of single board computers in a local network, which alows us to process generated data at the outer edge closer to producers and often consumers of the data. This solution addresses critical performance, but also trust concerns. We also look at cost concerns, important for the industrial application.

Single-board devices (SBD) such as Raspberry Pis have already been investigated for IoT and edge settings [25,33,43,47], but performance and trust for an industry-relevant setting still need to be better investigated. We introduce here an edge cloud architecture on SBDs [32] that builds on technologies commonly used in big data processing like Apache Hadoop and Apache Spark, which are characterised by high speed, high variety, and high volume. The software platform builds on Docker as the containerization technology. Docker Swarm is used as the mechanism of orchestrating application services on a device cluster.

We describe the implementation of the solution using a cluster of Raspberry Pis, a single board computer (SBC). We use Docker to deploy and orchestrate lightweight containers [35] in which we run an Apache Hadoop and Apache Spark cluster. In order to analyze the performance of the system [16] considering the resource constraints of the Raspberry Pi, system metrics are collected through a monitoring stack based on Prometheus, a monitoring and alerting tool, that we deployed on the cluster. Performance is evaluated experimentally, using a test application to process data. Furthermore, we demonstrate how the cluster can be used as test bed for such applications. We also look into trust, which we validate using a use case analysis.

2   State-of-the-Art Discussion

Many IoT-cloud integrations monitor and collect data at the IoT edge, but send this data directly to a centralized cloud where sufficient storage space and computational power is available. However, as a consequence of increasing numbers of IoT device and volume of data that is being generated, such centralised cloud infrastructures are not ideal from a latency, cost and reliability perspective [13].

The IoT domain gives rise to a number of use cases, where large amounts of data are generated and have to be processed. The ability to process data locally with a low-cost and low-power system opens up use cases in environments without large amounts of processing power at disposal on premise, which would benefit from a decreased traffic, like systems in remote areas. Also autonomous monitoring and automation systems, like remote localised power grids are sample applications. Possible application scenarios include autonomous power generation and distribution plants, such as smaller local energy grids. In smart city contexts, mobility applications need to support vehicles moving around that themselves have limited computational power.

Edge computing aims at migrating storage and computation to the remote layer close to the data producers and consumers [22]. Specifically low-cost and lightweight approaches based on the fog or edge cloud computing model are needed if the edge devices are somewhat resource-constrained or the need to use affordable devices exists. Functionally, the main requirement is to collect, process, and aggregate data locally. Quality-wise, the aim is reducing the overall amount of traffic and the need for a backing cloud infrastructure. The costs for acquisition, maintenance and operation of such a system and its suitability in an industrial setting will also need to be considered as well as the overall performance of the system with regards to the limited resource constraints. Another requirement is that a suitable platform needs to reflect a industry-relevant setting in terms of software deployment or big data processing. Yet another problem arises from the often cross-organisation setting. Often, no prior trust relationship exists between providers and consumers of devices, software and data.

Constrained edge systems benefit from the use of single board computers like the Raspberry Pi [24] to address cost or other constraints. The possibility of connecting sensors to the device's GPIO paired with the capability to perform more complex computations, thus creating a network of smart sensors capable of recording, filtering, and processing data is enabled here. The nodes can be joined together to a cluster to distribute the workload in the form of containers, having separate nodes responsible for different steps of the data pipeline from data generation and collection to evaluation for big data streaming and analytics.

Lightweight cluster infrastructure (Raspberry Pis), lightweight container-based software deployment and orchestration platform (Docker swarm) that hosts a big data streaming application architecture are introduced in the next section. This would lead towards a microservices-style architecture [19,42] allowing for flexible software deployment and management to be enabled. In this paper, we built on [1] by adding trust to the previous performance concern for evaluation. Furthermore, we better demonstrate the utility of our results by developing an automated vehicle and mobility use case and show how the proposed architecture can be utilised in this context.

3   Literature Review

Lightweight devices such as single-board devices and lightweight virtualization based on containers have continuously gained popularity. Lightweightness is a benefit for computing at the outer edge, where limited resources are available, but still data originating from the IoT layer needs to be processed. Lightweight devices result in lower costs and lower energy consumption.

We review literature in terms of three criteria: overhead, edge applicability and big data feasibility. Firstly, overhead: in comparison to native processes, according to [26,36] Docker container virtualization has been shown to not add significant overhead by leveraging kernel technologies like namespaces and control groups, allowing the isolation of processes from each other and an optimal allocation of resources such as CPU, memory and I/O device access. Secondly, IoT/Edge Applicability: according to [27,30], Docker is highly suitable as a platform for both IoT and Edge Computing. Here as a consequence of constraints imposed by low-power devices, it allows lightweight virtualization and facilitates the creation of distributed architectures. Thirdly, Big Data: [29] shows that Docker is suitable for provisioning Big Data platforms, for instance Hadoop and Pachyderm, thus helping overcome difficulties in installation, management, and usage of large data processing systems. Systems like Hadoop have been demonstrated in [12] to be a suitable platform for pre-processing large amounts of data even on small clouds with limited networking and computing resources.

In [46], it is pointed out that the recent development of low-cost SBDs allows the creation of low-power affordable IoT and edge clusters that offer the capability of pre-processing sensor data, while also reducing acquisition and maintenance costs [46]. SBDs such as the Raspberry Pi are particularly interesting for any system which gathers, processes, and reacts to environment data of some form. They allow technically to attach sensors and actuators to its GPIO pins. Their architecture enables smart infrastructures and smart sensor networks, see e.g.,[25,43] that describe the University of Glasgow Smart Campus project. HypriotOS [37,38] is a Linux-based operating system that makes the Docker platform available for ARM processor and thus for IoT networks. The Hypriot developers have demonstrated that container orchestration tools like Docker Swarm and Kubernetes can be run on Raspberry Pis to facilitate highly available and scalable clusters despite the given resource limits of SBDs. Trust is another open concern. While trust architectures exist [11] that address identity and integrity concerns for instance through distributed ledger technologies, their application to edge context is not sufficiently analysed.

Despite some acknowledgement of the principle suitability, an exploration of the performance limits resulting from a containerised big data streaming application on a lightweight cluster architecture is still lacking. Furthermore, trust platforms exist, but need to be better investigated regarding their edge suitability. Thus, we have built such an architecture and evaluated it in terms of cost, configuration, performance and trust concerns in the context of an industry-relevant choice of technologies such as container management (Docker), monitoring (Prometheus), stream process (Spark) and blockchain (Hyperledger Fabric).

Nowadays, the utilization of SBDs such as a Raspberry Pi with different techniques of lightweight virtualization attracts researchers from an industrial projects such as Carberry[1] and ODB-Pi[2] to academical research. In [28], a Docker container-based platform has been proposed as a lightweight virtualization solution for enabling a customized smart car application. According to the result, container-based virtualization is not an only a viable approach, although is more flexible and effective in terms of management of several parallel processes running on On-Board-Unit (OBU). In [40], a scaled validation of Connected and Automated Vehicles (CAV) has been studied for vehicle-to-vehicle and vehicle-to-infrastructure communications. Furthermore, the development of robotic devices such as Pololu Zumo[3] that combined with an on-board Raspberry

---

[1] http://www.carberry.it.

[2] http://www.instructables.com/id/OBD-Pi/.

[3] https://www.pololu.com/product/2506.

Pi 3 supports researchers to provide shorter gaps between theory and practical implementation scenarios to reduce the overall cost of the project. The possibility of cooperative automation through the cloud for distributed computing has been studied in [14,41] in the project CARMA (Cloud-Assisted Real-Time Methods for Autonomy). CARMA combines a 3-tier architecture, includes of Vehicle, Edge, and Cloud to address on-board and off-board computation as important necessities of cooperative automated driving technology. All 3 tiers are logically divided into CARMA Core Cloud, CARMA Edge and CARMA Vehicle, which have a possibility to work independently, therefore, they could enable ultra-Reliability and Low-Latency Communication (uRLLC) for 5G. Low-cost connected devices for measuring acceleration and assessing road surface friction during vehicle braking performance-wise have been studied in [2]. As reported in the study the measurements which obtained from the proposed prototype during some tests are comparable to their benchmark regarding all measurement parameters including sample frequency, acceleration values and triggering thresholds, on the other hand with 10 to 15-times fewer values for the material cost. Another implementation of an inexpensive Raspberry Pi for a real-time traffic jam on the road has been studied in [7]. An innovative prototype for control and management of a connected car is modeled in [45] which can be a remotely controlled connected car based on YANG/RESTCONF and cloud computing. In this demonstration, a RESTCONF server was installed on a Raspberry Pi, responsible for the sensors and actuators of the car and allowing for its remote control using SDN/NFV technology from a user terminal and through the cloud. In terms of safe driving system, [15] proposes a new model based on the plural sensors inside a car and on a driver's body which uses multiple edge computing nodes. This prototype consists of three edge computing nodes; first one is for monitoring the car and the driver. The second one acts as a controller and the last node is learning server for training a model for more sophisticated risk assessment. All these 3 distributed cooperative edge nodes are implemented based on the Raspberry Pi.

4   Platform Technologies

We propose a layered architecture of three platform technologies, with Raspberry Pis as the device layer, Docker containers and the software platform and Apache Hadoop/Spark as the data processing layer.

The Raspberry Pi (RPi) is a single-board computer, which was initially developed as an educational device, but soon attracted attention from developers due to the small size and relatively low price [39]. There have been multiple updates of the platform. The specifications are shown in Table 1. In this project, the Raspberry Pi 2 Model B, released in 2015, is used.

Docker is an open source software project that allows to run containerized applications [9]. A container is a runnable instance of a Docker image, a layered template with instructions to create such a container. A container holds everything the application needs to run, like system tools, libraries and

Table 1. Specification of the Raspberry Pi 2, Model B – see [1].

Architecture	ARMv7
SoC	Broadcom BCM2836
CPU	900 MHz quad-core 32-bit ARMCortex-A7
Memory	1 GB
Ethernet	10/100Mbit/s

resources, while keeping it in isolation from the infrastructure on which the container is running, thus forming a kind of virtualisation layer. Figure 1 illustrates Docker's architecture. Containers interact with their environment. Access to system resources can be configured for each container to access storage, or, in the case of the RPis, to the general-purpose input/output pins (GPIO) for interaction with its environment, e.g., for using sensors or actuators.

Technically, containers compartmentalize the container process and its children using Linux containers (LXC) and libcontainer technology provided by the Linux kernel via kernel namespacing and control groups (cgroups), in fact isolating the process from all other processes on the system, while using the hosts kernel and resources. The major difference between containers and VMs is that containers, sharing the hosts kernel, do not necessitate a separate operating system, resulting in less overhead and minimizing the needed resources.

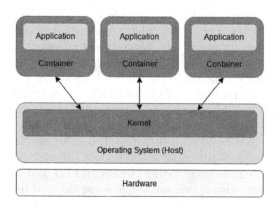

Fig. 1. Docker container architecture – see [1].

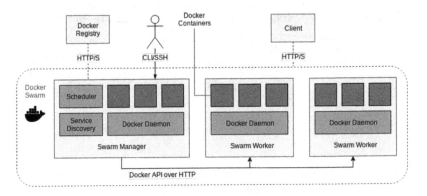

Fig. 2. Docker swarm configuration sample – see [1].

A central component is the Docker Engine[4]. The Docker daemon is the server that manages all Docker objects, i.e., images, containers, volumes and networks. The client, a command line interface (CLI), communicates with the daemon using a REST API. The Docker Swarm mode[5] allows natively to manage a cluster/swarm of Docker engines. Docker Swarm allows to use the Docker CLI to create and manage a swarm, and to deploy application services to it, without having to resort to additional orchestration software. A Docker swarm (cluster) is made up of multiple Docker hosts that run in swarm mode and act as either manager or worker nodes. A host can run as manager, worker, or both. When a service is created, the number of replicas, available network and storage resources, exposed ports, and other configurations are defined.

The state of a service is actively maintained by Docker. For example, if a worker node becomes unavailable, the tasks assigned to that node are scheduled on other nodes. This enables fault-tolerance. A task here refers to a running container that is run and managed by the swarm, as opposed to a standalone container. In Fig. 2, we illustrate a schematic Docker swarm configuration.

At the core is MapReduce, which is a programming model allowing to process big data sets. It is build on a distributed, parallel algorithm on clustered devices [8]. The name indicates that a MapReduce program contains (1) a map method for performing filtering/sorting of data and (2) also a Reduce method, to execute some associative operation. While being inspired by map and reduce methods common in functional programming, the main aim of MapReduce is the optimization of the underlying engine, thus achieving scalability and fault tolerance. The MapReduce process can be illustrated as follows:

---

[4] Docker Engine, https://docs.docker.com/engine.
[5] Docker Swarm, https://docs.docker.com/engine/swarm/.

```
1    Map(k1,v1) → list(k2,v2)
2    Reduce(k2, list(v2)) → list(v3)
```

Both the Map and Reduce operation are run on structured data in the form of (key, value) pairs. The Map function is applied to all pairs (k1, v1) of the input in parallel, producing a list of pairs (k2, v2). After this first step, all pairs with the same key k2 are collected by the framework, producing one group (k2, list(v2)) for each key. Then, the Reduce function is applied to each group in parallel, producing a list of values v3.

Apache Hadoop is an open source software library based on the MapReduce programming model [3] to process large datasets in a distributed way. The aim is to scale from single nodes to clusters with multiple thousands of machines [6]. The following modules are part of the Apache Hadoop core:

- Hadoop Common – common libraries & utilities;
- Hadoop Distributed File System (HDFS) – distributed file system to store data on cluster nodes;
- Hadoop YARN – manage/schedule computing resources and applications;
- Hadoop MapReduce – large scale MapReduce data processing.

Figure 3 illustrates a small cluster with a single master node and multiple worker nodes. The master node acts as a task and job tracker, NameNode (data index), and DataNode (data store). Worker nodes act as task tracker and DataNode.

At the core of the Hadoop architecture is the Hadoop Distributed File System (HDFS) together with the MapReduce processing component. Since the nodes manipulate the data they have access to, Hadoop allows for faster and more efficient processing of the dataset than more traditional supercomputer architectures [48]. Files are split into blocks of data and distributed across the DataNodes. Transferring a packaged application on the same nodes, Hadoop takes advantage of the principle of data locality.

Finally, Apache Spark is a distributed computing framework as an extension to the MapReduce paradigm that provides an interface for executing applications on clusters [4]. Based on resilient distributed datasets (RDD), a distributed and fault-tolerant set of read-only data items is processed. RDDs provide a limited form of Apache Spark generally reduces the latency, compared to an Apache Hadoop implementation by several orders of magnitude. Hadoop has a distributed shared memory for distributed programs, allowing a less forced dataflow compared to the MapReduce paradigm. Apache Spark requires a cluster manager – supported implementations are Spark native, Apache Hadoop YARN, and Apache Mesos clusters – and a distributed storage system. In extension to Apache Hadoop's batch processing model, Apache Spark provides an interface to perform streaming analytics.

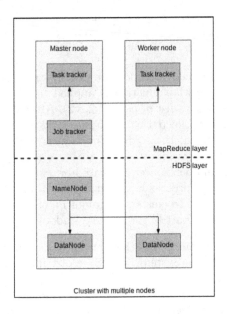

Fig. 3. Small Hadoop cluster – see [1].

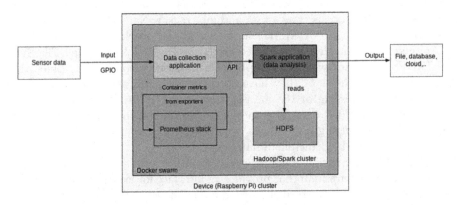

Fig. 4. Stream processing system architecture – see [1].

Spark supports distributed storage systems, TCP/IP sockets, and a variety of data feed providers such as Kafka and Twitter as streaming sources, thus making it interoperate well with common platforms.

5   A Lightweight Platform for Edge Data Processing

Our architecture builds on a Raspberry Pi cluster that hosts a Docker swarm to leverage the ease of container orchestration on multiple devices. Other applications, i.e., Apache Hadoop and Spark cluster, the Prometheus monitoring stack

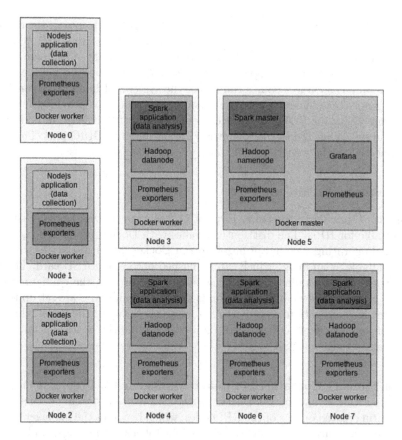

Fig. 5. Overview of the distribution of the service containers on the nodes – see [1].

and the applications used to simulate data collection, are executed inside Docker containers. In order to have a data producer, data is provided by a Nodejs[6] application that writes files to the HDFS via its API. The Hadoop distributed file system (HDFS) serves as data source for an Apache Spark streaming application. This simplifies the deployment and management of these applications. For instance, even partial hardware failure can be managed by Docker.

Our lightweight edge architecture is shown in Figs. 4 and 5. Figure 4 shows the processing in the architecture and the data flow during the experiments, while Fig. 5 shows an overview of the distribution of the services on the Raspberry Pis in the configuration that reflects our experimental setting.

5.1   Hardware Architecture

The Raspberry Pi cluster is made up of eight RPi 2 Model B, fitted with an 8 GB micro SDcard for the installation of the OS. The Raspberry Pis are connected

---

[6] Nodejs, https://nodejs.org.

to a Veracity Camswitch 8 Mobile switch[7]. This serves also to power the devices through Power over Ethernet (POE). The switch features ten 10/100Mbit/s ports, eight of which are 802.3 POE outputs. POE has the advantage of the setup being cleaner, since a separate power supply is not needed for the Raspberry Pis and as such less cables run across the system, although this is neither necessary nor cost efficient. Since the Raspberry Pi does not provide the necessary connectivity for POE, the devices need to be outfitted with an additional POE module, connected to the Raspberry Pis through the GPIO pins. The RPis are connected to the switch using category 5E SFTP cables.

5.2 Software Architecture

Hypriot - Operating System. Hypriot OS[8] is a specialized Debian distribution suitable for RPis. The distribution comes with Docker pre-installed, and is a minimal operating system optimized to run Docker on ARM devices. Hypriot OS is available as an image which can be flashed onto a micro SD card. The OS comes with a pre-installed SSH service, accessible through the configured credentials. Since password authentication is not secure, all nodes are set up to use public key authentication. In order to automate the setup of the nodes, the configuration management tool Ansible[9], is used to define the hosts and automate configuration tasks via SSH.

Docker Swarm - Container Setup and Management. In order to initialize and setup a Docker swarm, the Docker engine CLI is used, starting with a single node swarm created on one of the RPI nodes, which becomes the manager for the newly created swarm. The manager stores join tokens for manager and worker nodes, which can be used to join other machines to the swarm. In addition, different tags can be set through the Docker CLI on each node that can be used to constrain the deployment of services to specific nodes. For other swarm management tasks such as promotions, demotions and manage the membership of nodes, Docker engine commands can be issued to any define manager.

Application Services - Deployment. Docker stack deployment is used to deploy services to the swarm. To describe the stack, Docker uses a stack description in form of a Compose file, where multiple services can be defined. For each service part of the stack, the origin registry, ports and networks, mounted volumes, service name and replicas as well as deployment constraints, for example Docker node tags, can be specified. When deployed on a manager node, Docker will deploy each service in the stack to the nodes of the swarm, according to the constraints and definition, balancing out the containers on the available nodes.

---

[7] Veracity Global Camswitch 8, http://www.veracityglobal.com/products/networked-video-integration-devices/camswitch-mobile.aspx.

[8] Hypriot OS, https://blog.hypriot.com/about/.

[9] Ansible, https://www.ansible.com/.

To deploy the compose file to the swarm manager and to set up the nodes, e.g., for the preparation of configuration files and mounted directories, Ansible scripts can be used (or alternatively these actions can be performed manually). The table below describes the allocation of services to nodes[10], see also Fig. 5.

Node	Container
Node 0	Data collection, Prometheus exporters
Node 1	Data collection, Prometheus exporters
Node 2	Data collection, Prometheus exporters
Node 3	Spark worker 2, Prometheus exporters
Node 4	Spark worker 1, Prometheus exporters
Node 5	Spark master, Prometheus exporters, Prometheus, Grafana
Node 6	Spark worker 3, Prometheus exporters
Node 7	Spark worker 4, Prometheus exporters

Hadoop and Apache Spark - Deployment. Hadoop and Apache Spark are deployed to the cluster, together with the data collection application used to evaluate the implementation, through a Docker Compose file. Hadoop can be natively used to create clusters of computers, but Hadoop and also Apache Spark can also be deployed inside Docker containers. We chose the latter option to streamline the deployment process and avoid a tedious per-device installation of the software and the management of required dependencies.

We used a Docker image to install Hadoop and Apache Spark inside a container and also for the set-up of the environment. In the final set-up, one master node and four separate worker nodes are deployed. Since the worker nodes act as DataNodes for the cluster, each worker node container is provided with sufficient storage space, by means of a standard 3.5 inch. 1TB hard disk, mounted as a volume. Note that the three remaining cluster nodes act as data producers.

6   Data Processing and Monitoring at the Edge

The process of data production, collection and analysis is at the core and support by Hadoop/Spark. Additionally, monitoring is critical.

6.1   Edge Data Collection and Analysis

For the experimental evaluation of the architecture, we use two applications, one for simulating data production and collection on three nodes and a second one is deployed to the Apache Spark cluster to process the collected data. The applications are also used to gather data related to the performance of the system. Here, we focus on the data processing time.

---

[10] Prometheus exporters: Armexporter, Node exporter, cAdvisor.

- Data Collection. In order to simulate data collection, a Nodejs application sends a HTTP PUT request with the data content to the HDFS API creating a file in a specified interval of time. The data collection application is deployed on three cluster nodes. The experiment data are sample files exposed to and read by the application over the network allowing to change the size and the contents without having to modify the application and re-deploy it.
- Data Analysis. For collected data analysis, a Python application polls for newly created files every second and performs a count of single occurrences of words in the files. The application is derived, with some minor changes, from a sample application provided with the Apache Spark engine[11] in order to use a common benchmark. Our implementation follows the MapReduce model, i.e., creating a list of (key, value) pairs of the form (word, 1) for each occurrence of a word. This list is then grouped by keys (here words) and the Reduce step is then applied on each group, generating the sum of occurrences of each word. These last two steps are performed by one function, reduceByKey. The listing below illustrates the algorithm in pseudocode with the sample MapReduce implementation used as the test application.

```
1 lines
2 count :=
    lines.flatMap(lambda(line){line.split("_")})
3      .map(lambda(word){(word, 1)})
4      .reduceByKey(lambda(val, acc){val + acc})
5 counts.pprint()
```

Finally, the deployment of the application to the Spark cluster is done using the Spark CLI tool sparksubmit to send it to the master node, which then distributes the application to the workers.

6.2 Edge Monitoring

We deployed a Prometheus[12]-based monitoring stack to the cluster. Prometheus is an open source monitoring and alerting system, which uses a time series database and supports the integration with other software such as HAProxy, the ELK stack (Elasticsearch, Logstash and Kibana) or Docker. Since the task of Prometheus is to pull data from services, the stack uses a number of so-called exporters to collect data for different metrics and expose them to be collected by Prometheus. The Docker-related exporters that we used are cAdvisor[13], a daemon which collects and exposes container resource usage, and Node exporter[14], which exports hardware and system metrics exposed by the Linux kernel.

---

[11] Spark sample applications, https://github.com/apache/spark/tree/master/examples.
[12] Prometheus, https://prometheus.io/.
[13] Google cAdvisor, https://github.com/google/cadvisor.
[14] Node exporter, https://github.com/prometheus/node_exporter.

In order to visualize and analyse the collected data, we used Grafana[15]. Grafana allows to monitor and analyze metrics by creating dashboards exposed via a web user interface (UI). Grafana could be integrated with little configuration for monitoring of Docker containers on multiple Linux machines. The stack is deployed to the Docker cluster using a custom Compose file.

One instance each of the cAdvisor and Node exporter is deployed on every RPi. Prometheus and Grafana are both deployed on one of the node.

7 Trusted Orchestration Management for Edge Clouds

Besides performance, trust management is another key concern of edge architectures where often devices and software from different providers and consumers meet. In order to provide trust management, we propose here in this section a trust management component, the so-called Trusted Orchestration Management TOM, that we integrate with the container cluster architecture. Blockchain technologies shall be utilised here.

7.1 Blockchain Principles

Blockchains are shared distributed databases where the users can add to or read transactions with no one having full control, thus avoiding fraudulent manipulation. Thus, they form a distributed ledger and are also referred to as Distributed Ledger Technology DLT.

New transactions are signed digitally and timestamped, allowing operations to be traced, thus determining their provenance. Blockchains enhance security in untrusted environments. Often, security concerns can be remedied if autonomy and trust capabilities of decentralised blockchains are used to provide security functions that can operate without a central authority in unreliable networks.

Blockchains operate as follows. Blocks that represent transactions are added to the blockchain. An added transaction is cryptographically hashed and signed to ensure integrity and support non-repudiation. Smart contracts such as orchestration actions can also be attached to a blockchain. A problem with blockchains in general is massive data replication, requiring scalability and performance concerns to be addressed, specifically in constrained environment.

7.2 Blockchain-Based Trusted Orchestration

Orchestration is the key activity in clustered edge clouds that looks after the lifecycle management (create, run, delete) of data, software and hardware. In Fig. 6, we show the principles of a TOM architecture.

---

[15] Grafana, https://grafana.com/.

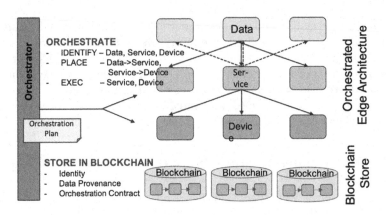

Fig. 6. Trusted orchestration management.

- the key entities to be looked after are data, service and device. Devices like RPis host software services. These software services are in our case container-ised. The containers process the data from the IoT layer, e.g., sensors.
- All entities need to be processed, which here means that the orchestrator needs to identify, place and orchestrate them (manage their lifecycle). Data is continuously produced, but needs to be identified when it enter the system at least in terms of its source. In dynamic environments, also software and device can join (or leave) the system and need to be identified, possibly more strictly in security terms. All need to be placed, i.e., transfered/connected to suitable host. These are containers for data processing or network nodes for hosting containers. Their lifecycle is then subsequently managed.
- In order to formalise this, our reference architecture builds on the W3C Prove-nance standard PROV. This standard introduces entities (here data, services, devices), agents (the orchestrator) and actions (identify, place, orchestrate in our case). The PROV standard then defines relationships between them: uses, is generated by, is followed by.

Trust management is a function added to the functional orchestration actions.

We aim to improve the trustworthiness of edge systems by recording identity, provenance and the actually executed orchestration actions in a tamper-proof, trustworthy infrastructure – the blockchain. We reflect the PROV relationships such as 'is generated by' or 'uses' in the records we enter into the blockchain.

The TOM Orchestrator is in our case placed in the Master node of the RPi cluster network as an additional function. Figure 7 shows the TOM reference architecture applied to the clustered edge cloud setting, with data, containers and devices as entities. The TOM orchestrator looks after the identification, placement and orchestration of these. Three types of information are entered in to the blockchain: 1) identity of the entity, 2) provenance data using the define relationships, and 3) orchestration action as a smart contract.

8   Evaluation and Discussion

We cover different aspects in our evaluation. We start with some operation concerns. Then, we look at performance in the following experimental performance evaluation. Subsequently, we discuss the trust management approach. Finally, we look at a use case to further demonstrate applicability.

8.1   Maintainability, Fault-Tolerance and Build Times

We can make some observations on some operations-oriented evaluation criteria:

- *Maintainability and Ease of Operation.* Using containerized services on a Docker swarm contributes significantly to achieving maintainability and ease of operation of the implementation.
- *Fault-Tolerance.* Using Docker requires only minimal overhead, but increases the overall fault tolerance of the system, since containers that have failed due to hardware or software problems can be restarted on any other node. This is managed by the cluster itself. Thus, Docker achieves high availability and increased fault tolerance.
- *Image Building and Build Times.* IA general limitation can be the lack of RPi (SBD) specific Docker images (for ARM architectures) that include applications such as Apache Hadoop and Apache Spark. Continuous integration and continuous delivery (CI/CD) services such as provided by Gitlab[16] can be

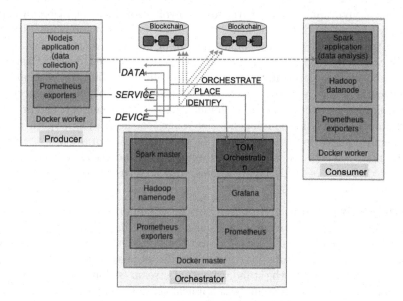

Fig. 7. TOM-enabled edge cluster architecture.

---

[16] Gitlab, https://about.gitlab.com/.

used to build necessary images. Since the containers used to build the images run on a different instruction set than the Raspberry Pis, we used a system emulator, QEMU[17] inside the Dockerfiles to cross-build images. Despite some problems due to the Java Virtual Machine (JVM) displaying bugs during the builds, requiring to run some preparatory commands manually on the already deployed services, we preferred this over building the images on one of the cluster nodes due to the longer build times. The table below shows the build times of one of the used images on a common notebook[18], compared to build times of the same image on a RPi used in the cluster, to which the time to distribute the image on the nodes has to be added.

Target architecture	Build architecture	Build time
armv7	x86_64	6 m 1 s
armv7	armv7	14 m 33 s

The pull of the image from the Gitlab registry took about 6 min. While these build times seem high, this is an activity that is not frequently needed and can generally be tolerated.

8.2 Experimental Performance Evaluation

A critical factor for small devices is to deliver the required performance in a constrained environment. The performance evaluation focus shall be on experimentally evaluating data processing time and resource consumption. Running the test applications required some fine tuning of the resources allocated to the Spark executors, influenced by the constraints imposed by the Raspberry Pis. The only relevant results were achieved by allocating 500 MB of memory to each executor, since the Spark process would generate out-of-memory exceptions when using less, while on the other hand, if given more memory, the processes would starve one of the components necessary for the Hadoop/Spark cluster. This memory allocation can be set during the submission of a job.

The main aspects are now file processing time and resource consumption, which we discuss separately before ending with a discussion of results.

File Processing Times. We based this on input data file sizes that reflect common IoT scenarios with common small-to-midsize data producers. The delay between the submission of a new file and the end of the analysis process was measured using time stamps by comparing the submission time with the time the output was printed to the standard output stream (stdout) of the submission shell. In both cases, the data analysis application was polling for new files every second, and files were submitted at a rate of one per second.

---

[17] QEMU, https://www.qemu.org/.
[18] The model used is a HP 355 G2, with AMD A8-6410 2 GHz CPU and 12 GB memory.

File size	Polling time	Delay
1.04 KB	1 s	236 s
532 B	1 s	61 s

The results in the table above shows the measurements for files with around 500 B and 1 KB, respectively, that were submitted once per second. This reflects, as already said, a common small-to-midsize data production volume. The test cases aimed at exploring the limits of the RPi-based container cluster architecture for certain IoT and edge computing settings. The delays shown above can be considered too high for some real-time processing requirements, e.g., for any application which relies on short times for immediate actuation, and are unexpectedly high considering the file size and the submission rates used during the test runs. However, if only storage and analysis without immediate reaction is required or the sensors produce a limited volume of data (such as temperature sensors), then the setting we outlines is adequate.

Resource Consumption. In our implementation, we had various services were distributed among the nodes of the cluster, see Fig. 5. The data recorded by the Prometheus monitoring stack deployed shows no increase of the used resources during file submission and analysis by the respective services. We detail this now for CPU and memory.

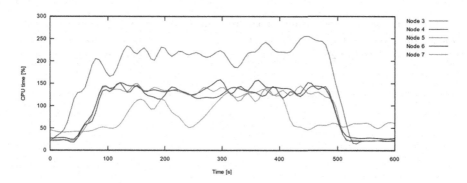

Fig. 8. Container CPU time, by node – see [1].

- **CPU.** In Fig. 8 we show the CPU time use (by node) during the execution of the test application, while Fig. 9 shows the same data, divided by container. The shown records are for the 532 Bytes test file.
  As expected, the graphs show an increase of CPU workload on all Apache Spark nodes, in particular on the worker nodes of the cluster. The analysis application was submitted from node 3 (Spark worker 2), which explains the

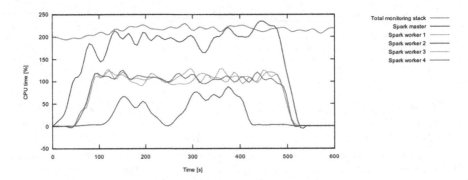

Fig. 9. Container CPU time, by container – see [1].

higher CPU use compared to the other nodes at point 0 in the graphs, while data collection was started two minutes in, at the 120 s mark, as can be seen by an increased CPU utilization by the Spark master node. Data collection and data analysis were stopped at 420 and 480 s, resp.

- **Memory.** Figures 10 and 11 show, similar to CPU, the memory use of the containers in Spark and the monitoring stack during the experiment divided by node and by container, respectively.

As expected, we observe that memory usage by the Spark node is higher than on the other nodes, as it is used to submit the application and therefore acts as controller for the execution and collects the results from all other nodes.

Note that the resource usage by the remaining system is not shown (e.g., the Docker daemons and system processes), which were constant during the test, with CPU time below 2% and memory use around 120 MB on each node stable.

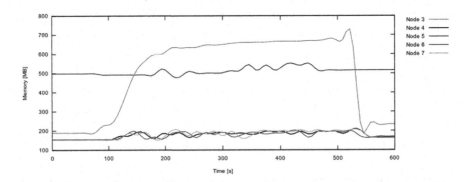

Fig. 10. Container memory use, by node – see [1].

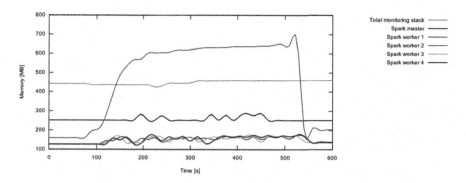

Fig. 11. Container memory use, by container – see [1].

Performance Analysis and Discussion. The experimental results demonstrate that the system resources are not used optimally, with capacities both at the CPU and in particular for the memory of the devices. The results suggest that the delay is due to how the distribution and replication of small files is performed by HDFS (a typical block size used to split files by HDFS is 64 MB), causing a non-optimal use of system resources as well as Spark streaming capabilities. Besides the rather high delays and suboptimal resource usage, the recorded data shows an uneven CPU utilization by the Spark master container, reaching 0% around the 250 s mark, which was consistently irregular throughout all the test runs. This might be due to the file system, or rather HDFS, starving the process due to high I/O times. Here, further experiments with alternative sources might be better able to confirm reasons.

Raspberry Pi 2 has now been replaced by RPi 3, which would allow some performance improvements. While in comparison the CPU only gains 300 MHz, it also updates its architecture from a Cortex-A7 set to a Cortex-A53, i.e., an architecture improvement from 32-bit to 64-bit. This should result in much better performance of a factor 2 to 3[19]. In terms of RAM and tact rate, where the Raspberry Pi 2 has 450 MHz, the Pi 3 has 900 MHz RAM.

In order to summarise, the objective here was to determine some of the limits of the proposed infrastructure. Depending on the concrete application in question, our configuration could however still be sufficient, or could otherwise be improved through better hardware or software configuration.

In order to utilise resources better, a controller allowing self-adaptation [20] to address performance and resource utilisation anomalies of the platform configuration [17,18] is a solution that could address suboptimal resource utilisation.

---

[19] https://www.jeffgeerling.com/blog/2018/raspberry-pi-3-b-review-and-performance-comparison.

8.3 Trust Management Review

As such, containers can provide a degree of security through the in-build process isolation. However, in an open and often cross-organisation setting, more is need to secure the infrastructure and provide an additional degree of trust, particularly between partners that need to cooperate. For this situation, we introduced and applied the TOM reference model earlier on.

The application of the TOM principles in a blockchain-supported architecture demonstrates that a degree of trust can be achieved. In more concrete terms, we mapped the PROV-based TOM model to Hyperledger Fabric [11]. Hyperledger Fabric is an open-source implementation of a permissioned distributed, decentralized ledger. It relies on a modular architecture, which enables pluggable components and implementations of different functionality (e.g., consensus and encryption mechanisms). Differently from many widely used blockchain platforms where all nodes of the network can carry all the operations, fabric distinguishes between two types of nodes: worker nodes and peer nodes. Peer nodes are responsible for coordinating the consensus mechanism, validating transactions and committing transactions to the blockchain. Each peer maintains a copy of the blockchain.

In our architecture a Hyperledger fabric is used as the PROV chain storing all the three block types (identity, provenance, orchestration). Each block contains thus transactions specifying the identity, provenance records, smart orchestration contracts of the interactions taking place in the network.

- Identity: Hyperledger fabric relies on public key infrastructures (PKI), which provide verifiable identities through a chain of trust to identify each entity (i.e., device, container and data).
- Provenance: One of the main features of the proposed architecture is the implementation of the W3C-PROV standard. Being able to track the origin of every piece of data in the system is at the core of blockchain technology. In the proposed architecture each asset has an attribute (i.e., derivedFrom) that connects it with its origin. Once the system is in place, starting from a data object, a recursive call would provide the complete chain of provenance.
- Orchestration: To support the orchestration requirements of the reference scenario, a high degree of nodes management is required. The proposed architecture takes advantage of Docker Swarm to dispatch services on remote nodes as well as start containers to run different services.

8.4 Cooperative, Connected and Automated Mobility Use Case

In order to validate the usefulness of our architecture for concrete application settings, we discuss in this section its application to a use case.

Cooperative, Connected and Automated Mobility (CCAM) is a context in which for instance vehicles are connected using a network. Often, compute and storage capabilities in this application area are limited and largely similar to the capabilities of RPis, see [26, 27]. These compute capabilities are often spread

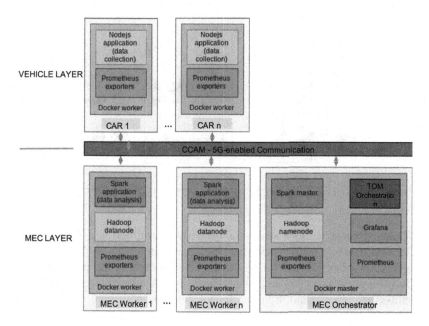

Fig. 12. CCAM scenario: 5G-enable MEC-to-vehicle coordination.

between in-vehicle and road-side computation and edge clouds. Often the term MEC is used here, standing for Mobile Edge Computing or Multi-Access Edge Computing (in 2017, the ETSI standardisation body officially changed the name from Mobile Edge Computing to Multi-Access Edge Computing). MEC often refers to communication using mobile phone networks. Lightweight MECs provide computational and storage services close to the vehicles.

Figure 12 shows a MEC architecture that supports direct vehicular coordination. Here, the cars are data producers (providing position or car status data) and the MEC nodes are data consumers that provide e.g. lane change support (or other coordinated, cooperative maneouvres). The orchestrator for this coordination between vehicles and road-side devices is a dedicated MEC node.

In Fig. 13, we detail further how the orchestrator enables virtualised network functions or application services, e.g., for the lane change scenario. Other services for similar CCAM usage scenarios could be video streaming, where different MEC nodes will buffer video content close to the position of the vehicle.

As a consequence of the dynamic nature here, vehicles move and might connect differently over time. The different services such as lane changing or video streaming have different quality requirements (lane changing is latency critical, but not high volume in data, whereas video streaming is more of the opposite). An important function here is the placement engine that assigns suitable nodes for virtual functions (in container format) to cluster nodes depending on their capabilities and capacities. Figure 14 shows a layered orchestration and management stack for this, which includes placement, lifecycle management (LCM) and

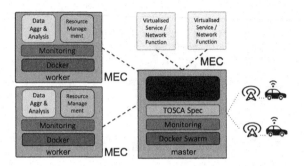

Fig. 13. CCAM architecture: lightweight MEC cluster.

quality management engines as central orchestration functions. We refer here to TOSCA as the service specification and orchestration format, but other semantic description notations [23, 34] for description and matching are possible.

What this short use case discussion shows is that our containerised RPi cluster architecture is a typical architecture for common edge computing scenarios.

- Virtual Network Functions VNFs for CCAM (lane change, video streaming)
- independent deployment in container

- Placement engine selects node for a VNF depending on node capabilities and available resources
- LCM runs deployment and management

VNF (CCAM)   VNF (CCAM)

TOSCA-based service/function discovery/selection

| onboard, place, migrate PLACEMENT ENGINE | create, delete LCM ENGINE | monitor, scale QoS/SLA ENGINE |

Orchestration

Monitoring

Docker + Docker Swarm to deploy, operate, scale containers

Management

Lightweight MEC   Infrastructure RPi network/cluster

Fig. 14. CCAM layered light management and orchestration stack for MEC.

9   Conclusions

Leveraging the lightweight containerization and orchestration capabilities offered by Docker, allows for an edge computing architecture that is simple to manage and has high fault-tolerance. A lightweight containerised cluster platform can be suitable for a common range of IoT data processing applications at the edge.

Due to the Docker swarm actively maintaining the state of the services, we gain high availability of services, making the cluster self-healing, while also making scaling simple. In practical terms, for our platform configuration, most of the images used were created from scratch, or at least heavily customized from similar implementations to meet the requirements. Nonetheless, the number of projects targeting ARM devices are growing in popularity. The monitoring stack, which we used in a performance test bed for the implementation and applications, was available as a ready-to-use Docker compose file.

Further benefits apply. Low energy and cost are properties of single board devices, that are still able to run complex infrastructures by means of clustering, are promising with regards to the overall reduction of infrastructure costs even in the presence of high volumes of data. We have shown that it is possible to implement a data streaming processing system on device clusters with strict constraints on networking and computing resources like the Raspberry Pis to create a low-cost and low-power cluster capable of processing large amounts of data. Though, the actual performance of our prototype system has limits. For instance, a performance limitation of the prototype implementation was caused by the choice of the Hadoop distributed file system (HDFS) as source for data streams of small files, indicating that not all components are suitable for the constained environment. Trust [10,31] has been an equally important aspect that we included in our discussion.

The presented lightweight edge architectures are important for many new application areas. Autonomous driving is an example where mobile edge clouds are required. Vehicles need to coordinate their behaviour, often using modern telecommunications technologies such as 5G mobile networks. This requires onboard computing capability as well as local edge clouds in addition to centralised clouds in order to guarantee the low latency requirements. SBC clusters are an example of computational infrastructure close the outer edge that can support these scenarios as our use case analysis has shown.

In the future, we will explore different configuration options of Apache Spark, e.g., using the network as a data source. This would allow the use of IoT data transmission protocols like MQTT, while Hadoop and HDFS might be used on pre-processed and aggregated data. Furthermore, the model used to evaluate the implementation could be extended in order to verify the actual performance of the system in more scenarios. Here, alternative data stream sources could also be considered as part of future work. In this work, we only looked at identifying performance problems. An opportunity is using machine learning [21] to implement autonomous configuration and resource management [5].

Acknowledgements. This work has received funding from the EU's Horizon 2020 research and innovation programme under grant agreement 825012 - Project 5G-CARMEN.

References

1. Scolati, R., Fronza, I., El Ioini, N., Samir, A., Pahl, C.: A containerized big data streaming architecture for edge cloud computing on clustered single-board devices. In: International Conference on Cloud Computing and Services Science (2019)

2. Ambroz, M., Hudomalj, U., Marinsek, A., Kamnik, R.: Raspberry pi-based low-cost connected device for assessing road surface friction. Electronics **8**(3), 341 (2019)
3. Apache: Hadoop (2019). https://hadoop.apache.org. Accessed June 2019
4. Apache: Spark (2019). https://spark.apache.org. Accessed June 2019
5. Arabnejad, H., Pahl, C., Jamshidi, P., Estrada, G.: A comparison of reinforcement learning techniques for fuzzy cloud auto-scaling. In: 17th IEEE/ACM International Symposium on Cluster, Cloud and Grid Computing (2017)
6. Baldeschwieler, E.: Yahoo! launches world's largest hadoop production application (2018). http://yahoohadoop.tumblr.com/post/98098649696/ yahoo-launches-worlds-largest-hadoop-production. Accessed September 2018
7. Baumgartl, R., Muller, D.: Raspberry pi as an inexpensive platform for real-time traffic jam analysis on the road. In: Federated Conference on Computer Science and Information Systems (2018)
8. Dean, J., Ghemawat, S.: Mapreduce: simplified data processing on large clusters. In: OSDI 2004 Symposium on Operating System Design and Implementation (2004)
9. Docker (2018). https://docs.docker.com/. Accessed September 2018
10. El Ioini, N., Pahl, C.: A review of distributed ledger technologies. In: Panetto, H., Debruyne, C., Proper, H.A., Ardagna, C.A., Roman, D., Meersman, R. (eds.) OTM 2018. LNCS, vol. 11230, pp. 277–288. Springer, Cham (2018). https://doi.org/10.1007/978-3-030-02671-4_16
11. El Ioini, N., Pahl, C.: Trustworthy orchestration of container based edge computing using permissioned blockchain. In: Fifth International Conference on Internet of Things: Systems, Management and Security (IoTSMS) (2018)
12. Femminella, M., Pergolesi, M., Reali, G.: Performance evaluation of edge cloud computing system for big data applications. In: 5th IEEE International Conference on Cloud Networking (Cloudnet), pp. 170–175 (2016)
13. Fowley, F., Pahl, C., Jamshidi, P., Fang, D., Liu, X.: A classification and comparison framework for cloud service brokerage architectures. IEEE Trans. Cloud Comput. **6**(2), 358–371 (2018)
14. Gillam, L., Katsaros, K., Dianati, M., Mouzakitis, A.: Exploring edges for connected and autonomous driving. In: Conference on Computer Communications WS (2018)
15. Haramaki, T., Nishino, H.: A safe driving support system based on distributed cooperative edge computing. In: International Conference on Consumer Electronics (2018)
16. Heinrich, R., et al.: Performance engineering for microservices: research challenges and directions. In: Proceedings of the 8th ACM/SPEC on International Conference on Performance Engineering Companion (2017)
17. Jamshidi, P., Sharifloo, A., Pahl, C., Arabnejad, A., Metzger, A., Estrada, G.: Fuzzy self-learning controllers for elasticity management in dynamic cloud architectures. In: 12th International ACM Conference on Quality of Software Architectures (2016)
18. Jamshidi, P., Sharifloo, A., Pahl, C., Metzger, A., Estrada, G.: Self-learning cloud controllers: Fuzzy q-learning for knowledge evolution. arXiv preprint arXiv:1507.00567 (2015)
19. Jamshidi, P., Pahl, C., Mendonca, N.C., Lewis, J., Tilkov, S.: Microservices: the journey so far and challenges ahead. IEEE Softw. **35**(3), 24–35 (2018)
20. Jamshidi, P., Pahl, C., Mendonca, N.C.: Managing uncertainty in autonomic cloud elasticity controllers. IEEE Cloud Comput. **3**, 50–60 (2016)

21. Jamshidi, P., Pahl, C., Chinenyeze, S., Liu, X.: Cloud migration patterns: a multi-cloud service architecture perspective. In: Toumani, F., et al. (eds.) ICSOC 2014. LNCS, vol. 8954, pp. 6–19. Springer, Cham (2015). https://doi.org/10.1007/978-3-319-22885-3_2

22. Jamshidi, P., Pahl, C., Mendonca, N.C.: Pattern-based multi-cloud architecture migration. Softw.: Practice Experience **47**(9), 1159–1184 (2017)

23. Javed, M., Abgaz, Y.M., Pahl, C.: Ontology change management and identification of change patterns. J. Data Semant. **2**(2–3), 119–143 (2013)

24. Johnston, S.J., et al.: Commodity single board computer clusters and their applications. Future Gen. Comput. Syst. **89**, 201–212 (2018)

25. Hentschel, K., Jacob, D., Singer, J., Chalmers, M.: Supersensors: Raspberry pi devices for smart campus infrastructure. In: IEEE International Conference on Future Internet of Things and Cloud (FiCloud) (2016)

26. Morabito, R.: A performance evaluation of container technologies on internet of things devices. In: IEEE Conference on Computer Communications Workshops (2016)

27. Morabito, R., Farris, I., Iera, A., Taleb, T.: Evaluating performance of containerized iot services for clustered devices at the network edge. IEEE Internet Things J. **4**(4), 1019–1030 (2017)

28. Morabito, R., Petrolo, R., Loscri, V., Mitton, N., Ruggeri, G., Molinaro, A.: Lightweight virtualization as enabling technology for future smart cars. In: Symposium on Integrated Network and Service Management, pp. 1238–1245. IEEE (2017)

29. Naik, N.: Docker container-based big data processing system in multiple clouds for everyone. In: International Systems Engineering Symposium (ISSE), pp. 1–7 (2017)

30. Pahl, C., Lee, B.: Containers and clusters for edge cloud architectures - a technology review. In: IEEE International Conference on Future Internet of Things and Cloud (2015)

31. Pahl, C., El Ioini, N., Helmer, S., Lee, B.: An architecture pattern for trusted orchestration in IoT edge clouds. In: International Conference Fog and Mobile Edge Computing (2018)

32. Pahl, C., Jamshidi, P., Zimmermann, O.: Architectural principles for cloud software. ACM Trans. Internet Technol. (TOIT) **18**(2), 17 (2018)

33. Pahl, C., Helmer, S., Miori, L., Sanin, J., Lee, B.: A container-based edge cloud PaaS architecture based on raspberry pi clusters. In: IEEE International Conference on Future Internet of Things and Cloud Workshops (2016)

34. Pahl, C.: An ontology for software component matching. In: Pezzè, M. (ed.) FASE 2003. LNCS, vol. 2621, pp. 6–21. Springer, Heidelberg (2003). https://doi.org/10.1007/3-540-36578-8_2

35. Pahl, C., Brogi, A., Soldani, J., Jamshidi, P.: Cloud container technologies: a state-of-the-art review. IEEE Trans. Cloud Comput. **7**, 677–692 (2017)

36. Renner, T., Meldau, M., Kliem, A.: Towards container-based resource management for the internet of things. In: International Conference on Software Networking (2016)

37. Renner, M.: Testing high availability of docker swarm on a raspberry pi cluster. https://blog.hypriot.com/post/high-availability-with-docker. Accessed 09 2018

38. Renner, M.: Evaluation of high availability performance of kubernetes and docker swarm on a raspberry pi cluster. In: Highload++ Conference (2016)

39. Raspberry Pi Foundation (2018). https://www.raspberrypi.org/products/raspberry-pi-2-model-b/. Accessed Sept 2018

40. Stager, A., Bhan, L., Malikopoulos, A., Zhao, L.: A scaled smart city for experimental validation of connected and automated vehicles. IFAC **51**(9), 130–135 (2018)
41. Stevens, A., et al.: Cooperative automation through the cloud: the CARMA project. In: Proceedings of 12th ITS European Congress (2017)
42. Taibi, D., Lenarduzzi, V., Pahl, C.: Architectural patterns for microservices: a systematic mapping study. In: International Conference, Cloud Computing and Services Science (2018)
43. Tso, F.P., White, D.R., Jouet, S., Singer, J., Pezaros, D.P.: The glasgow raspberry pi cloud: a scale model for cloud computing infrastructures. In: IEEE 33rd International Conference on Distributed Computing Systems Workshops (2013)
44. Turner, V.: The digital universe of opportunities: rich data and the increasing value of the internet of things. IDC Report (2014)
45. Vilalta, R., et al.: Control and management of a connected car using YANG/RESTCONF and cloud computing. In: International Conference on the Network of the Future (2017)
46. von Leon, D., Miori, L., Sanin, J., El Ioini, N., Helmer, S., Pahl, C.: A performance exploration of architectural options for a middleware for decentralised lightweight edge cloud architectures. In: International Conference Internet of Things, Big Data & Security (2018)
47. von Leon, D., Miori, L., Sanin, J., El Ioini, N., Helmer, S., Pahl, C.: A lightweight container middleware for edge cloud architectures. In: Fog and Edge Computing: Principles and Paradigms, pp. 145–170. Wiley (2019)
48. Wang, Y., Goldstone, R., Yu, W., Wang, T.: Characterization and optimization of memory-resident mapreduce on HPC systems. In: IEEE 28th International Parallel and Distributed Processing Symposium (2014)

Data Flows Mapping in Fog Computing Infrastructures Using Evolutionary Inspired Heuristic

Claudia Canali and Riccardo Lancellotti[✉]

Department of Engineering "Enzo Ferrari",
University of Modena and Reggio Emilia, Modena, Italy
{claudia.canali,riccardo.lancellotti}@unimore.it

Abstract. The need for scalable and low-latency architectures that can process large amount of data from geographically distributed sensors and smart devices is a main driver for the popularity of the fog computing paradigm. A typical scenario to explain the fog success is a smart city where monitoring applications collect and process a huge amount of data from a plethora of sensing devices located in streets and buildings. The classical cloud paradigm may provide poor scalability as the amount of data transferred risks the congestion on the data center links, while the high latency, due to the distance of the data center from the sensors, may create problems to latency critical applications (such as the support for autonomous driving). A fog node can act as an intermediary in the sensor-to-cloud communications where pre-processing may be used to reduce the amount of data transferred to the cloud data center and to perform latency-sensitive operations.

In this book chapter we address the problem of mapping sensors over the fog nodes with a twofold contribution. First, we introduce a formal model for the mapping model that aims to minimize response time considering both network latency and processing time. Second, we present an evolutionary-inspired heuristic (using Genetic Algorithms) for a fast and accurate resolution of this problem. A thorough experimental evaluation, based on a realistic scenario, provides an insight on the nature of the problem, confirms the viability of the GAs to solve the problem, and evaluates the sensitivity of such heuristic with respect to its main parameters.

Keywords: Fog computing · Optimization model · Evolutionary programming · Genetic algorithms · Smart cities

1 Introduction

Cyber-physical systems are producing an ever-growing amount of data through the presence of a large number of geographically-distributed sensors. This ever-increasing amount of data needs to be filtered and processed to support advanced

© Springer Nature Switzerland AG 2020
D. Ferguson et al. (Eds.): CLOSER 2019, CCIS 1218, pp. 177–198, 2020.
https://doi.org/10.1007/978-3-030-49432-2_9

applications that can monitor complex systems. However, as the data size grows, the traditional cloud paradigm becomes inadequate and can result in poor performance, due to the risk of high latency in the responses or due to the risk of creating congestion on the network links of the cloud data centers.

An approach that can increase the scalability and can reduce the latency is the *fog computing* paradigm. Fog computing moves some services from the cloud data center (located on the network core) towards a set of *fog nodes* located on the network edge, that is the location where the data sources connect to the network. The services that are typically deployed on the fog layer involve data filtering, validation, aggregation, alarm triggering and other pre-processing tasks that can reduce latency and the amount of data transferred towards the cloud data centers. This paradigm has been proposed in [11,13] as an enabling architecture in different areas. Examples include:

- Applications such as gaming and videoconferencing that need very low and predictable latency
- Geo-distributed monitoring applications like pipeline monitoring or environmental sensing
.- Fast mobile applications such as smart connected vehicles and connected rails
- Large-scale distributed control systems including smart grid, smart traffic monitoring, and support for autonomous driving

In this book chapter, we focus mainly on an environmental monitoring application for a smart city, where multiple sensors are deployed over a geographic area to monitor air pollution and traffic. We assume that the infrastructure is structured as in Fig. 1 and is composed of three layers: a first *sensor layer* that produces data (the sensors are represented at the bottom of the figure as a set of wireless devices), an intermediate *fog layer* that carries out the preliminary processing of data from the sensors, and a *cloud layer* that is composed by one or more data centers (at the top of the figure) and that is the final destination of the data. Sensors collect information about the city status, such as traffic intensity or air quality [16]. Such data should be collected at the level of a cloud infrastructure to provide value-added services such as traffic or pollution forecast. The proposed fog layer intermediates the communication between the sensors and the cloud to provide scalability and reliability in the smart city services.

Our problem is centered on the management of data flows in a fog infrastructure, that is, distributing the data from the sensors among the fog nodes taking into account both the load balancing issues at the level of each fog node, and the latency in the sensors-to-fog links. This problem is rather new, because most literature on fog infrastructures takes the sensor-to-fog mapping as a fixed parameter depending on the system topology [8], while we assume that, at least on a city-scale scenario, there are degrees of freedom that can be leveraged. As this problem is complex and may present scalability issues, we also introduce an heuristic, based on Genetic Algorithms, to solve the problem. A preliminary version of this research appeared in [5]; however, in this chapter we improve the theoretical model, supporting a more detailed analysis of the problem, and we

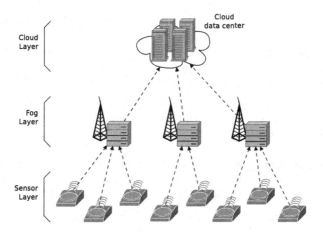

Fig. 1. Fog infrastructure.

introduce a more detailed experimental evaluation of our proposal to provide a better insight on the problem and on its solution.

Specifically, our contribution can be summarized as follows: (1) we present an innovative approach to model fog infrastructures, defining an optimization problem for the sensor-to-fog mapping problem; (2) we introduce a GAs-based heuristic to solve this new problem (other approaches based on this heuristics were applied only to traditional cloud data centers [20] and/or to Web Service composition [10]); (3) we provide a thorough experimental analysis of the problem, with the aim to give insight on the nature of the problem and on the performance of the proposed heuristic solution.

The book chapter is organized as follows. Section 2 discusses the related work, while Sect. 3 formalizes as an optimization problem the model of the considered application. Section 4 presents the heuristic algorithms proposed to solve the problem. Section 5 introduces the experimental testbed and discusses the results that confirms the viability of our approach. Finally, Sect. 6 concludes the paper with some final remarks.

2   Related Work

The significant increase in the amount of data generated by modern infrastructures, joined to the need of processing the same data to provide value-added services, motivates the research community to explore the edge-based solutions (such as the so-called *fog computing*) as an evolution of the traditional cloud-based model. Indeed, when we have a large amount of data originated at the border of a network, a centralized cloud model becomes inefficient, while an approach that pushes some operation (such as filtering or aggregation of the data) towards the network edge has been demonstrated to be viable alternative in several papers [8,15,17,18].

In [18], Yi *et al.* propose a survey with significant application scenarios (and the corresponding design and implementation challenges) of fog computing. A more wide- spread discussion of open issues, open research directions and challenges of fog computing for IoT services and smart cities is proposed in [17]. This vision is consistent with the reference scenario proposed in this chapter. Indeed, we refer to a similar smart-city sensing application and we consider, as the main challenge, the combined goal of reducing communication latency, while preserving load balancing.

Some studies focus on the allocation of services that process data from the fog nodes over a distributed cloud infrastructure. For example, Deng et al. [8] investigate how power consumption and transmission delay can be balanced in fog-to-cloud communication, proposing an optimization model. Another interesting study [19] focuses on minimizing the service delay in a IoT-fog-cloud scenario, where fog nodes implement a policy based on fog-to-fog load sharing. It is noteworthy to consider that, in both these studies, the mapping of data sources over the fog nodes is not taken into account. Indeed, [8] assumes single-hop wireless links between sensors and fog nodes, while communication in [19] is based on application-specific domains. Our research is complementary with respect to these issues, as we consider a network layer capable of multi-hop links so that each sensor can communicate with each fog node, motivating our sensors-to-fog mapping.

Another area that is close to our research is that of fog computing infrastructures supporting smart cities. For example, Tang *et al.* [15] propose a hierarchical 4-layer fog computing system for smart cities. This layering leverages the nature of a geographic distribution in a large set of sensors that carry out latency-sensitive tasks, where a fast control loop is required to guarantee the safety of critical infrastructure components. Moreover, unlike our research, also this paper assumes that the sensors-to-fog nodes mapping is fixed so that a fog node communicates only with a local set of sensors that are deployed in the neighborhood.

A different research [6] is more focused on the vision of Data Stream Processing (DSP) applications. In particular, the paper addresses the operator placement problem: DSP operators must be mapped on the fog nodes with the goal of maximizing the QoS. The problem is described as an Integer Linear Programming (ILP) problem. However, the authors of [6] assume that the incoming data flow can be split to support parallel processing. Our research considers a more generic application scenario where this assumption may not be acceptable. Research on genetic algorithms (GAs) have been proposed in the area of cloud computing. In particular, Yusoh et al. [20] rely on GAs to propose a solution of Software as a Service (SaaS) Placement Problem that is scalable. Another significant example is [10] where a QoS-aware service composition problem in cloud systems is solved using GAs.

Finally, this chapter extends a previous research [5], where a similar problem is considered. However, in the present study improves both the model, with a more effective and simplified presentation of the problem model, and the exper-

imental section, introducing a thorough discussion of the parameters characterizing the problem and their impact on the ability of commercial solvers and of
the proposed solution to reach a high quality solution for the problem.

3   Problem Definition

3.1   Problem Overview

The reference architecture in Fig. 1 is used as the basis of our problem modeling.
In particular, we consider a set of sensors S distributed over an area and we
assume that these sensors are producing data with a known intensity, such that
the generic sensor $i \in S$ produces a packet of data with a frequency λ_i (the
reader may refer to Table 1 for a summary of the symbols used in the model).
In our model, we introduce some simplifying assumptions that is, we consider a
stationary scenario where the data rate of sensors remains stable over time and
where sensors do no move. Furthermore, we anticipate that, in the experiments
we will consider sensors to be homogeneous, that is λ_i is the same for every
sensor, even if the model is capable to capture an heterogeneous scenario as
well.

The fog layer is composed by a set of nodes $\mathcal{F}$ that collect the data from
the sensors and carry out tasks such as validation, filtering and aggregation on
them, to guarantee a fast and scalable processing of data even in the case where
data processing is computationally demanding. In our model we consider that
the generic fog node $j \in \mathcal{F}$ can process a data packet from a sensor with an
average service time equal to $1/\mu_j$. The fog nodes send their output to one or
more cloud data centers where additional processing and data storage is carried
out.

Since the problem of managing a cloud data center has been widely discussed
in literature [14], we do not consider the details of the internal management of
the cloud resources but we focus instead on the issue of mapping the sensors over
the fog nodes. In particular, we aim to model the QoS of the fog infrastructure
in terms of response time, taking into account the following two contributions
for the infrastructure performance:

- Network-based latency. This delay is due to the communication between the
  sensors and the fog nodes. We denote the latency as $\delta_{i,j}$ where i is a sensor
  and j is a fog node.
- Processing time. The processing time on the fog node can be modeled using
  the queuing theory. It depends on $1/\mu_j$, the service time or a packet of data
  from a sensor on fog node j, and on the incoming data rate λ_j that is the sum
  of the data rates λ_i of the sensors i that are sending data to the fog node j.

The reader may refer to Table 1 where we summarize the symbols used in
the model.

3.2   Optimization Model

In the considered fog scenario, we aim to map the data flows from the sensors on the fog nodes. Hence, we introduce an optimization problem where the decision variable represents this mapping as a matrix of boolean values $X = \{x_{i,j}, i \in \mathcal{S}, j \in \mathcal{F}\}$. Considering the values on the matrix, $x_{i,j} = 1$ if sensor i sends data to fog node j, while $x_{i,j} = 0$ if this data exchange does not occur. To support some stateful pre-processing (even a simple moving window average function would fall in this category), we assume that all the data of a sensor should be sent to the same fog node. Hence, for a given value of i, there is only one value of j such that $x_{i,j} = 1$.

We now introduce a formal model for the previously-introduced optimization problem. The basis is similar to the request allocation problem in a distributed infrastructure, such as the allocation of VMs on a cloud data center [9,12,14]. As previously pointed out, we rely on a decision variable represented as a matrix of boolean values X. The values in the matrix determine if a sensor i is sending data to fog node j. Furthermore, we introduce an objective function and a set of constraints as follows:

Table 1. Notation [5].

Symbol	Meaning/role
Decision variables	
$x_{i,j}$	Sending data flow from sensor i to fog node j
Model parameters	
$\mathcal{S}$	Set of sensors
$\mathcal{F}$	Set of Fog nodes
λ_i	Outcoming data rate from sensor i
λ_j	Incoming data rate at fog node j
$1/\mu_j$	Service time at fog node j
$\delta_{i,j}$	Communication latency between sensor i to fog node j
Model variables	
i	Index of a sensor
j	Index of a Fog node

$$\min Obj(X) = Obj_{net}(X) + Obj_{proc}(X) \tag{1.1}$$

where:

$$Obj_{net}(X) = \sum_{i \in \mathcal{S}} \sum_{j \in \mathcal{F}} x_{i,j} \cdot \delta_{i,j} \tag{1.2}$$

$$Obj_{proc}(X) = \sum_{i \in \mathcal{S}} \sum_{j \in \mathcal{F}} x_{i,j} \cdot \frac{1}{\mu_j - \lambda_j} \tag{1.3}$$

$$\lambda_j = \sum_{i \in S} x_{i,j} \cdot \lambda_i \quad \forall j \in \mathcal{F}, \tag{1.4}$$

subject to:

$$\sum_{j \in \mathcal{F}} x_{i,j} = 1 \quad \forall i \in \mathcal{S}, \tag{1.5}$$

$$\lambda_j < \mu_j \quad \forall j \in \mathcal{F}, \tag{1.6}$$

$$x_{i,j} = \{0,1\}, \quad \forall i \in \mathcal{S}, j \in \mathcal{F}, \tag{1.7}$$

In the problem formalization, the objective function 1.1 is composed by two components (Obj_{net} and Obj_{proc}, respectively) that represent the total (and hence the average) latency and processing time, respectively. The computation of the latency component is rather straightforward and aims to capture the communication delay in a geographically distributed infrastructure based on the latency values $\delta_{i,j}$, as detailed in Eq. 1.2. The processing time used for the component Obj_{proc} of the objective function is detailed in Eq. 1.3. The definition is consistent with other papers that focus on a distributed cloud infrastructure such as [3]. In particular, the processing time is derived from Little's result applied to a M/G/1 system and takes into account the average arrival frequency λ_j and the processing rate μ_j of each fog node j. Equation 1.4 defines the incoming load λ_j on each fog node j as a function of the mapping of sensors in the infrastructure.

The objective function is combined with a set of constraints. In particular, constraint 1.5 means that, for each sensor i, its data is sent to one and only one fog node. Constraint 1.6 guarantees that, for each fog node j, we avoid a congestion situation, that is we need to avoid the case where, for a generic node j, the load λ_j is higher than the processing capability μ_j. Finally, constraint 1.7 describes the boolean nature of the decision variables $x_{i,j}$.

4   Heuristic Algorithm

To solve the optimization problem defined in the previous section we consider an evolutionary inspired heuristic based on the Genetic Algorithms (GAs), with the aim to evaluate its effectiveness in solving the problem by comparing the heuristic performance with the one of commercial solvers.

The main idea behind GAs is to operate on a *population* of *individuals*, where each individual represents a possible solution of the problem. The solution is encoded in a *chromosome* that defines the individual and the chromosome is composed by a fixed number of *genes* that represent the single parameters characterizing a specific solution of the problem.

A population of individuals is typically initialized randomly. A *fitness function*, that describes the objective function of the optimization problem is applied to each individual. The evolution of population through a set of *generations* aims at improving the fitness of the population using the following main operators:

Mutation is a modification of a single or a group of genes in a chromosome describing the individual of the population. Figure 2 presents an example of such operator where the ith gene of the rightmost individual in the Kth generation undergoes a mutation. The main parameter of this operator is the probability of selecting an individual to perform a mutation on one of its genes. In the sensitivity analysis in Sect. 5.4, we will refer to this probability as P_{mut}.

Crossover is a merge of two individuals by exchanging part of their chromosomes. Figure 2, again, provides an example of this operator applied to the two individuals composing the population at the Kth generation. In particular, in Fig. 2 the child individual is characterized by a chromosome containing the genes from c_0 to c_{i-1} from the rightmost parent and the genes from c_i to c_S from the leftmost parent. The main parameter of this operator concerns the selection of the parents. In the sensitivity analysis in Sect. 5.4, we will refer to the probability of selecting an individual for a crossover operation as P_{cross}.

Selection concerns the criteria used to decide if an individual is passed from the Kth generation to the next. The typical approach in this case is to apply the fitness function to every individual (including new individuals generated through mutation and crossover) and to consider a probability of being selected for the next generation that is proportional to the fitness value. The selection mechanism ensures that the population size remains stable over the generations.

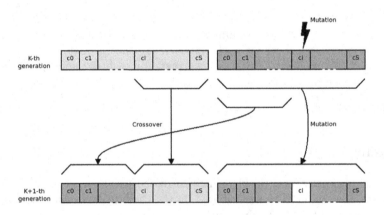

Fig. 2. Examples of genetic algorithms operators [5].

When applying a GAs approach to the problem of mapping sensors over the fog nodes of a distributed architecture, we must encode a solution as a gene. In particular, we aim to formalize the relationship between the model in Sect. 3.2 and the GA chromosome encoding. Hence, we define a chromosome as a set of S genes, where $S = |\mathcal{S}|$ is the number of sensors. Each gene is an integer number from 1 to F, where $F = |\mathcal{F}|$ is the number of fog nodes in our infrastructure. The generic i^{th} gene in a chromosome c_i can be defined as: $c_i = \{j : x_{i,j} = 1\}$. Due to constraint 1.5 in the optimization model, we know that only one fog node will receive data from sensor i, so we have a unique mapping between a solution of the problem expressed using the decision variable $x_{i,j}$ and the GA-based representation of a solution. As we can map each chromosome into a solution of the original optimization problem, we can use the objective function 1.1 as the basis for fitness function of our problem. Constraints 1.5 and 1.7 are automatically satisfied by our encoding of the chromosomes. The only constraint we have to explicitly take into account is constraint 1.6 about the fog node overload. As embedding the notion of unacceptable solution in a genetic algorithm may hinder the ability of the heuristic to converge towards a solution, we prefer to insert this information into the fitness function, in such a way that the individual providing a solution where one or more fog nodes are overloaded is characterized by a high penalty and is unlikely to enter in the subsequent generation.

Multiple optimization algorithms have been considered before adopting the choice of a genetic algorithm. On one hand, greedy heuristics tend to provide performance that heavily depends on the inherent nature of the problem. For example, the non-linear objective function may hinder the application of some greedy approaches, while the number of sensors that may be supported by each fog node may have significant impact on the performance of branch and bound heuristics. As we aim at providing a general and flexible approach to tackle this problem, we prefer to focus on meta-heuristics that are supposed to be better adaptable to a wider set of problem instances [4]. Among these solution, we focus on evolutionary programming in general and on genetic algorithms in particular as this class of heuristics has been proven a viable option in similar problems such as the problem of allocating VMs on a cloud infrastructure [20].

5 Experimental Results

5.1 Experimental Testbed

To evaluate the performance of the proposed solution, we consider a realistic fog computing scenario where geographically distributed sensors produce data flows to be mapped over a set of fog nodes, which are nodes with limited computational power and devoted to tasks such as aggregation and filtering of the received data; then, the pre-processed data are sent to the cloud data center.

To evaluate our proposal in a realistic scenario, we modeled the geographic distribution of all the components of the system according to the real topology of the small city of Modena in Italy (counting almost 180.000 inhabitants). Our reference use case is a traffic monitoring application where the wireless sensors are located on the main streets of the city and collect data about the number of cars passing on the street, their speed and other traffic related measures together with environmental quality indicators (an example of this application can be found in the Trafair Project [16]). Figure 3 shows the map of sensor nodes, fog nodes and cloud data center for the considered smart city scenario. To build the map of sensors, we collected a list of the main streets in Modena and we geo-referenced them. We assume that in each main street we have at least one sensor producing data. We selected a group of 6 buildings hosting the offices of the municipality and we use them as the location of the fog nodes – this assumption is consistent with the current trend of interconnecting the main public building of each city with high bandwidth links. Our final scenario is composed of 89 sensors and 6 fog nodes. The interconnection between fog nodes and sensors is characterized by a delay that we model using the euclidean distance between the nodes. The average delay is in the order of 10 ms, that is consistent with a geographic network. Finally, we assume that the cloud data center is co-located with the actual location of the municipality data center.

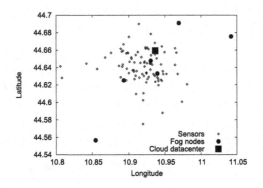

Fig. 3. Smart city scenario [5].

Concerning the traffic and processing models, we rely on two main parameters to evaluate different conditions: the first metric ρ represents the average load of the system; the second parameter $\delta\mu$ represents the ratio between the average network delay (δ) and the service time $(1/\mu)$. Specifically, we define the two parameters as:

$$\rho = \frac{\sum_{i \in \mathcal{S}} \lambda_i}{\sum_{j \in \mathcal{F}} \mu_j} \tag{2}$$

$$\delta\mu = \frac{\sum_{i \in \mathcal{S}} \sum_{j \in \mathcal{F}} \delta_{i,j}}{|\mathcal{F}||\mathcal{S}|} \cdot \frac{\sum_{j \in \mathcal{F}} \mu_j}{|\mathcal{F}|} \tag{3}$$

In our experiments, we consider several scenarios corresponding to different combinations of these parameters, in order to analyze the performance of the GAs-based solution for the sensor mapping problem.

In order to solve the problem of mapping data flows over the sensor nodes, we implemented the optimization model with the AMPL language [2] and then we use the commercial solver K-NITRO [1]. Specifically, the AMPL definition is directly based on the optimization problem discussed in Sect. 3. Due to the nature of the problem, we were not able to let the solver run until the convergence. Instead, we placed a walltime limit of 120 min, with a 16 core CPU and 16 concurrent threads. Due to this limitation, we also consider a case where we remove the constraint 1.5, thus allowing each data flow to be split over more fog nodes: the best solution achieved in this case represents a theoretical optimal bound for our problem.

The genetic algorithm is implemented using the Distributed Evolutionary Algorithms in Python (DEAP) framework [7] based on the details provided in Sect. 4. In the evaluation of the genetic algorithm approach, we run the experiments 5 times and we average the main metrics. In particular, for each run of the genetic algorithm, we consider the best achieved solution at each generation. The algorithm maintains a population of 200 individuals and we force a stop of the algorithm after 300 generations. Moreover, the genetic algorithm considers for the main parameters the following default values, that have been selected after some preliminary experiments: mutation probability $P_{mut} = 0.8$ and crossover probability $P_{cross} = 0.5$.

In order to analyze the performance of the evolutionary inspired proposal for the sensor mapping problem, we compare the best solution found by the GA heuristic (Obj^{GA}) with the best solution found by the solver for the walltime limited AMPL problem (Obj^{AMPL}) and with the theoretical optimal bound (Obj^*), considering as the main performance metric the *discrepancy* ϵ between the solutions, as it will be defined in the rest of the section. Furthermore, we evaluate the convergence speed of the GA algorithm, considering as the convergence criteria the case of a fitness value within 2% of the theoretical optimal bound. To this aim, we measure the number of generations needed by the GA heuristic to converge. Finally, we consider also the computation time as a function of the population size.

5.2   Evaluation of Genetic Algorithm Performance

The first analysis in our experiments compares the difference between the solution found by the GA and the theoretical optimal bound obtained by the solver in the case the constraint 1.5 is removed. To this aim, we consider as performance metric the discrepancy ϵ^{GA} defined as follows:

$$\epsilon^{GA} = \frac{Obj^{GA} - Obj^*}{Obj^*} \tag{4}$$

In this experiment, we consider several scenarios by varying the values of the parameters ρ and $\delta\mu$. Figure 4 shows as an heatmap the value of ϵ^{GA} for ρ ranging from 0.2 to 0.9 and $\delta\mu$ ranging from 0.01 to 10. To better understand the results, let us briefly discuss the impact of the considered parameters. For example, a scenario where $\rho = 0.9$ and $\delta\mu = 0.01$ (corresponding to the bottom right corner of Fig. 4) represents a case where network delay is much lower than the average job service time, while the processing demand on the system is high. This means that the scenario is CPU-bound because managing the computational requests is likely to be the main driver to optimize the objective function. On the other hand, a scenario where $\rho = 0.2$ and $\delta\mu = 10$ (top left corner of Fig. 4) is a scenario characterized by a low workload intensity and a network delay comparable with service time of a job, where it becomes important to optimize also the network contribution to the objective function.

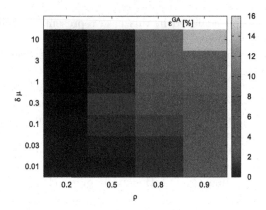

Fig. 4. Performance of GA.

In the color coded representation of ϵ^{GA} in the figure, black hues refer to a better performance of the genetic algorithm, while yellow hues correspond to a worse performance. From this comparison, we observe that the value of ρ has a major impact on the performance of the GA heuristic. Indeed, the heatmap clearly shows good performance for low values of ρ (for $\rho = 0.2$, we have ϵ^{GA} below 1% for all the values of $\delta\mu$). On the other hand, when the average load of the system is high ($\rho = 0.9$) the GA algorithm shows a higher discrepancy with respect to the theoretical optimal bound: the risk of overloading the nodes is higher and the value of the objective function is highly variant with respect to the considered solution. In this case, the value of $\delta\mu$ shows its impact on the final performance: indeed, until the ratio between the average network delay (δ) and the service time ($1/\mu$) is low ($\delta\mu = 0.01$) the discrepancy still remains limited to few percentage points, while for high values of this ratio ($\delta\mu = 10$) it goes up to almost 15%.

We now present an in-depth analysis where we separately measure the discrepancy regarding the individual contributions of the two main components of the objective function, related to the total network latency Obj_{net} and to processing time Obj_{proc} (defined in Eqs. 1.2 and 1.3, respectively) with respect to the corresponding optimal values. To this aim, we define the discrepancies ϵ_{net}^{GA} and ϵ_{proc}^{GA} defined as follows:

$$\epsilon_{net}^{GA} = \frac{Obj_{net}^{GA} - Obj_{net}^*}{Obj_{net}^*} \tag{5}$$

$$\epsilon_{proc}^{GA} = \frac{Obj_{proc}^{GA} - Obj_{proc}^*}{Obj_{proc}^*} \tag{6}$$

Figure 5 shows as heatmaps the values of ϵ_{net}^{GA} and ϵ_{proc}^{GA} for the considered scenarios with varying ρ and $\delta\mu$. Both the figures confirm that the difficulty to achieve a solution close to the optimum for high values of ρ. Furthermore,

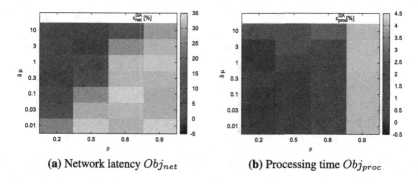

(a) Network latency Obj_{net} **(b)** Processing time Obj_{proc}

Fig. 5. Components of the objective function.

we observe high discrepancies (between 30% and 35%) regarding the network latency in the bottom right part of Fig. 5a. The reason of this result is that the network latency contribution to the overall object function is very small when $\delta\mu$ is low with respect to the processing time, hence the network latency component is not optimized, thus showing high discrepancies with respect to the corresponding optimal value.

To have a confirmation of the observed result, we directly measure the weight of the contribution of the two main components (network latency and processing time) to the overall value of the objective function in the case of the solution corresponding to the theoretical optimal bound. To this aim, we define W_{net} and W_{proc} as follows:

$$W_{net} = \frac{Obj^*_{net}}{Obj^*} \tag{7}$$

$$W_{proc} = \frac{Obj^*_{proc}}{Obj^*} \tag{8}$$

Figure 6 show as heatmaps the weight of the two components expressed as percentages of the total value of the objective function, for varying values of ρ and $\delta\mu$. In the figures, black hues refer to a low percentage of the component, while yellow hues correspond to a higher weight.

Figure 6a confirms the motivation of the previous result, showing how small the contribution of the network latency can get with respect the overall objective function for low values of $\delta\mu$: as show in the lower part of the heatmap, for $\delta\mu = 0.01$ the weight of latency is close to 1% of the objective function. On the other hand, Fig. 6b shows that the weight of the processing time contribution always never decreases below the 30% in the considered scenarios, reaching values between 90% and 100% in all the cases with $\delta\mu$ lower than 0.3.

We now evaluate the performance of the solution of the AMPL model obtained by the solver (Obj^{AMPL}) with respect to the theoretical optimal bound (Obj^*) and to the GA heuristic (Obj^{GA}). To this aim, we consider ϵ^{AMPL} and

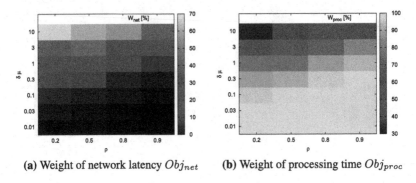

(a) Weight of network latency Obj_{net} **(b)** Weight of processing time Obj_{proc}

Fig. 6. Weight of components of objective function. (Color figure online)

$\epsilon^{GA-AMPL}$ defined as follows:

$$\epsilon^{AMPL} = \frac{Obj^{AMPL} - Obj^*}{Obj^*} \tag{9}$$

$$\epsilon^{GA-AMPL} = \frac{Obj^{GA} - Obj^{AMPL}}{Obj^{AMPL}} \tag{10}$$

Figure 7a compares the performance of the solver with the theoretical optimal bound in the form of a heatmap. We observe that for the majority of the scenarios identified by the considered values of ρ and $\delta\mu$ the discrepancy ϵ^{AMPL} is quite low (below 7%), while it significantly increases up to almost 40% for very high average system load ($\rho = 0.9$) and $\delta\mu \leq 1$. The high discrepancy is due to the non-linear nature of the objective function, and in particular to the presence of several local minima that the solver is not able to overcome within the time limitation of 120 min. This clearly evidences that, in case of very high average system load, also the solver is not able to guarantee good performance due to the fact that the risk of overloading the fog nodes is high and the value of the objective function is highly variant with respect to the considered solution.

On the other hand, Fig. 7b, comparing the performance of the solver and of the proposed GA heuristic, shows that the GA achieves solutions very similar to the solver ($\epsilon^{GA-AMPL}$ close to 0%) for the majority of the scenarios, while differences can be observed for high values of average system load ($\rho \geq 0.8$). In these cases, the behavior of the GA heuristic shows significant differences. When the system is processing bound ($\delta\mu \leq 1$) the GA algorithm tends to perform much better that the solver, with the discrepancy $\epsilon^{GA-AMPL}$ reaching negative values close to -25% for $\rho = 0.9$. This is an important result showing that the GA is not only able to reach an efficient solution even in presence of a complex problem with integer programming and a non-linear objective function, but can also outperform the solver in a challenging case of highly loaded system. On the other hand, in the top right part of the heatmap ($\rho \geq 0.8$ and $\delta\mu = 10$) the GA shows worse performance than the solver, with a discrepancy $\epsilon^{GA-AMPL}$ between 7% and 15%. In this case, where the system is network bounded and with a high average load, finding an optimal solution would require to explore a wider space of solutions that the GA cannot explore being limited to 300 generations in our experiments.

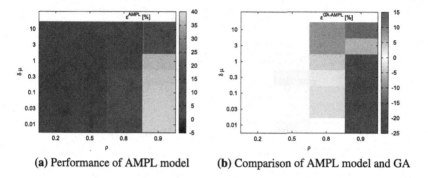

(a) Performance of AMPL model   (b) Comparison of AMPL model and GA

Fig. 7. Performance of AMPL model.

5.3   Convergence Analysis of GAs

A critical analysis concerns the impact of the number of generations on the performance of the GA heuristic, in particular on its capability to reach convergence. To carry out this analysis (and the following sensitivity analysis), we select two specific intermediate scenarios corresponding to points of interest: the first scenario, characterized by $\rho = 0.5$ and $\delta\mu = 1$, represents a case of intermediate average system load and where the two main contributions (network latency and processing time) of the objective function have a similar weight; the second scenario, characterized by $\rho = 0.8$ and $\delta\mu = 0.3$, represents a processing bound case with a high average system load where finding a good solution for mapping data flows over the fog nodes reveals more challenging, as shown by the previous results. The motivation of this choice can be supported by the graph in Fig. 8, showing the behavior of the Obj_{proc} component of the objective function for different values of ρ. Specifically, we consider the theoretical curve of Obj_{proc} for the case of one fog node and $1/\mu = 1$. The graph confirms how the value of $\rho = 0.8$ represents a point where the problem is ill-conditioned: due to the high risk of overload in the fog nodes, little variations in ρ can cause significant oscillations of the objective function. On the other hand, for $\rho = 0.5$ this risk is low, as shown by the slopes of the tangents to the load curve in the corresponding points.

In the following convergence analysis we consider the previously introduced discrepancy ϵ^{GA} between the GA and the theoretical optimal bound. The value of ϵ^{GA} is measured at every generation for the GA (and compared with the final optimal bound). This allows us to evaluate whether the population is converging over the generations to an optimum.

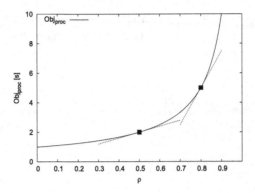

Fig. 8. Load curve of Obj_{proc}.

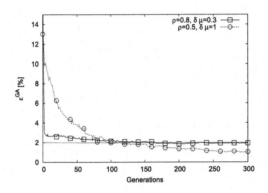

Fig. 9. Convergence analysis.

Figure 9 presents the results of the analysis. Specifically, we consider the evolution of ϵ^{GA} for the two considered scenarios through 300 generations of the GA. The graph shows also an horizontal line at the value of 2%: we consider that the GA has reached convergence when $\epsilon \leq 2\%$ and we consider the generation when this condition is verified as a metric to measure how fast the algorithm is able to find a suitable solution.

Comparing the two curves we observe a different behavior. On one hand, for the curve characterized by $\delta\mu = 1$ we have a clear descending trend. On the other hand, for the $\delta\mu = 0.3$, the value of ϵ^{GA} is very low even with few generations and remains quite stable over the generations. The reason for this behavior can be explained considering the nature of the problem, where the objective function depends on two main contributions: the processing time (that depends mainly on the ability of the algorithm to distribute fairly the sensors among the fog nodes) and the network latency (that depends on the ability of the algorithm to map the sensors on the closest fog node). When $\delta\mu = 0.3$, the impact of the second contribution is quite low, so, any solution that provides a good level of load sharing will be very close to the optimum. As the genetic algorithm initializes the chromosomes with a random solution, it is likely to have one or more individuals right from the first generation that provides good performance: this explains the more stable values of ϵ^{GA} over the generations. On the other hand, when $\delta\mu = 1$ the two contributions to the objective function are similar: hence, the genetic algorithm must explore a wider space of solutions before finding good individuals, and this requires more generations before reaching convergence.

As a final observation, we note that for both the scenarios, convergence is quite fast, with the objective function almost reaching the optimal value in little more than 75 generations. This result is interesting because it means that the genetic algorithm is able to explore the solution space in a small amount of time, reaching the proximity of the optimum (even if the actual optimum value may require more generations to be found). In terms of execution time, the time for the genetic algorithm to reach a value within 2% of the optimum is in the order of 15 s.

5.4 Sensitivity to Mutation and Crossover Probability

As a further important analysis, we carry out a sensitivity of the genetic algorithm with respect to the two probabilities that define the evolution of the population (the mutation probability P_{mut} and the crossover probability P_{cross}) to understand whether the capability of the genetic algorithm to rapidly reach optimal solutions just occurs for a properly tuned algorithm or if the property of fast convergence is stable.

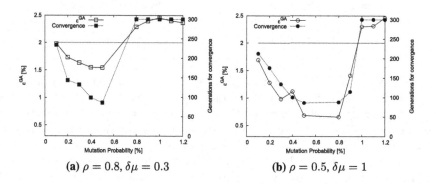

(a) $\rho = 0.8, \delta\mu = 0.3$ **(b)** $\rho = 0.5, \delta\mu = 1$

Fig. 10. Sensitivity to mutation probability.

The first analysis evaluates the impact of the mutation probability P_{mut} in the two considered scenarios. The results are shown in Fig. 10, reporting the value of the discrepancy ϵ^{GA} between the GA best fitness and the theoretical optimal bound as a function of the mutation probability. The graph also shows the number of generations necessary to reach the convergence, that means a value of ϵ^{GA} below 2%, represented through the horizontal line. For both scenarios, we observe U-shaped curves, where both low values and high values of P_{mut} result in the algorithm reaching higher value of ϵ^{GA}. In particular, the major challenges are encountered for high values of P_{mut}, when the GA is not able to reach convergence. On the other hand, values in the range $0.4\% \leq P_{mut} \leq 0.8\%$ provide good performance. This behavior is explained considering the two-fold impact of mutations. On one hand, a low value of P_{mut} hinders the ability to explore the solutions space by creating variations in the genetic pool. On the other hand, an higher mutation rate may simply reduce the ability of the algorithm to converge, because the population keeps changing too rapidly and good genes cannot be passed through the generations. If we now compare the results for the two different scenarios, we observe that they lead to a similar message, with the only difference of having a smaller range of intermediate P_{mut} values giving good performance. However, this is consistent with the major challenges posed by the scenario with high system load ($\rho = 0.8$).

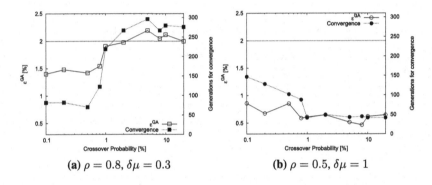

(a) $\rho = 0.8$, $\delta\mu = 0.3$ **(b)** $\rho = 0.5$, $\delta\mu = 1$

Fig. 11. Sensitivity to crossover probability.

The second analysis shown in Fig. 11 evaluates the impact of the probability of selecting an individual for a crossover operation P_{cross}. Again we show both ϵ^{GA} and the number of generations to reach convergence as a function of this parameter. Since we change the crossover probability over a large range of values (from 0.1% to 20%), we use a logarithmic scale for the x-axis. First of all, we observe that also the crossover probability has a major impact on the performance of the GA. However, in this case the results show two very different behaviors for the considered scenarios. In the scenario with $\rho = 0.5$ (Fig. 11b) the algorithm reaches convergence quite fast showing very low values of ϵ^{GA} for every value of P_{cross}. On the other hand, in the scenario with $\rho = 0.8$ (Fig. 11a) the crossover probability has a very significant impact on the GA performance, hindering the capability to converge for high values of P_{cross}. This is due to the fact that with a high value of ρ, little variations in the solutions can cause significant oscillations of the objective function due to the high risk of overload in the fog nodes, as already pointed out in the comment of Fig. 8. Hence, the high crossover probability, that is likely to increase fast changes in the population, may lead to oscillations that hinder the convergence capability. To underline this effect, we analyze the convergence of the GA heuristic in the case with for $\rho = 0.8$ and $\delta\mu = 0.3$ for different values of the crossover probability. The results are shown in Fig. 12. We can clearly observe as different values of P_{cross} lead to completely different behaviors: while for $P_{cross} = 0.8$ the continuous oscillations in the solutions do not allow to converge, for $P_{cross} = 0.5$ the behavior is quite stable and stable to reach convergence, as already noticed in Fig. 9.

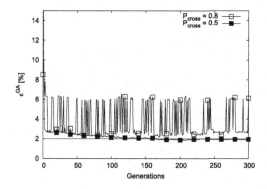

Fig. 12. Convergence analysis for different values of crossover probability.

This sensitivity analysis confirms that, when the average system load is very high, reaching an optimal solution is challenging both for the GA heuristic and the solver. Anyway, the GA approach is in many cases able to achieve performance close, or even better, compared to the solver, even in this challenging scenario. However, we need to take into account that in this case the GA heuristic becomes more sensible to its main parameters, such as the crossover probability. Hence, in the most challenging scenarios, an approach based on specifically designed ad-hoc heuristics can be worth to investigate.

5.5   Sensitivity to Population Size

As a final analysis, we evaluate how the population size affects the performance of the genetic algorithm. To this aim, we change the population size from 50 to 500 individuals and we measure the execution time, the difference in the objective function ϵ^{GA}, and the number of generations required to reach the convergence.

The first significant result, shown in Fig. 13, shows the execution time of the genetic algorithm for 300 generations. Specifically, we observe a linear growth in the execution time with respect to the population size for both considered scenarios. This result is expected, as the core of the genetic algorithm iterates, for every generation, over the whole population to evaluate the individuals and for every operation, such as crossover, mutation, and selection for the next generation. The message from these experiments is that every benefit from an increase of the population should be weighted against the additional computational cost we may incur in.

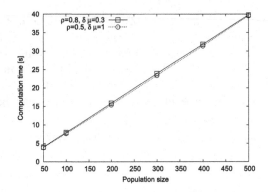

Fig. 13. GA execution time *vs.* population size.

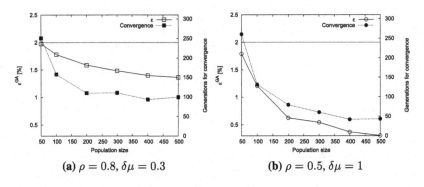

(a) $\rho = 0.8$, $\delta\mu = 0.3$ **(b)** $\rho = 0.5$, $\delta\mu = 1$

Fig. 14. Sensitivity to population size.

Another interesting result comes from the evolution of ϵ^{GA} and of the number of generations required to reach convergence in the considered scenarios, shown in Figs. 14a and 14b. The two scenarios show similar behaviors, even if for the more challenging case of $\rho = 0.8$ we observe higher discrepancy and number of generations needed for convergence, as expected. In general, the results show that increasing the population provides a benefit as it can both reduce the minimum value of ϵ^{GA} and reduce the number of generations required for the convergence. This can be explained considering that increasing the population allows the algorithm to explore a larger portion of solution space with each generation, thus accelerating the convergence. Furthermore, it is worth to note that the benefit from increasing the population decreases as the population grows, while the execution time grows linearly, as previously discussed. For this reason, in our experiments we choose a population of 200 individuals, that is a value close to the knee where the benefit form a larger population decreases rapidly.

6   Conclusions

In the present chapter we discussed the design of a typical sensing application in a smart city scenario. We consider a set of sensors or other smart devices that are distributed in a geographic area and produce a significant amount of data. A traditional cloud-based scenario would send all these data on a centralized data center, with the risk of network congestion and high latency. This is clearly unacceptable for several classes of applications, that require a fast and scalable management of data packets (critical examples are the support for automatic traffic management and autonomous driving or the data collection in a widespread array of sensors). Hence, it is common to move the tasks of data aggregation, filtering and, in general, pre-processing towards the edge of the network, where a layer of computing nodes called *fog nodes* is placed.

The introduction of the fog layer in an infrastructure motivates our study, that concerns the mapping of data flows from the sensors to the fog nodes. We tackle this problem, providing a formal model as an optimization problem that aims to minimize the average response time experienced in the system taking into account both network latency and processing time. Furthermore, we present an heuristic approach that leverages the evolutionary programming paradigm to solve the problem.

Using a smart city scenario based on a realistic testbed, we validate our proposal. First, we analyze the problem using a solver to explore the impact of the parameters that affect the problem solution. Next, we demonstrate the ability of the proposed heuristic to solve the problem in a fast and scalable way. Finally, we provide a sensitivity analysis to the main parameters of the genetic algorithm to explore the limits of its stability.

References

1. Knitro Website. https://www.artelys.com/solvers/knitro/. Accessed 10 July 2019
2. AMPL: Streamlined modeling for real optimization (2018). https://ampl.com/. Accessed 10 July 2019
3. Ardagna, D., Ciavotta, M., Lancellotti, R., Guerriero, M.: A hierarchical receding horizon algorithm for QoS-driven control of multi-IaaS applications. IEEE Trans. Cloud Comput. 1 (2018). https://doi.org/10.1109/TCC.2018.2875443
4. Binitha, S., Sathya, S.S., et al.: A survey of bio inspired optimization algorithms. Int. J. Soft Comput. Eng. **2**(2), 137–151 (2012)
5. Muñoz, V.M., Ferguson, D., Helfert, M., Pahl, C. (eds.): CLOSER 2018. CCIS, vol. 1073. Springer, Cham (2019). https://doi.org/10.1007/978-3-030-29193-8
6. Cardellini, V., Grassi, V., Lo Presti, F., Nardelli, M.: Optimal operator placement for distributed stream processing applications. In: Proceedings of the 10th ACM International Conference on Distributed and Event-based Systems, DEBS 2016, pp. 69–80. ACM, New York (2016). https://doi.org/10.1145/2933267.2933312
7. DEAP: Distributed Evolutionary Algorithms in Pyton (2018). https://deap.readthedocs.io
8. Deng, R., Lu, R., Lai, C., Luan, T.H., Liang, H.: Optimal workload allocation in fog-cloud computing toward balanced delay and power consumption. IEEE Internet Things J. **3**(6), 1171–1181 (2016)

9. Duan, H., Chen, C., Min, G., Wu, Y.: Energy-aware scheduling of virtual machines in heterogeneous cloud computing systems. Future Gen. Comput. Syst. **74**, 142–150 (2017). https://doi.org/10.1016/j.future.2016.02.016. http://www.sciencedirect.com/science/article/pii/S0167739X16300292
10. Karimi, M.B., Isazadeh, A., Rahmani, A.M.: QoS-aware service composition in cloud computing using data mining techniques and genetic algorithm. J. Supercomput. **73**(4), 1387–1415 (2017). https://doi.org/10.1007/s11227-016-1814-8
11. Liu, J., et al.: Secure intelligent traffic light control using fog computing. Future Gen. Comput. Syst. **78**, 817–824 (2018). https://doi.org/10.1016/j.future.2017.02.017. http://www.sciencedirect.com/science/article/pii/S0167739X17302157
12. Noshy, M., Ibrahim, A., Ali, H.: Optimization of live virtual machine migration in cloud computing: a survey and future directions. J. Netw. Comput. Appl. **110**, 1–10 (2018). https://doi.org/10.1016/j.jnca.2018.03.002
13. Sasaki, K., Suzuki, N., Makido, S., Nakao, A.: Vehicle control system coordinated between cloud and mobile edge computing. In: 2016 55th Annual Conference of the Society of Instrument and Control Engineers of Japan (SICE), pp. 1122–1127, September 2016
14. Helfert, M., Ferguson, D., Méndez Muñoz, V., Cardoso, J. (eds.): CLOSER 2016. CCIS, vol. 740. Springer, Cham (2017). https://doi.org/10.1007/978-3-319-62594-2
15. Tang, B., Chen, Z., Hefferman, G., Wei, T., He, H., Yang, Q.: A hierarchical distributed fog computing architecture for big data analysis in smart cities. In: Proceedings of the ASE BigData & Social Informatics 2015, ASE BD&SI 2015, pp. 28:1–28:6. ACM, New York (2015). https://doi.org/10.1145/2818869.2818898
16. Trafair Project Staff: Forecast of the impact by local emissions at an urban micro scale by the combination of Lagrangian modelling and low cost sensing technology: the trafair project. In: Proceedings of 19th International Conference on Harmionisation within Atmospheric Dispersion Modelling for Regulatory Purposes. Bruges, Belgium, June 2019
17. Wen, Z., Yang, R., Garraghan, P., Lin, T., Xu, J., Rovatsos, M.: Fog orchestration for internet of things services. IEEE Internet Comput. **21**(2), 16–24 (2017). https://doi.org/10.1109/MIC.2017.36
18. Yi, S., Li, C., Li, Q.: A survey of fog computing: concepts, applications and issues. In: Proceedings of the 2015 Workshop on Mobile Big Data, Mobidata 2015, pp. 37–42. ACM, New York (2015). https://doi.org/10.1145/2757384.2757397
19. Yousefpour, A., Ishigaki, G., Jue, J.P.: Fog computing: towards minimizing delay in the internet of things. In: 2017 IEEE International Conference on Edge Computing (EDGE), pp. 17–24, June 2017. https://doi.org/10.1109/IEEE.EDGE.2017.12
20. Yusoh, Z.I.M., Tang, M.: A penalty-based genetic algorithm for the composite SaaS placement problem in the cloud. In: IEEE Congress on Evolutionary Computation, pp. 1–8, July 2010. https://doi.org/10.1109/CEC.2010.5586151

MPI to Go: Container Clusters for MPI Applications

Luiz Angelo Steffenel[1]([⊠])(iD), Andrea S. Charão[2](iD), Bruno Alves[2],
Lucas R. de Araujo[2], and Lucas F. da Silva[2]

[1] CREsTIC Laboratory, Université de Reims Champagne Ardenne, Reims, France
angelo.steffenel@univ-reims.fr
[2] Universidade Federal de Santa Maria, Santa Maria, Brazil
andrea@inf.ufsm.br, {bdalves,lraraujo,lferreira}@inf.ufsm.br

Abstract. Container-based virtualization has been investigated as an
attractive solution to achieve isolation, flexibility and efficiency in a wide
range of computational applications. In High Performance Computing,
many applications rely on clusters to run multiple communicating processes using MPI (Message Passing Interface) communication protocol.
Container clusters based on Docker Swarm or Kubernetes may bring
benefits to HPC scenarios, but deploying MPI applications over such
platforms is a challenging task. In this work, we propose a self-content
Docker Swarm platform capable of supporting MPI applications, and
validate it though the performance characterization of a meteorological
scientific application.

Keywords: Container-based virtualization · High Performance
Computing · Performance evaluation · MPI

1 Introduction

1.1 Motivation

High performance computing (HPC) is a generic term for computationally or
data-intensive applications of a [25] nature. While most HPC platforms rely on
dedicated and expensive infrastructures such as clusters and grids, other technologies such as cloud computing are becoming attractive. Recent developments
on the virtualization domain have considerably reduced the performance overhead of these new platforms. Furthermore, traditional HPC infrastructures must
often struggle with administration and development issues as the installation and
maintenance of HPC applications often leads to library incompatibilities, access
rights conflicts or simply dependencies problems for legacy software.

© Springer Nature Switzerland AG 2020
D. Ferguson et al. (Eds.): CLOSER 2019, CCIS 1218, pp. 199–222, 2020.
https://doi.org/10.1007/978-3-030-49432-2_10

The arrival of efficient virtualization techniques such as container-based virtualization has set a new landmark towards the maintainability of computing infrastructures. Concepts such as isolation and packaging of applications now allow a user to create its own execution environment with all required libraries, to distribute this environment and to reproduce the same install everywhere with almost no effort.

When considering HPC applications, the MPI (Message Passing Interface) protocol [21] is often used for data exchange and task coordination in a cluster. Despite recent advances in its specification, the deployment of an MPI application is still too rigid to be easily deployed on more dynamic environments such as cloud or container clusters. Indeed, the starting point of an MPI execution is the definition of a list of participant nodes, which requires a prior knowledge of the runtime environment.

Deploying an MPI cluster on containers clusters is also difficult task because the internal overlay network from popular environments such as Docker Swarm is designed for load balancing and not for addressing specific nodes, as in the case of MPI. As a consequence, only a few works in the literature try to offer support MPI on Docker, and most fail to develop a simple and stand-alone solution that does not require manual or external manipulation of the MPI configuration.

In this paper we address the lack of elegant deployment solutions for MPI over a Docker Swarm cluster. We extend the preliminary results presented on [27], demonstrating the interest of our platform through the deployment of a meteorological simulation software and its evaluation thanks to execution benchmarks and trace analysis on both cloud and container environments. In addition, we expand the analysis by comparing the performance on traditional x86 processors and ARM processors represented by clusters of Raspberry Pi machines.

1.2   Background

Considering all current virtualization technologies, we can highlight two of them: hardware virtualization, which makes use of Virtual Machine Monitors (VMMs), better known as **hypervisors**, and OS-level virtualization (**containers**).

Hardware virtualization can be classified as Type I or Type II. Each type considers where the hypervisor is located in the system software stack. Type I hypervisors (Fig. 1a) execute directly over hardware and manage the guest OSs. This way, the access to the hardware (and the isolation between different host OS) must be aware of the underlying VMM to access the hardware (both through the hypervisor or through paravirtualization interfaces).

The Type II (Fig. 1b) virtualization, on the other hand, relies on a hypervisor working inside the host OS, with the later one ensuring the access to the hardware. Type II allows creating complete abstractions and total isolation from the hardware by translating all guest OS instructions [18]. This type of virtualization is also known as *full virtualization*. As drawback, it imposes a high overload that penalizes most HPC applications [33]. While these performance penalties can be mitigated by the use of hardware-assisted virtualization (a set of specific instructions present in most modern processors), other virtualization strategies are often preferred when dealing with HPC applications.

As hypervisor-based solutions are considered heavy-weighted, the development of OS-level virtualization is becoming much more popular (Fig. 1c). This approach uses OS features that partition the physical machine resources, creating multiple isolated user-space instances (containers) on top of a single host kernel. Another advantage of container-based virtualization is that it does not need a hypervisor, incurring much less overhead [12]. Hence, popular OS-level virtualization systems include Linux Containers (LXC), RKT and Docker.

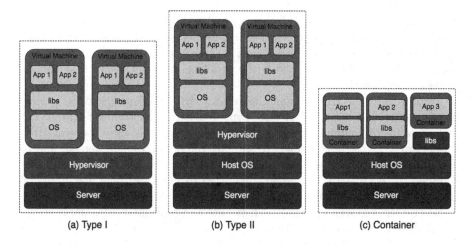

Fig. 1. Main virtualization types.

In all those systems, the container shares the kernel with the host OS, so its processes and file system are completely visible from the host, but thanks to the OS isolation, the container only sees its file system and process space [31]. The also use *namespaces* to isolate the containers and ensure that they access only their subsets of resources. Namespaces are also used to control the network and inter-process communication capabilities, and allow containers to be checkpointed, resumed or even migrated.

One of the most popular container solutions is Docker[1]. In addition to managing containers at the OS level, Docker allows the users to create personalized images that can be saved and used as a base to the deployment of many concurrent containers. Docker also provides a registry-based service named *Docker Hub*[2], allowing users to share their images.

More recently, Docker provides a basic orchestrator service called **Docker Swarm**, that enables the deployment of a cluster of Docker nodes. While Docker

---

[1] https://www.docker.com/.

[2] https://hub.docker.com/.

Swarm is not as modular as other orchestrators like Kubernetes [7], it is simple to use, and Swarm services can be easily adapted to operate under Kubernetes.

It is also interesting to note that although Docker was initially developed for x86 platforms, it now contemplates other processor architectures. For example, the adaption to the ARM processors family started around 2014, with an initial work made by Hypriot[3] for Raspberry Pi machines. More recently, Docker started to officially support ARM, and several base images on Docker Hub are now published with both x86 and ARM versions.

1.3 Related Work

HPC applications often search to solve problems that are hard to compute in a single machine due to capacity (memory, storage) or performance limitations. Distribute these applications on a cluster is often a way to increase the available resources all while trying to divide the problems in small pieces that can be processed in parallel.

Traditionally, the HPC community refuses virtualization due to the performance overheads from Type II and Type I hypervisors. However, the recent dissemination of container virtualization is changing this view. Several HPC centers favor the use of containers to simplify the resources management and to guarantee compatibility and reproducibility for the users' applications [23]. For example, the NVidia DGX servers[4], dedicated to Deep Learning and Artificial Intelligence applications, use Docker containers to deploy the user's applications.

Several strategies can be used to distribute and coordinate HPC applications over a cluster, and one of the most popular ones is the use of message passing through the MPI (Message Passing Interface) communication protocol. Indeed, MPI provides standard operations for data exchange and task coordination, including single and multi-point communications, synchronous and asynchronous primitives, parallel I/O, etc. While recent advances have improved several performance aspects, the MPI specification is still based on "stable" HPC clusters, which may hinder the deployment of an MPI application on new dynamic environments such as clouds and virtualized clusters. Indeed, MPI requires a well-known execution environment, characterized by a list of participating nodes (often known as the `hostfile`). Please note that while some fault-tolerance has been included in the last MPI specification (see [21]), it only serves to handle nodes that go down, not to manage a dynamic list of nodes.

As a consequence, deploying MPI applications over a container cluster such as Docker Swarm or Kubernetes is a challenging task. In the specific case of Docker Swarm (which we consider in this work), the overlay network connecting the containers is designed to perform replication and load balancing, not to manage node lists as required by MPI. This problem can be found on the literature, where most works trying to deploy MPI application over Docker require manual

---

[3] https://blog.hypriot.com/.

[4] https://www.nvidia.com/content/dam/en-zz/Solutions/Data-Center/dgx-1/dgx-1-rhel-centos-datasheet-update-r2.pdf.

or external manipulation of MPI elements to deploy applications. One of our aims is therefore to propose a self-content Docker Swarm platform capable of supporting MPI applications.

Among the related works, we can cite [5], which focus on the automation of the deployment of the MPI application over a Docker Swarm cluster (i.e., scripts to copy and launch the application), but requires the user to provide the list of available nodes at launch time. More often, the literature describes an external management for the nodes in the container cluster. For example, [32] suggests two architectural approaches to be used with Docker, all relying on an external script that feeds information to the containers through SSH. The same approach is used by [13], where the containers are launched separately by PBS, a resource manager, and a set of scripts helps deploying and connecting the containers together. The same strategy is used by [3], using Slurm. In both cases, the authors connect isolated containers "by hand", instead of relying on the Docker Swarm orchestrator.

Not all solutions rely on scripts, but sometimes they depend on solutions specifically tailored for MPI. This is the case of Singularity [16], a container manager developed for HPC applications. As these applications often rely on MPI, Singularity automatically sets up an MPI hostfile with the host names.

An extreme case of external dependency is that of [8], where even MPI tools (mpirun, mpiexec) are absent from the containers. Instead, both the application, data and libraries are imported from the host OS, with the containers playing simply the role of isolated execution environments. Such approach makes the execution totally dependent on the hosting platform, preventing the usage of any generic platform such as the cloud.

To our knowledge, only the work from [22] approaches the minimal requirements for the automatic deployment of MPI applications on a Docker Swarm cluster. This platform includes scripts for the deployment of the Docker Swarm service and creates list of nodes for the hostfile by inspecting active network connections (using **netstat**). Nonetheless, the use of **netstat** proved to be too unstable, and recent patches to the code try to correct this issue.

1.4   Our Contributions

In this paper, we consider the problem of developing a container environment capable of supporting MPI applications in both server and cluster configurations. As expressed before, we search to propose a self-content solution based on Docker Swarm, a well known tool that adds clustering capabilities to Docker containers, including distribution, load balance and overlay networking.

When regarding the solutions presented in the literature, we consider that they are too dependent on external scripts, making them inelegant and unreliable. Instead, we propose a simpler solutions that integrate well to the deployment of a Docker Swarm cluster.

The second contribution of this work is an extensive performance evaluation of a real application in both cloud and container environments. We selected the WRF (Weather Research and Forecast) model as it is both an application that relies on MPI for distributed computing, but also because it has several install issues that favorize its distribution as a container image. The benchmarks and execution traces performed on this work allow us to better understand the impact of the container environment and the Docker Swarm overlay network, but also to identify performance bottlenecks from the WRF software that may be addressed in a future work. This extensive analysis is also an addition to the preliminary results we presented in [27].

Our final contribution is the adaption of the environment to support the execution on ARM processors, and another set of benchmarks and analysis in a cluster of Raspberry Pi. The main interest of supporting this family of processors lies on its potential and relative low cost. We performed new experiments in a Raspberry Pi 3 cluster, experimentally demonstrating that applications such as WRF can be deployed over ARM processors and produce results within acceptable time intervals and for a fraction of the cost of a traditional HPC platform.

2   Supporting MPI on a Docker Swarm Cluster

As we indicated before, most works aiming at supporting MPI on Docker rely on the users to complete the information in the `hostfile`, or require external tools to reach such objective. Only the work from [22] tries to create an automated process, but it does not works reliably enough.

Such difficulty is due to the fact that Docker Swarm was not conceived as an HPC environment, but rather as a self balancing/fault tolerant environment to deploy applications. This can be observed if we analyze the different execution modes Docker support: in the "individual" mode (i.e., the "original" mode that does not depend on Docker Swarm), a container is launched as a standalone application. In this mode, no additional interconnections to other instances is required, even if this can be made possible. In the "service" mode, which is part of the Docker Swarm configuration, instances are interconnected by a routing overlay. This overlay includes a naming service that allows services to locate each other easily (instead of using hard-coded IP addresses), but it also includes a load balance mechanism to redirect messages among instance replicas or to restart faulting instances.

As the own Docker Swarm documentation illustrates (see Fig. 2), replicas of a service instance, even if located in different nodes, can be addressed by the same name, with messages being rerouted by the "Ingress" overlay network. In this example, two *my-web* instances exist, and they can be contacted through any of the nodes from the service. This naming service simplifies the development of applications (the code only needs to indicate a *my-web* address), and the overlay performs the redirection of the messages and the eventual load balancing among the instances of a service.

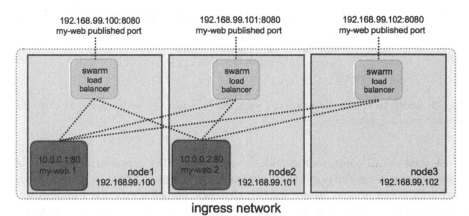

Fig. 2. Docker routing mesh [11].

In the case of MPI applications, the "replication and redirection" approach from Docker does not apply conveniently, as the MPI `hostfile` requires the list of the computing servers. The `hostfile` can be composed by hostnames or IP addresses, but obtaining the hostnames is not an easy task in Docker Swarm because the overlay hides the instances under the same "umbrella" name (for example, *my-web* in the previous example). For this reason, we need to discover the instances' IP addresses inside the overlay network. As the approach used by [22] is not reliable as it depends on open network connections between the instances (which may be transient or even non existent), we chose to query the naming service of Docker with the *dig* DNS lookup tool. More exactly, Docker Swarm allow us to contact all instances of the same service under the *tasks.XXXX* nickname, where *XXXX* is the name of the service. By using *dig*, we can obtain detailed information sent by the DNS server and, in the case of umbrella names, get the list of the IP addresses from all instances associated with that name.

The `hostfile` also allows the users to indicate a few more information about the computing resources, like the number of processes (or slots) a node can run simultaneously. As most recent processors have multiple computing cores, we can consider that each machine in a Swarm cluster is able to run more than one process. To obtain this extra information, we call the *nproc* application on each machine, obtaining therefore the number of available processing cores.

Therefore, these two discovery steps (IP addresses and computing capabilities) can be elegantly arranged in a few lines of scripts as presented in the snippet from Fig. 3, where we compose the `hostfile` with the list of all *worker* nodes (i.e., instances of the "worker" service on Swarm) and the number of computing cores from each node.

```
iplists=`dig +short tasks.workers A`
for i in $iplists; do
    np=`ssh $i "nproc --all"`
    echo "$i:$np" >> hostfile
done
```

Fig. 3. Script to create the `hostfile` with the IP addresses and number of cores for Docker Swarm instances.

A final detail concerns the nodes' *ranks*. Most HPC applications rely on a node or process rank to perform specific tasks or to segment data to be processed, and MPI is not an exception. In MPI, the node launching the MPI application uses the order of the nodes in the `hostfile` to set the ranks and to launch the application on the other nodes. This "master" node, known as "rank 0", is often used as a frontend node for the cluster, where the user can execute preprocessing steps, setup the application parameters or simply run the code before deploying it over the cluster. Because of this, it is important to allow users to access this node using SSH, for example. Even if most of the MPI application deployment can be automated through scripts, we believe that this improves the usability of our environment. In addition, we must consider that a Docker Swarm cluster remains an isolated environment, and accessing it via SSH is a simple way to import and export data.

Because of the load balancer in the Docker network, we cannot simply add an SSH server to each worker replica as the connection will not always be directed to the same node. Therefore, we have to create a "master" service that can be correctly identified and accessed from the outside. As the SSH port must be published, the master node cannot simply use the Ingress routing network, but needs to be executed under the special `global` deployment mode. Some other attributes in the service definition file (`docker-compose.yaml`) ensure that the master will be easy to contact (by deploying it on the manager node from the Swarm cluster), open the ports for SSH and also mount correctly all external volumes required for the application. Therefore, Fig. 4 presents the main elements of the `docker-compose.yaml` file used to define and deploy the Swarm service for our application. All these files are available at our Github repository[5] and the images are available on Docker Hub.

---

[5] https://github.com/lsteffenel/swarm_mpi_basic.

```
version: "3.3"
services:
  master:
    image: lsteffenel/swarm_mpi_basic
    deploy:
      mode:
        global
      placement:
        constraints:
          - node.role == manager
    ports:
      - published: 2022
        target: 22
        mode: host
    volumes:
      - "./input:/input"
      - "./output:/output"
    networks:
      - mpinet
  workers:
    image: lsteffenel/swarm_mpi_basic
    deploy:
      replicas: 2
      placement:
        preferences:
          - spread: node.labels.datacenter
    volumes:
      - "./input:/input"
      - "./output:/output"
    networks:
      - mpinet
networks:
  mpinet:
    driver: overlay
    attachable: true
```

Fig. 4. Excerpt of the Swarm service definition.

3 Profiling and Tunning an Application

In order to assess the performance our virtualized, container-based cluster platform, we decided to benchmark Weather Research and Forecasting (WRF) model
[24], a well-known numerical weather prediction model. In the next sections we
will describe the WRF suite in greater details, and conduct several performance
measurements and analysis to identify performance overheads and bottlenecks
on both virtual cluster and application levels.

3.1   WRF - Weather Research and Forecasting

The Weather Research and Forecasting (WRF) Model [24] is a state-of-the-art numerical weather prediction software widely used for both operations, research and education. It is one of the most known meteorological forecast tools, with users numbering in the tens of thousands. Indeed, it is one of the main tools used in our MESO project[6], an international collaboration to explore stratospheric events that affect the Ozone layer.

In spite of its popularity, WRF developers still do not offer it in binary packages ready to be installed, but instead the user needs to configure and compile the software, which may be a challenge for beginners or for users that do not have administration rights on their computing infrastructures. Today, WRF has more than 1.5 million lines of code in C and Fortran, and presents many dependencies on external software packages for input/output (I/O), parallel communications, and data compression. Many of these external libraries are becoming obsolete or unsupported by recent Linux distributions, forcing the users to download and compile these libraires too.

We believe that running WRF on containers is a way to mitigate many of the problems cited above, simplifying its deployment for both education and research usages. Indeed, containers allow the packaging of a working WRF install, ready to be used in local machines but also on the cloud.

Execution Steps. In addition to the configuration complexity, running the WRF model requires several steps to preprocess, compute and visualize the results. Indeed, the typical workflow to execute the WRF model is made of 5 phases, represented in Fig. 5 and detailed in the list below:

1. Geogrid - creates terrestrial data from static geographic data (external files with around 60 GB of data);
2. Ungrib - unpacks GRIB meteorological data obtained from an external source and packs it into an intermediate working format;
3. Metgrid - horizontally interpolates the meteorological data onto the model domain;
4. Real - vertically interpolates the data onto the model coordinates, creates boundary and initial condition files, and performs consistency checks;
5. WRF - generates the model forecast.

The three first steps belong to the WRF Preprocessing System (WPS), a subset of applications that is configured and compiled separately from the remainder of the tool. During its configuration, WPS allows two execution modes: serial or dmpar, the later one providing distributed memory parallelism through the use of MPI.

The second part of the configuration, which compiles and install the WRF model, offers four execution modes: serial, smpar (shared memory parallelism), dmpar (distributed memory parallelism) and sm+dmpar. The smpar option is

---

[6] http://meso.univ-reims.fr.

based on OpenMP, while the dmpar uses MPI as communication overlay. The last option (sm+dmpar) combines OpenMP and MPI, but several user reports point out that dmpar usually outperforms the mixed option [9,17] and should be preferred.

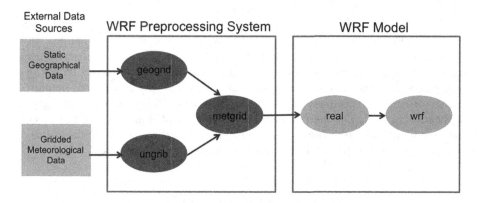

Fig. 5. WRF workflow [27].

3.2   Performance Evaluation

Computer researchers have been dedicated to investigating the impact of containers on HPC applications. The use of containers facilitates dependency management by providing a solid environment for running applications. [12,15] have shown that the use of containers generates negligible performance payloads in a single server. In the case of Docker Swarm, however, the overlay network is created with the help of VXLAN tunnels, and this encapsulation has a payload that may represent about 6% of the transmitted data [14] and therefore a potential performance issue. Hence, in order to test the impact generated by Docker Swarm, we designed two scenarios to compare the performance of the WRF application.

To perform the tests, we used three machines configured as c4.large instances in the Amazon AWS service. Each machine featured a 2.9 GHz Intel Xeon E5-2666 v3 processor, 2 cores, 3.75 GiB of RAM and a network connection with moderate performance (300 Mb/s). Two scenarios were considered. In scenario (a), WRF was run on baremetal with the number of processes varying as follows: 1 (1 machine), 2 (2 machines), 4 (2 machines), 6 (3 machines). In scenario (b) the same test was performed, however, using containers with an Ubuntu OS image and with WRF installed and configured. For the execution of scenario (b), a Docker overlay network was also created so that instances could communicate, sending and receiving TCP packets used by MPI for synchronization and execution of distributed tasks. The tests on both scenarios were performed 10 times, with the average of the times presented below.

The benchmarks used a dataset concerning an area covering Uruguay and the south of Brazil and allowing a 12-h forecasting from October 18, 2016. This small dataset is used as training example for meteorology students at Universidade Federal de Santa Maria, who can modify the parameters and compare the results to the real observations. The entire dataset is accessible at the Github repository we created for the WRF container images[7].

From the Fig. 6 chart it is possible to see that as the number of processes grows, the impact on performance from Docker is higher. This difference can be caused by the overhead generated by the overlay network, so that containers on different hosts can communicate. Nevertheless, the overall impact on performance is still reduced, reaching 7.8% when 6 processes were used. Therefore, the use of containers remains interesting, facilitating the deployment of a given application or tool. The next section conducts a detailed analysis on the execution traces of WRF, allowing us to better understand the reasons for the reduced speedup observed in both baremetal and container environments.

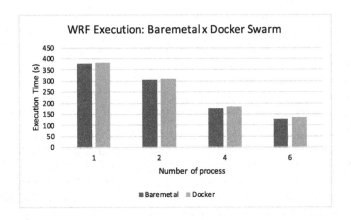

Fig. 6. WRF performance on AWS: baremetal versus Docker.

3.3   Going Deeper: Tracing MPI Communications

Parallel applications have their own circumstances when it comes to analyzing its execution behavior. Beyond the individual flow of each process, it is essential to monitor how the processes communicate with each other and how this communication affects the overall performance. The tracing tools and its outcome enables this evaluation to be done, as the traces are valuable resources to find unexpected behaviors or bottlenecks during the execution. Along with this investigation, trace visualization tools will also be helpful. These tools are crucial when it comes to realizing the *post-mortem* analysis, facilitating to identify

---

[7] https://github.com/lsteffenel/wrf-container-armv7l-RaspberryPi.

events that might be affecting the performance. Lastly, it is desirable to connect these events with the code to implement improvements.

Currently, there is a variety of tracing tools available, along with a variety of trace visualization tools. Among the existent tracing tools, EZTrace appears as a tool designed for providing a generic way to analyze an application without impacting its execution [28]. Besides that, EZTrace was commonly adopted in previous works and provides runtime instrumentation. Since these characteristics fit our needs, EZTrace was chosen to trace the executions of the case study application, described in Sect. 3. The version chosen for EZTrace was version 1.1-6, that is compatible with the `binutils-dev` package, version 2.26.1-1, available on Ubuntu 16.04. This package is a requirement and its version impacts which EZTrace version to choose. To the current case study, it was necessary to include the MPI module, as we are meant to collect data in this context during the execution.

The tracing analysis was performed on the same cloud environment as the previous performance tests, using three `c4.large` on Amazon Web Services (AWS). Two cases were executed to generate traces, the first with 4 WRF processes distributed over two nodes, and the second with 6 processes distributed over three nodes, just like in Sect. 3.2. Were realized five executions for each case, and EZTrace was instrumented to collect MPI related events (`eztrace -t mpi`).

As the executions finished and the data was collected, we converted it into two trace formats: Pajé and OTF. To visualize these trace formats, ViTE[8] (Pajé) and Vampir[9] (OTF) were the visualization tools utilized. Each one of these tools provides specific resources to explore the traces and its data.

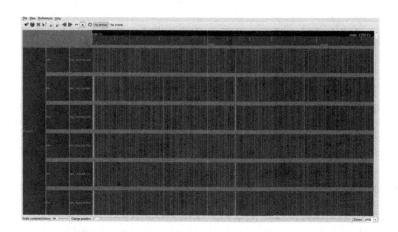

Fig. 7. ViTE tool interface.

---

[8] http://vite.gforge.inria.fr/.

[9] https://vampir.eu/.

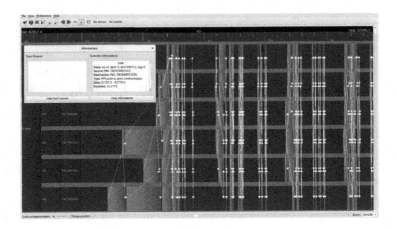

Fig. 8. ViTE zoom on communications.

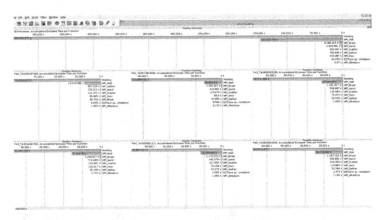

Fig. 9. Communication matrices.

Firstly, the view on ViTE tool is presented in Fig. 7, illustrating the communications between 6 WRF processes. The ViTE interface allows us to zoom in and see the messages' flow along with more details about a specific event or arrow, as the user double clicks it (Fig. 8). The tool also has a statistical plugin that presents the data collected in charts shape.

Another visualization tool utilized was Vampir. Its interface provides multiple resources to investigate the trace. These resources include most of what is available on ViTE and some extra. For instance, in Fig. 9, a function summary is shown. With this resource, it is possible to view how much utilized is each MPI function, in general, and for each process. Another resource presented, shown in Fig. 10 is a communication matrix. It enables to visualize how many times a process has sent and received messages from another process. It also shows

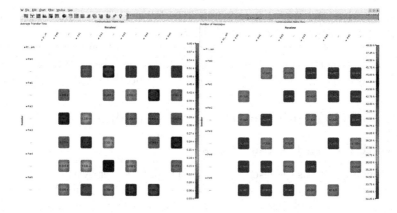

Fig. 10. Resources available on Vampir tool.

the shortest, longest, and average transfer time for each specific combination of sender and receiver process.

Looking these traces, we see that MPI_Wait events represent an important part of the execution time. MPI_Wait is a primitive used when non-blocking functions as MPI_Isend and MPI_Irecv, are called. Indeed, it indicates that a process is waiting for the arrival of a message, evidencing a lack of synchronization between processes. Even though the time spent during this invocation is inconvenient, non-blocking messages are usually an improvement over blocking messages, since non-blocking calls are used to overlap communication and computation. This behavior allows processing between the time that the process sends the message and the MPI_Wait instance but, in the case of the WRF application, it seems too important and therefore affect the overall performance.

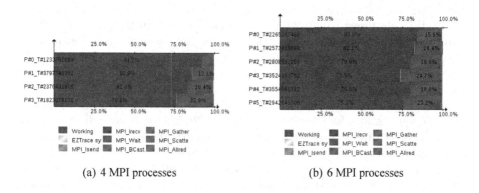

(a) 4 MPI processes   (b) 6 MPI processes

Fig. 11. Performance statistics.

Hence, the time occupied by MPI_Wait increases with the number of processes, as we observe in the statistical details obtained with 4 and 6 processes on Fig. 11. Also, the time expended in MPI_Wait is not equally distributed, evidencing a load balance issue inside WRF.

While this analysis does not uncovers any special problem with the container environment, it helps concluding that scalability issues observed in Sect. 3.2 are due to the own WRF code, whose solution is beyond the scope of this work.

4   Supporting Different Processor Architectures

4.1   WRF on ARM Architectures

In the previous sections we described the design of a Docker Swarm platform supporting MPI applications, and we perform benchmarks using the WRF meteorological model as a testing subject. Those benchmarks were performed in classical x86 processors, which are popular among the HPC community.

In recent years, however, we have seen the arrival of computing platforms based on ARM processors. Most ARM computers are based in the Sytem-on-a-Chip (SoC) model that encapsulates CPU, GPU, RAM memory and other components on the same chip [30], including the popular single-board computers like Raspberry Pi, but also cellular phones and tablets.

ARM processors are currently used for a large range of applications, from Computer Science teaching [1] to Internet of Things [19]. They have an active role in Fog and Edge computing [26], bringing computation closer to the user and therefore offering proximity services that otherwise would be entirely deployed on a distant infrastructure. All naturally, many cloud providers such as Amazon and Google start to propose servers running on ARM processors.

The HPC community has demonstrated an increasing interest in this architecture, with many projects on the way. If the choice for ARM processors was initially driven by energy and cost requirement, nowadays this family of processors presents several improvements that allow the construction of computing infrastructures with a good computing power and a cost way inferior to traditional HPC platforms [10,20,29]. Furthermore, a SoC cluster can substitute a traditional HPC cluster in some situations, as SoC are relatively inexpensive and have low maintenance and environmental requirements (cooling, etc.). Of course, this is only valid as long as the SoC infrastructure provides sufficient Quality of Service (QoS) to the final users.

The use of Docker on SoCs represent also an interesting solution to deploy scientific applications for educational purposes [2]. Indeed, if virtualization (and especially **container-based virtualization**) contributes to simplify the administrative tasks related to the installation and maintenance of scientific applications, it also enables a rich experimental learning for students, which can test different software and perform hands-on exercises without having to struggle with compilers, operating systems, and DevOps tasks. Furthermore, by developing solutions for both x86 and ARM architectures, we try to simplify the deployment of applications on personal computers, classrooms, dedicated infrastructures or even the cloud, seamlessly. While the MPI support is almost identical in both architectures, we faced some additional difficulties when adapting

WRF. When we started to configure WRF for the ARM platform, we had to address a few additional issues besides the availability of some libraries, a problem already observed during the configuration on x86. Indeed, the configuration of WRF supports several compilers (gcc, Intel, Portland, etc.) and architectures, but ARM processors are not listed among the supported ones. Fortunately, some researched had the same problem before and documented their experiences, like for example the work from [4]. While the adaption requires the editing of the configuration files in order to find a match to the ARM platform, the configuration differences for both ARM or x86 are minimal, and most of the process is simple and straightforward.

In addition, we have changed how to access input data, from a fixed Docker volume to a mounted file system. This gives more flexibility to develop workflows to execute the application regularly, like for example in a daily forecast schedule. This also helps to fix the problems due to the storage of the *geogrid* geographical database. As the full database reaches 60 GB when uncompressed, the users can attach an external storage drives to their nodes instead of having all the database in the Docker image.

In order to assess the interest running meteorological simulations on ARM processors, we conducted a series of experiments to evaluate the performance of each step of the WRF application. The next sessions describe the experiments and present our first insights.

4.2 Environment Description

In these benchmarks we deployed our virtual cluster over a network of three **Raspberry Pi 3 model B** (Broadcom BCM2837 processor, ARM Cortex-A53, 4 cores, 1.2 GHz, 1 GB RAM). The interconnection between devices is by a Fast Ethernet switch (100 Mbps). As the goal of the cluster is to run an application that demands considerable computing resource, for reduce the effects of limited RAM memory, to provide a Swap memory, a USB drive (1.8 GB) has been connected to each device. The WRF dataset is the same used on the experiments from Sect. 3.2.

All measures presented in this section correspond to the average of at least 5 runs. Furthermore, as the WRF workflow is composed by 5 steps, we computed the execution time of each step individually, in order to determine the best deployment strategy. Therefore, the next sections present the separate analysis of the preprocessing steps (all three steps from WPS and the real step from WRF) and the forecast step (WRF).

4.3 Performance of WPS and Real Steps

In traditional x86 environments, the execution of the WRF workflow is dominated by the WRF model: all WPS preprocessing steps (geogrid, ungrib, metgrid) and the real steps represent only a small fraction of the computing time. On ARM processors (and especially on SoCs) this is not necessarily true, and we need to identify the constraints we can face during the usage of those machines.

One of the first issues concern the access to the geographical database required by the geogrid step. As indicated in Sect. 3.1, this database has more than 60 GB, which is a potential problem for the internal storage of a typical SoC that relies on SD cards. Indeed, in our experiments, we had to attach an external USB storage device to a Raspberry Pi node to accommodate this WPS_GEOG database.

As the ARM processors used in our experiments are less powerful than x86 processors, we decided to study the performance of each workflow step separately, trying to identify whether the use of MPI would benefit each one of the WPS steps (as well as the real step). For such, we measured the execution time of each step when varying the number of computing cores (using the mpirun -np option).

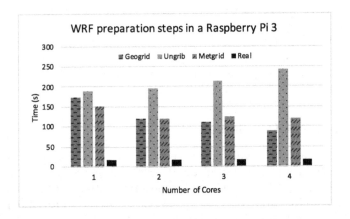

Fig. 12. Performance of WPS steps when varying the number of cores [27].

Table 1. Relative performance of WPS steps on a single machine (in seconds) [27].

Cores	1	2	3	4
Geogrid	173.81	119.59	111.56	88.54
Ungrib	188.78	196.15	212.97	241.57
Metgrid	151.42	120.47	123.56	119.26
Real	16.437	16.54	16.59	16.69

The result of this benchmark, illustrated in Fig. 12 and detailed in Table 1, indicates that only the *Geogrid* step effectively benefits from a multi-core execution. Even though, the acceleration is under-optimal (we need 4x cores to obtain only a 50% performance improvement). Associated with the storage limitations cited before and its relatively small impact to the overall execution time (when comparing with the forecast step, see Sect. 4.4), we advise against running *Geogrid* cluster-wide. Instead, we suggest assigning a single node (the `master`) who can preprocess the data for the forecast model.

For all the other steps, a parallel execution is not an interesting option. The *Metgrid* step shows a small performance gain when parallelizing but the execution time stabilizes for 2 or more cores, and the *Real* step shows no evidence of improvements. In the case of *Ungrib*, the parallel execution even penalizes the algorithm. Additional benchmarks on the network performance, such as those conducted by [32], may also help tuning the different steps.

From these results, we suggest organizing the deployment of the preprocessing steps as follows:

- *Geogrid* - parallel execution with `mpirun`, preferentially only in the machine hosting the WPS_GEOG database (the `master` node);
- *Ungrib* - serial execution in a single core;
- *Metgrid* - serial execution or at most parallel execution with `mpirun` in a single machine;
- *Real* - serial execution in a single core.

4.4   WRF Execution

Even in an ARM processor, the preprocessing steps listed before represent only a small part of the execution. This is not the case of the WRF forecast step, which can have a much larger duration, especially inn "production" environments with larger datasets and more than a simple 12-h forecast to be computed.

As expected, the forecasting step of WRF does benefit from multicore and cluster scenarios. Figure 13 shows the average execution time of this step when running on one, two or three nodes in the Raspberry Pi cluster.

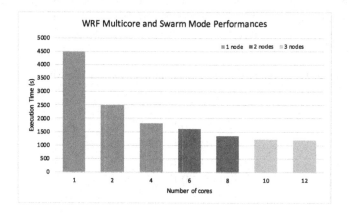

Fig. 13. Performance of WRF in multicore and Swarm cluster mode.

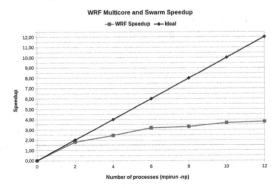

Fig. 14. Speedup of WRF execution in multicore and Swarm cluster mode.

If the multicore execution allows an important performance gain, the Swarm cluster execution shows more mitigated results. Indeed, the performance gain when passing from one to two nodes (4 to 8 process) is only 25%, and when passing from two to three nodes (8 to 12 process) it is barely 12%. As shown in Fig. 14, this is really far from a linear speedup, but can be explained both by the poor performance of WRF on `dmpar` mode (MPI) identified in Sect. 3.3. In addition, we suspect that the network performance on the Raspberry Pis also play a role. Indeed, as observed by [6], the access to the communication bus in the Raspberry Pi is known by its "low" speed interconnection card (10/100 Mbps only) that penalizes all communication interfaces.

Tables 2 and 3 detail these results, and also present a performance comparison with a the x86 processors from the AWS cloud used in Sect. 3.2. Please note that the x86 column is limited to a single `c4.large` instance from AWS as it has only two available vCPUs. Without surprise, the x86 processors are faster, but the execution time on the Raspberry Pis is still acceptable. Indeed, the processing time is fair enough for education and training. Even a production environment can be considered, if we expect WRF to deliver daily or even hourly forecasts. Furthermore, if we consider the material and environmental cost of the SoC solution, it is clearly an interesting alternative.

Table 2. WRF relative performance on a single machine (in seconds).

Cores	R Pi 3	AWS c4.large
1	4469.8374	539.05
2	2503.3624	314.69
3	2194.1872	–
4	1823.8314	–

Table 3. Performance on a Raspberry Pi 3 swarm cluster (in seconds).

Machines	Cores	Pi Swarm
1 × Pi 3	1	4469.8374
	2	2503.3624
	4	1823.8314
2 × Pi 3	6	1401.0106
	8	1352.72
3 × Pi 3	10	1218.7158
	12	1183.2734

5   Conclusions and Future Work

This work focuses on the design of a container-based platform for HPC applications based on MPI. Indeed, container virtualization enables the packaging of complex applications and their seamless deployment. As most traditional scientific applications rely on MPI for scalability, we were surprised by the lack of a proper support for MPI, neither on popular container managers like Docker, nor on other works from the literature. We therefore propose, in a first moment, a service specification to deploy a Docker Swarm cluster that is ready for MPI applications.

Later, we evaluate the proposed platform through the performance analysis of the WRF meteorological forecast model. Through performance benchmarks on both baremetal and container environments, we were able to separate performance overheads related to the use of the container environment from those related to the own application. For instance, the analysis of the execution traces from WRF allowed us to identify performance bottlenecks that affect the scalability of the application.

Finally, we conducted a few more experiences to evaluate the performance and the interest of using containers over SoC (System-on-Chip) clusters. These results indicate that if popular the ARM processors in SoCs such as Raspberry Pi cannot compete in performance with x86 processors, they still are able to deliver results within an acceptable delay.

Future improvements to this work include the execution of additional benchmarks to validate the scalability of the platform with other MPI-based applications. Also, the bottlenecks we identified during the analysis of the execution traces of WRF will be the subject of a performance tuning project that we shall conduct in the next months.

Acknowledgements. This research has been partially supported by the French-Brazilian CAPES-COFECUB MESO project (http://meso.univ-reims.fr) and the GREEN-CLOUD project (http://www.inf.ufrgs.br/greencloud/) (#16/2551-0000 488-9), from FAPERGS and CNPq Brazil, program PRONEX 12/2014.

References

1. Ali, M., Vlaskamp, J.H.A., Eddin, N.N., Falconer, B., Oram, C.: Technical development and socioeconomic implications of the Raspberry Pi as a learning tool in developing countries. In: Computer Science and Electronic Engineering Conference (CEEC), pp. 103–108. IEEE (2013)
2. Alvarez, L., Ayguade, E., Mantovani, F.: Teaching HPC systems and parallel programming with small-scale clusters. In: 2018 IEEE/ACM Workshop on Education for High-Performance Computing (EduHPC), pp. 1–10, November 2018. https://doi.org/10.1109/EduHPC.2018.00004
3. Azab, A.: Enabling Docker containers for high-performance and many-task computing. In: 2017 IEEE International Conference on Cloud Engineering (IC2E), pp. 279–285, April 2017. https://doi.org/10.1109/IC2E.2017.52
4. Barker, D.: Setting up an ARM-based micro-cluster and running the WRF weather model, March 2014. http://supersmith.com/site/ARM.html
5. de Bayser, M., Cerqueira, R.: Integrating MPI with Docker for HPC. In: 2017 IEEE International Conference on Cloud Engineering (IC2E), pp. 259–265, April 2017. https://doi.org/10.1109/IC2E.2017.40
6. Beserra, D., Pinheiro, M.K., Souveyet, C., Steffenel, L.A., Moreno, E.D.: Performance evaluation of OS-level virtualization solutions for HPC purposes on SOC-based systems. In: 2017 IEEE 31st International Conference on Advanced Information Networking and Applications (AINA), pp. 363–370, March 2017. https://doi.org/10.1109/AINA.2017.73
7. Burns, B., Grant, B., Oppenheimer, D., Brewer, E., Wilkes, J.: Borg, omega, and kubernetes. Commun. ACM 59(5), 50–57 (2016). https://doi.org/10.1145/2890784
8. Chung, M.T., Quang-Hung, N., Nguyen, M., Thoai, N.: Using docker in high performance computing applications. In: 2016 IEEE Sixth International Conference on Communications and Electronics (ICCE), pp. 52–57, July 2016. https://doi.org/10.1109/CCE.2016.7562612
9. HPC Advisory Council: Weather research and forecasting (WRF): performance benchmark and profiling, best practices of the HPC advisory council. Technical report, HPC Advisory Council (2010). http://www.hpcadvisorycouncil.com/pdf/WRF_Analysis_and_Profiling_Intel.pdf
10. Cox, S.J., Cox, J.T., Boardman, R.P., Johnston, S.J., Scott, M., O'brien, N.S.: Iridis-pi: a low-cost, compact demonstration cluster. Cluster Comput. 17(2), 349–358 (2014). https://doi.org/10.1007/s10586-013-0282-7
11. Docker Inc.: Use swarm mode routing mesh. https://docs.docker.com/engine/swarm/ingress/
12. Felter, W., Ferreira, A., Rajamony, R., Rubio, J.: An updated performance comparison of virtual machines and Linux containers. IBM technical report RC25482 (AUS1407-001), Computer Science (2014)
13. Higgins, J., Holmes, V., Venters, C.: Orchestrating docker containers in the HPC environment. In: Kunkel, J.M., Ludwig, T. (eds.) ISC High Performance 2015. LNCS, vol. 9137, pp. 506–513. Springer, Cham (2015). https://doi.org/10.1007/978-3-319-20119-1_36
14. Iveson, S.: TCP/IP over VXLAN bandwidth overheads, March 2014. https://packetpushers.net/vxlan-udp-ip-ethernet-bandwidth-overheads/
15. Joy, A.M.: Performance comparison between Linux containers and virtual machines. In: International Conference on Advances in Computer Engineering and Applications (ICACEA), pp. 342–346. IEEE (2015)

16. Kurtzer, G.M., Sochat, V., Bauer, M.W.: Singularity: scientific containers for mobility of compute. PLoS ONE **12**(5), 1–20 (2017). https://doi.org/10.1371/journal.pone.0177459

17. Langkamp, T., Böhner, J.: Influence of the compiler on multi-CPU performance of WRFv3. Geosci. Model Dev. **4**(3), 611–623 (2011). https://doi.org/10.5194/gmd-4-611-2011. https://www.geosci-model-dev.net/4/611/2011/

18. Manohar, N.: A survey of virtualization techniques in cloud computing. In: Chakravarthi, V., Shirur, Y., Prasad, R. (eds.) VCASAN-2013. LNEE, vol. 258, pp. 461–470. Springer, Cham (2013). https://doi.org/10.1007/978-81-322-1524-0_54

19. Molano, J.I.R., Betancourt, D., Gómez, G.: Internet of Things: a prototype architecture using a Raspberry Pi. In: Uden, L., Heričko, M., Ting, I.-H. (eds.) KMO 2015. LNBIP, vol. 224, pp. 618–631. Springer, Cham (2015). https://doi.org/10.1007/978-3-319-21009-4_46

20. Montella, R., Giunta, G., Laccetti, G.: Virtualizing high-end GPGPUS on ARM clusters for the next generation of high performance cloud computing. Cluster Comput. **17**(1), 139–152 (2014). https://doi.org/10.1007/s10586-013-0341-0

21. MPI Forum: MPI: A message-passing interface standard version 3.1. https://www.mpi-forum.org/docs/

22. Nguyen, N., Bein, D.: Distributed MPI cluster with Docker Swarm mode. In: 2017 IEEE 7th Annual Computing and Communication Workshop and Conference (CCWC), pp. 1–7, January 2017. https://doi.org/10.1109/CCWC.2017.7868429

23. Ruiz, C., Jeanvoine, E., Nussbaum, L.: Performance evaluation of containers for HPC. In: HunoldHunold, S., et al. (eds.) Euro-Par 2015. LNCS, vol. 9523, pp. 813–824. Springer, Cham (2015). https://doi.org/10.1007/978-3-319-27308-2_65

24. Skamarock, W.C., et al.: A description of the advanced research WRF version 3. NCAR technical note. National Center for Atmospheric Research, Boulder, Colorado, USA (2008)

25. Somasundaram, T.S., Govindarajan, K.: CLOUDRB: a framework for scheduling and managing High-Performance Computing (HPC) applications in science cloud. Future Gen. Comput. Syst. **34**, 47–65 (2014)

26. Steffenel, L.A., Kirsch Pinheiro, M.: When the cloud goes pervasive: approaches for IoT PaaS on a mobiquitous world. In: Mandler, B., et al. (eds.) IoT360 2015. LNICST, vol. 169, pp. 347–356. Springer, Cham (2016). https://doi.org/10.1007/978-3-319-47063-4_36

27. Steffenel., L.A., Charão., A.S., da Silva Alves., B.: A containerized tool to deploy scientific applications over SOC-based systems: the case of meteorological forecasting with WRF. In: Proceedings of the 9th International Conference on Cloud Computing and Services Science - Volume 1: CLOSER, pp. 561–568. INSTICC, SciTePress (2019). https://doi.org/10.5220/0007799705610568

28. Trahay, F., Rue, F., Faverge, M., Ishikawa, Y., Namyst, R., Dongarra, J.: EZTrace: a generic framework for performance analysis. In: 2011 11th IEEE/ACM International Symposium on Cluster, Cloud and Grid Computing, pp. 618–619. IEEE (2011)

29. Weloli, J.W., Bilavarn, S., Vries, M.D., Derradji, S., Belleudy, C.: Efficiency modeling and exploration of 64-bit ARM compute nodes for exascale. Microprocess. Microsyst. **53**, 68–80 (2017). https://doi.org/10.1016/j.micpro.2017.06.019. http://www.sciencedirect.com/science/article/pii/S0141933116304537

30. Wolf, W., Jerraya, A.A., Martin, G.: Multiprocessor system-on-chip (MPSoC) technology. IEEE Trans. Comput.-Aided Des. Integr. Circ. Syst. **27**(10), 1701–1713 (2008)

31. Xavier, M.G., Neves, M.V., Rossi, F.D., Ferreto, T.C., Lange, T., De Rose, C.A.F.: Performance evaluation of container-based virtualization for high performance computing environments. In: 2013 21st Euromicro International Conference on Parallel, Distributed, and Network-Based Processing, pp. 233–240, February 2013. https://doi.org/10.1109/PDP.2013.41
32. Yong, C., Lee, G.W., Huh, E.N.: Proposal of container-based HPC structures and performance analysis. J. Inf. Process. Syst. 14(6), 1398–1404 (2018)
33. Younge, A.J., Henschel, R., Brown, J.T., von Laszewski, G., Qiu, J., Fox, G.C.: Analysis of virtualization technologies for high performance computing environments. In: IEEE 4th International Conference on Cloud Computing, CLOUD 2011, pp. 9–16. IEEE Computer Society, Washington, DC (2011)

Evolving Adaptation Rules at Runtime for Multi-cloud Applications

Kyriakos Kritikos[1]($\boxtimes$), Chrysostomos Zeginis[1], Eleni Politaki[2], and Dimitris Plexousakis[1]

[1] ICS-FORTH, 70013 Heraklion, GR, Greece
{kritikos,zegchris,dp}@ics.forth.gr
[2] Department of Computer Science, University of Crete, Heraklion, Greece
politaki@csd.uoc.gr

Abstract. Cloud computing is the most prevailing computing paradigm as it has led to a proliferation of cloud-based applications, either through the migration of existing legacy or the development of novel ones from scratch. In fact, nowadays, there is also a move towards adopting multi-clouds due to the main benefits they introduce, including vendor lock-in avoidance and optimal application design and provisioning via different cloud services. Unfortunately, multi-cloud applications face the challenge that even a single cloud environment exhibits a certain level of dynamicity and uncertainty. As such, a suitable service level cannot be handed over to their customers, which leads to SLA penalty costs and application provider reputation reduction. To address this challenge, we have previously proposed a cross-level and multi-cloud application adaptation architecture. Towards realising such an architecture, this paper focuses on supporting cross-level application adaptation through the modelling of adaptation rules that enact adaptation workflows but also on evolving such an adaptation to address both the application and exploited cloud services evolution as well as the provisioning environment's dynamicity. The modelling of such rules and their execution history is accommodated through corresponding extensions to a state-of-the-art cloud modelling language called CAMEL. Further, a specific selection algorithm for those alternative adaptation rules able to address the current problematic situation is suggested which takes into account their execution history and especially their performance.

Keywords: Adaptation · Evolution · Execution · Selection · History · Rule performance · Meta-model · DSL

1 Introduction

The way applications are developed, deployed and provisioned has been revolutionised through the advent of cloud computing. In fact, the wide adoption of this computing paradigm has led to a proliferation of cloud applications and services. These applications were either migrated from on-premise to public cloud

D. Ferguson et al. (Eds.): CLOSER 2019, CCIS 1218, pp. 223–246, 2020.
https://doi.org/10.1007/978-3-030-49432-2_11

environments or developed from scratch by adopting existing or new, cloud-based software engineering technologies. Cloud computing paradigm's success relies on the benefits it delivers, which include cost reduction, flexible resource management and resource elasticity allowing applications to infinitely scale on demand.

Traditional web service, e-commerce and infrastructure providers as well as new ones have rushed to offer cloud services at different abstraction levels. From those providers, the biggest also have attempted to lock-in their customers by offering particular added-value secondary services as well as related technologies and platforms to assist the development and provisioning of cloud-based applications. To avoid this vendor lock-in, the academia and nowadays also the industry seems to endorse multi-cloud computing. Apart from dealing with the aforementioned issue, deployment at multi-clouds is quite promising as it delivers extra benefits, which include selecting the best possible cloud services to optimally realise an application based on its requirements, increasing the application security level by adopting different security services as well as bypassing scaling hurdles in single-cloud environments.

However, multi-cloud applications face now the challenge of increased dynamicity and uncertainty, which is inherent even in a single cloud. This challenge jeopardises their ability to keep up with their promises through the delivery of the right service level to their customers. It is further hardened by the fact that real-world applications span multiple levels which depend on each other and involve the use of different cloud service types. As such, multi-cloud applications are negatively affected by the variation exhibited in the quality of all these services which propagates from lower to higher abstraction levels. In addition, both services and applications can evolve over time, e.g., due to market competition and advent of new technologies. Thus, even if multi-cloud applications are optimally realised through suitable cloud services, this realisation will be surely invalidated over time due to this dynamicity.

The aforementioned gap can be closed through our already proposed architecture [13] of an advanced, cross-level and multi-cloud application adaptation framework. This framework will feature the following capabilities, which are currently being implemented: (a) semi-automatically infer new adaptation rules [24] by considering the application structure and the dependencies at the different abstraction levels; (b) dynamically transform such rules into adaptation workflows to be enacted via workflow execution engines; (c) dynamically evolve adaptation rules based on their execution history, performance and successability to completely address an actual event ("problematic situation") that has caused their triggering.

This paper provides support to the realisation of the aforementioned capabilities through three main contributions where the first focuses on the third capability and the rest cross all capabilities. Our first contribution, by considering the existence of multiple adaptation rules that can confront the same event, attempts to dynamically select the best possible one by considering all these rules' execution history, especially in terms of their performance, cost and successability. Such a dynamic selection relies on the fact that one adaptation rule might not always be successful in addressing a certain event, especially also in case that application requirements and cloud service capabilities evolve over time. As such, all adaptation rules addressing the same event need to be continuously assessed over time in order to always promote the one which has the best current quality. In this way, the adaptation behaviour of the application concerned is continuously evolved to always select the right adaptation rules that best confront all possible problematic events as well as the increased levels of dynamicity and uncertainty.

The second and third paper contributions concentrate on the modelling side. In particular, this paper suggests two meta-model extensions to a state-of-the-art cloud modelling language [20] called CAMEL. The first extension specialises in the modelling of advanced adaptation rules. This modelling is quite rich as it re-uses elements from Complex Event Pattern (CEP) languages (e.g., the Esper's[1] one), to specify complex event patterns via the logical or time-based composition of simpler events. To also complete the adaptation rule specification, this extension enables associating such events patterns with workflow-language-independent adaptation workflows, including actions at any possible abstraction level (infrastructure, platform, software and workflow). To the best of our knowledge, such adaptation rules cannot be specified by any other meta-model or language [4,16,17,23]. This modelling contribution benefits the first two capabilities of the envisioned adaptation framework. In particular, workflow language independence leads to implementation flexibility as our adaptation framework could re-use any workflow engine, which might specialise in using only a certain workflow language.

Our last contribution focuses on extending CAMEL's execution meta-model to capture not only the application execution but also its adaptation history by specifying: (a) which adaptation rules and their respective adaptation actions were enacted and (b) how well these rules addressed the respective problematic event according to which quality level. This extension benefits the third capability of the envisioned adaptation framework as follows. First, it enables analysing the appropriateness of both single and composite adaptation actions (i.e., workflows), so as to allow their prospective substitution when the respective need arises. It can also determine those places where the application adaptation behaviour needs to be improved through the detection of situations where all automatically-generated alternative adaptation workflows for the same event do not exhibit the right quality level any more. To this end, this extension provides support to our first contribution as it assists in the automatic evolution of the application adaptation behaviour over time through the assessment of the quality of adaptation actions and subsequently of the adaptation rules that include them. To the best of our knowledge, this third paper contribution is also novel as no other approach seems to exist that is able to record the cloud application adaptation history.

---

[1] www.espertech.com/esper/.

This paper enhances the one in [14] as follows: (a) first, it includes the contribution of the automatic selection of the right adaptation rule for the handling of the respective problematic event; (b) second, it supplies a more complete use case example on which our work is applied to showcase its suitability; (c) third, it reviews the related work on both adaptation rule modelling and evolution; (d) it supplies some interesting directions for further improving the proposed work; (e) it slightly extends the analysis of the proposed application adaptation framework architecture while it also unveils its current realisation level.

The rest of the paper is structured as follows. The next section shortly details our envisioned adaptation framework architecture. Sections 3 and 4 elaborate on the modelling extensions conducted on CAMEL. Section 5 explicates our proposition towards the evolution of adaptation rules at runtime. Section 6 showcases the application of the proposed work on an example use case. Section 7 reviews the related work. Finally, the last section concludes the paper and draws directions for further research.

2 Multi-cloud Application Adaptation Framework

Our suggested, holistic multi-cloud application adaptation framework is depicted in Fig. 1. This framework will feature the following capabilities: (a) infer new from existing adaptation rules; (b) transform such rules into adaptation workflows able to be executed by workflow engines; (c) dynamically change the adaptation workflows associated with problematic events to better address them and thus evolve the application's adaptive behaviour; (d) edit adaptation rules, which is a suitable capability when automatically generated rules must be adjusted or so as to rapidly deal with cases not covered by the existing adaptation rule set; (e) browse the adaptation history to check the successfulness and performance of adaptation rules. As already indicated, all these five capabilities are enabled by the paper's main contributions.

We now shortly explain the adaptation framework architecture and especially the components its encloses as well as their interactions. The *Adaptation UI* enables experts to edit adaptation rules as well as to enact them (e.g., manually specified rules to rapidly react to unanticipated situations) while it is able to visualise both the application adaptation history and the results of its analysis. The expert could then approve the analysis results so as to evolve the application adaptation behaviour, if needed.

Edited or automatically generated rules are passed to the *Transformer* who transforms them from CAMEL into the format expected by the *Rule Engine*. Further, enacted rules pass through this component in order to transform their workflow part into the workflow language expected by the *Adaptation Engine*.

The *Rule Engine* is the component responsible to trigger the enactment path of rules. In particular, it is responsible to select those rules that must be triggered due to the occurrence of input monitoring events, which are retrieved from the *Monitoring Framework*. The selected rules are then passed to the *Transformer* so as to enact their adaptation workflows. This component internally utilises a *Rule Base* to support adaptation rule storage.

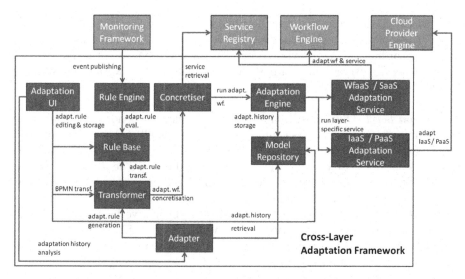

Fig. 1. The envisioned adaptation framework architecture [14].

The *Rule Engine* is also responsible for realising our first contribution. In particular, it continuously assesses all adaptation rules able to confront a certain event and selects the best possible one according to its current quality level. As such, the engine's rule base incorporates both selected rules for events as well as alternative, back up ones for the same events which might be promoted in the next assessment iteration. The assessment is facilitated through the content of the *Model Repository* (a placeholder for all CAMEL models produced and manipulated) and especially the execution history being recorded for the adaptation rules. The selection is carried out by executing a certain algorithm per each event of interest which is detailed in Sect. 5.

The enacted rule's workflow part is transformed into an abstract workflow representation that must be concretised. Such a concretisation is required due to the fact that the adaptation framework capabilities can be enriched over time such that a certain adaptation task could be realised by two or more alternatives. To this end, there is a need for a component, the *Concretiser*, which should construct and solve a constraint optimisation problem so as to select the best possible adaptation task alternative according to the user requirements and preferences.

The *Adaptation Engine* takes the form of a workflow execution engine able to execute the concretised adaptation workflows. It is also responsible for storing information related to the adaptation workflow execution in the *Model Repository* by exploiting the proposed CAMEL's execution meta-model extension. The actual workflow execution incorporates the invocation of level-specific services (e.g., a WfaaS/SaaS adaptation service) that represent service-based realisations of adaptation tasks.

New adaptation rules are generated while existing ones are adapted via the *Adapter* component. In the first case, the generation is semi-automatically conducted according to our previous work [24], which associates the patterns of events being discovered with all possible combinations of adaptation tasks able to address them.

Realisation Level. Our envisioned adaptation framework is not yet complete as the implementation level of its component varies while all of them have not been yet integrated into a coherent whole. The *Adaptation UI* is able to edit adaptation rules but does not yet offer the other two capabilities. The *Transformer* and *Concretiser* have not been realised yet. The *Rule Engine* is almost complete but it cannot yet promote rules based on the rule evaluation results. The *Adaptation Engine* and the *Adapter* are those components which have been fully realised. Finally, the two higher abstraction levels (WfaaS and SaaS) have been already mapped to the respective adaptation functionality while for the other two lower levels, the facilities of an existing cloud orchestration engine will be exploited.

3   CAMEL Adaptation Meta-model Extension

3.1   Background

CAMEL originally included a scalability meta-model dedicated to the modelling of scalability rules in form of mappings from events to scaling actions. The event modelling part of CAMEL was already quite rich and was not enhanced in any way. However, as we will see in the sequel, the scaling part was greatly adapted. In the following, we explicate the original way scalability rules were modelled via CAMEL before we enter into the details of such adaptation.

Events (see Fig. 2) in CAMEL can be simple or composite. Metric conditions are mainly used to specify simple events. On the other hand, composite events are specified as patterns of events by applying time-based (e.g., PRECEDES) and logical operators (e.g., AND) over simpler events. Thus, event patterns actually represent event trees or hierarchies.

Both vertical and horizontal scaling actions can be modelled in CAMEL. Horizontal scaling actions are specified by indicating the number of instances to be added or removed for an application component. Vertical scaling actions specify the VM to be scaled as well as the update in the size or number of certain VM features like the number of cores.

3.2   Extension

CAMEL has been extended in the context of this work (see Fig. 3) to transform its scalability meta-model to an adaptation one so as to cover the whole adaptation possibilities of a multi-cloud application at different levels of abstraction.

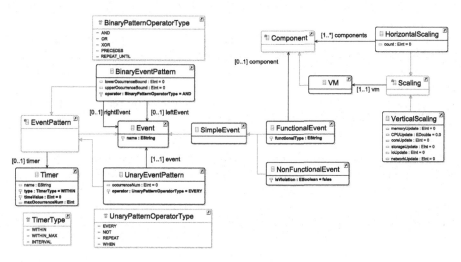

Fig. 2. The representation of events in CAMEL [14].

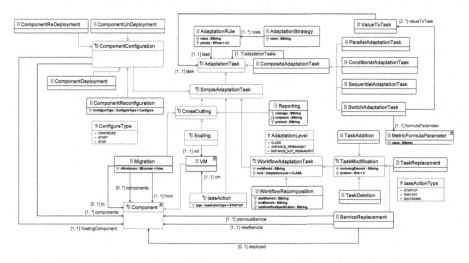

Fig. 3. The adaptation meta-model in CAMEL [14].

Adaptation Rules and Strategies. CAMEL's adaptation meta-model incorporates the topmost *AdaptationModel* element, which acts as a container for all adaptation-related elements. It also includes the key concept of an *Adaptation-Rule*, which enables to associate events with adaptation actions.

As it has been already stated, a problematic situation, i.e., an event can be alternatively confronted by multiple adaptation rules. As such, an adaptation system must choose the best from these rules. In particular, the rule with highest *priority*, i.e., a dynamically-modifiable attribute, should be selected. This could mean that an already selected rule might be unsuitable for selection in the near future as it might not have a sufficient successability level, such that its priority is reduced, or a better rule is discovered that more completely addresses the respective event, having a higher priority than the existing ones. The collection of all these rules that confront such an event is represented by the *Adaptation-Strategy* concept. As such, the application's current adaptive behaviour as well as the way such a behaviour can evolve over time can be represented then by the collection of all adaptation strategies.

Adaptation Tasks. Adaptation tasks represent the way problematic events can be addressed. They can be classified as either simple or composite. A simple task represents a single, level-specific action (e.g., a scaling action), while a composite task represents an adaptation workflow, i.e., a composition of adaptation tasks controlled by well-known control flow constructs.

Composite Adaptation Tasks. A composite task can be regarded as a tree incorporating tasks with lower complexity. As any kind of workflow can be constructed by four main types of basic control flows, we have created respective sub-concepts of *CompositeAdaptationTask* to represent them.

A sequential and parallel execution of adaptation tasks is represented by *SequentialAdaptationTask* and *ParallelAdaptationTask*, respectively. A conditional construct predicated over a certain referenced event is represented by *ConditionalAdaptationTask*. If that event occurs, then the first task associated with this composite task must be executed; otherwise, the second associated task must be executed. On the other hand, to cover a conditional branch with multiple alternatives, the *SwitchAdaptationTask* has been modelled, which is associated with a certain *MetricFormulaParameter*, i.e., a metric or a metric formula. As multiple values can be produced by monitoring this metric or computing this formula, these values can be mapped (see *ValueToTask* concept) to respective adaptation tasks that need to be executed.

Simple Adaptation Tasks. Various abstract sub-classes of simple adaptation task have been created to cover adaptation actions in different abstraction levels, with the exception of the *Cross-Cutting* abstract concept, representing cross-cutting adaptation actions.

The abstract class of *IaaSAction* covers all possible actions (startup, shutdown and restart) at the IaaS level by referring to the VM to be adapted and the action type to be performed on it (see *IaaSActionType* enumeration).

At the SaaS level, we have modelled two adaptation tasks covering the replacement of SaaS services and their reconfiguration. In the former case, we need to specify the SaaS to be replaced as well as the replacement SaaS. In the latter case, an abstract concept has been modelled (*ComponentConfiguration*) which can be further distinguished into more concrete reconfiguration actions:

- *ComponentDeployment*: references the SaaS components that must be deployed in a PaaS or IaaS component. As such, it could be useful in the context of deploying components, such as load balancers, only after the second instance of an application component is created.

– *ComponentUnDeployment*: references the components that need to be undeployed from their hosting component, which is also referenced. This could be handy in hybrid cloud bursting, where the public VMs for a certain application component are not needed any more.
– *ComponentReDeployment*: references those components that must be redeployed. This could facilitate migrating the components to a new version, e.g., to address certain permanent bugs.
– *ComponentReconfiguration*: references those components that must be reconfigured by either stopping, starting (e.g., to bypass the potential transient error occurred) or redeploying them (e.g., when the error is not transient).

At the workflow/WfaaS level, all possible adaptation tasks are encapsulated by the *WorkflowAdaptationTask*. These can be further distinguished into *WorkflowRecomposition* and *TaskModication* ones.

WorkflowRecomposition expresses the need to recompose a workflow, from the current execution point until the final workflow task, by replacing the remaining workflow content with another (sub-)workflow description. On the other hand, a *TaskModification* task expresses a single, low-level workflow modification at the task level by pointing to the respective workflow part (i.e., workflow task) to be modified. Such an adaptation task can be further distinguished into:

– *TaskAddition*: represents the addition of a workflow task (represented by an *ApplicationTask* encapsulating the respective task description) at the point referenced.
– *TaskDeletion*: signifies the deletion of the workflow task pointed.
– *TaskReplacement*: expresses the replacement of the workflow task pointed by another one also referenced.

Workflow level changes can be permanent or temporary. The *level* attribute in *WorkflowAdaptationTask* signifies this by covering 3 possible cases: (a) *Class*: the change is permanent – case of workflow evolution; (b) *InstancePermanent*: the change is permanent for the current instance but does not impact the other workflow instances; (c) *InstanceNonPermanent*: this special kind of an instance-level change needs to be modelled when a task instance in a workflow loop must be adapted only once in the context of the current loop repetition.

Cross-cutting adaptation tasks are either level-independent tasks or tasks that can be realised in different or across levels. These can be further distinguished into:

– *EventCreation*: enables creating an event that can be consumed by the adaptation system and possibly lead to an adaptation rule triggering. This nice mechanism facilitates, e.g., dealing with the uncertainty in executing an adaptation rule. In particular, the failure of a rule to address the current event could lead to the creation of a new event that signifies this failure. This allows formulating more advanced adaptation rules, accounting for the possibility of adaptation-related exceptions.

- *Reporting*: in some cases, it is possible that a particular critical event is raised which potentially also causes the triggering of an adaptation rule. Such event should then be notified to particular kinds of users, like admins. This could be handy for, e.g, enabling the admin to complete the partial addressing of the current problem by the adaptation rule.
- *Scaling*: this adaptation task can be alternatively performed in different levels (IaaS or PaaS) and is already covered by the original version of CAMEL.
- *Migration*: signifies the migration of one or more components into a different hosting component of the same or different cloud provider. The hosting components can be certain PaaSes or IaaSes. This means that we can cover different possible migration cases (e.g., from PaaS to IaaS or IaaS to PaaS). We can also indicate via this task whether all instances of the component(s) to be adapted must be migrated or only the affected one. The former could be suitable in case the current hosting could be deemed problematic for all the component(s) instances and not just a single one.

4   CAMEL Execution Meta-model Extension

4.1   Background

CAMEL's execution meta-model captures historical information related to executing a multi-cloud application. Such information is partitioned into groups called *ExecutionContexts*, representing different deployment episodes for the same application, where a deployment episode covers the overall provisioning session that involves the application initial deployment, its continuous reconfiguration and its final decommissioning. The collection of all these deployment episodes over time for this application is then called an *ExecutionModel*, which also represents the top-level container for execution history-oriented elements.

The coverage of execution history information can be considered as quite important for various reasons. First, it enables to explore an application's performance capabilities over time. Second, it can support reasoning over the best deployments of an application or its components. The respective facts inferred can enable accelerating the application deployment reasoning time [11] as certain application components can be directly as- signed to particular cloud offerings. Third, it can be exploited by, e.g., a Reinforcement Learning deployment reasoning algorithm [8] to avoid inspecting deployments which have failed in the past (either leading to errors or SLO violations). Fourth, it can support traceability analysis for identifying those requirements that have led to not only producing particular application deployment models but also transiting from one to the other at the instance level.

To accommodate for achieving the above benefits, CAMEL has been designed to capture all necessary information that can enable deriving the aforementioned knowledge types. In this respect, the execution context encapsulates information associated with: (a) what was the application's overall execution period during the deployment episode; (b) its overall provisioning cost in that period; (c) which deployment and requirement models drove the application deployment and adaptive provisioning. Further, all other execution history-related elements which can be modelled via CAMEL should be bound to a specific execution context. These elements will be now shorty explained.

A *Measurement* is an abstract class that represents a measurement that has been produced by a metric instance. Such a measurement is associated with its respective value as well as the point in time it was generated. Further, it can be associated with those SLOs that can be assessed based on it. Depending on the type of object that this measurement concerns, measurements can be further distinguished into application, internal component, VM, PaaS and communication measurements. The latter measurement kinds refers to network-based measurements produced for metrics related to a couple of components that communicate with each other.

The concept of *SLOAssessment* represents an assessment of a certain SLO, i.e., a hard, non-functional application requirement. Such an assessment is associated with a certain outcome (SLO was violated or not) as well as the point in time where this outcome has been produced. The SLO assessments not only enable to track over time which SLOs have been violated but also to trigger the respective adaptation of the affected application.

Finally, a scalability rule's enactment is represented by the *RuleTrigger* class, which is associated with the point in time this enactment was conducted as well as the respective instances of events that have caused it.

4.2 CAMEL Enhancements

While CAMEL captured well the execution history of applications, it did not enable to completely cover information related to an application's actual adaptive behaviour. Thus, CAMEL was decided to be extended with the ability to cover both adaptation rule triggering as well as measurability and successability aspects related to this triggering. As already stated, this extension aimed to facilitate the assessment of adaptation rules within a certain adaptation strategy and the dynamic modification of their priority according to the information that has been recorded.

As such, we have enhanced CAMEL's execution meta-model (see Fig. 4) according to the following three ways. First, *RuleTriggering* was extended to cover all information relevant to the triggering of adaptation rules, i.e., the generic replacement of scalability rules, including the realisation of adaptation tasks that took place in this triggering. The latter gave rise to the modelling of a new concept called *TaskRealisation*.

Through this new concept, we cover the following details about how an adaptation task was realised in the context of an adaptation rule: (a) when the task execution started and ended so as to compute the task's execution time, (b) the task's unit cost and its respective currency unit; (c) the task execution result. The latter maps to the following *AdaptationResult* enumeration members:

- *SUCCESSFUL*: the adaptation task was able to achieve its main adaptation goal

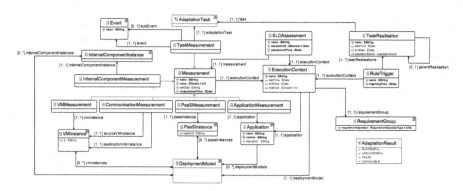

Fig. 4. The extended execution meta-model in CAMEL [14].

- *UNSUCCESSFUL*: the task, while successfully executed, was unable to achieve its adaptation goal
- *FAILED*: a certain error or failure occurred when executing the adaptation task
- *UNAVAILABLE*: the adaptation task was not available or accessible when it was attempted to execute it

The first two enumeration members enable evaluating the successability of an adaptation task, which could be, e.g., measured by the percentage of times the task was able to attain its goal. The third member facilitates evaluating the task reliability, while the last member enables evaluating task availability. As such, it becomes clear that through just two time-based and two cost-based attributes as well as a single enumeration one, we are able to assess various quality parameters for an adaptation task. Further details about the exact way these quality parameters can be computed and how they could be utilised to dynamically calculate the priority of an adaptation task will be supplied in the next section.

A task's realisation also refers to the realisation of its parent task. This could be useful for traceability reasons as it enables to assess how many times one or more sub-tasks can be blamed for the failure of a parent task. This could facilitate discovering those parent adaptation tasks which are doomed to fail in addressing a "problematic" event due to the "bad" combination of included sub-tasks. For instance, it could be possible that the component tasks combination is either overlapping or wrong, thus always leading to the parent task's unsuccessfulness.

The adaptation task realisation specification is completed through a reference to the event being coped with. This also guarantees the correct aggregation of measurements for the current task realisation at hand in the context of the same adaptation strategy. This is also necessary in case an adaptation task can be used to deal with more than one event (which could be the overall event or a component of such an overall event) in the context of the same or different adaptation strategies. This will offer an additional insight of, e.g., an adaptation task's successability across the multiple adaptation strategies in which it is potentially re-used.

5   Adaptation Rule Selection

In order to enable evolving the adaptive behaviour of a cloud application, we have devised a specific algorithm which is able to compute the priority of all adaptation rules that formulate a certain adaptation strategy (and thus confront the same 'problematic' event). Such a computation is conducted by evaluating a certain mathematical formula. Before going into the details of this formula and of the respective algorithm that computes it, we present the main components of this formula, which map to certain parameters that correspond to the quality of the composite adaptation task at hand.

5.1   Quality Parameters and Their Computation

We consider that the quality of an adaptation task comprises certain well-known, domain-independent non-functional parameters. Such parameters have been selected not only due to their wide recognition and application but also due to the ease of their computation in terms of respective metrics. In the following, we explain all these parameters and how they can be actually computed from the information stored in the respective application's execution model.

Execution Time. The *execution time* of an adaptation task can be considered as an important factor that can influence its selection due to the timeliness in the way an application can be adopted. In particular, as it has been already highlighted in the literature, the higher is the delay introduced in the adaptation process, the more difficult it is to properly address the current problematic situation and the more costlier this addressing can become. As such, it is always preferred to select adaptation actions that are fast enough as well as suitable to confront such a situation.

By considering the current information stored for a certain adaptation task's realisation in CAMEL's execution model for a specific event, the raw execution time raw_rt_{ij} of this task i can be computed easily from the two time-based fields as follows: $raw\_rt_{ij} = endTime_{ij} - startTime_{ij}$, where $startTime_{ij}$ and $endTime_{ij}$ are the starting and ending time points for the j-th recorded execution of this task in the context of the same event addressing, respectively.

However, the raw execution time metric offers just an insight about one task realisation. Thus, a more meaningful metric maps to the statistical handling of the former metric. In particular, we should compute the mean execution time $mean\_et_i$ of an adaptation task i in the context of the same event by averaging all the raw execution time recordings of this task for that event as follows: $mean\_et_i = \frac{\sum_{j=1}^{N} raw\_rt_{ij}}{N}$, where N is the number of recordings/realisations of this task for the same event.

Availability. We take the position that a certain adaptation action is realised in the form of a service. In this respect, the availability of such a service should be high in order to be eligible for selection for application adaptation. This is especially true in the context of applying that service across multiple adaptation strategies for one or even more cloud applications.

Due to the information recorded for an adaptation task realisation, the computation of availability can be easily performed as the percentage of times the task was available. This can be easily mapped to the following formula: $avail_i = 1 - \frac{\sum_{j=1}^{N}(adaptationResult_{ij}==\text{UNAVAILABLE})}{N}$, where $adaptationResult_{ij}$ is the adaptation outcome of task i with respect to its j-th recording/task realisation for the same 'problematic' event. In other words, we subtract from one (ideal availability) the percentage of times the adaptation task was unavailable in order to compute this metric.

Reliability. An adaptation workflow should always comprise tasks which are quite reliable, i.e., they do not fail and deliver an expected outcome. Otherwise, the successability of such a workflow cannot be actually guaranteed. Fortunately, in the context of the execution meta-model proposed, there is a certain way an adaptation task's reliability can be measured. This maps to the *success rate* metric which assesses the percentage of times the respective task execution did not end up to a certain kind of failure. As such, the following formula has been utilised for computing this metric: $succRate_i = 1 - \frac{\sum_{j=1}^{N}(adaptationResult_{ij}==\text{FAILED})}{N}$, which is quite similar to the one concerning availability with the sole exception that we now count the number of times the task failed and not that it was unavailable.

Successability. This is one of the most important factors for selecting an adaptation task which affects directly the main task's goal, which is to completely address the current problematic situation. In this sense, it is always critical to select adaptation tasks which are as much successful as possible. In the context of the extended CAMEL execution model, the successability $succ_i$ of an adaptation task i can be computed by the following formula: $succ_i = \frac{\sum_{j=1}^{N}(adaptationResult_{ij}==\text{SUCCESSFUL})}{N}$.

Cost. Cost represents an important business factor that always influences any kind of selection that relates to the management of a cloud application. More importantly, in the context of application provisioning, by considering a certain budget for a particular reference time period that can be afforded by the application provider, we should always attempt to adapt the respective application in such a way that the corresponding budget is never surpassed, (i.e., the sum of actual provisioning and adaptation cost should be less than this budget). This highlights the need for selecting adaptation tasks which are less costly but still effective enough to completely address the current problematic situation.

As stated before, adaptation actions can be considered as services which could be launched and executed on-demand (see new serverless computing paradigm) or continuously offered in a micro-service form. As such, there will be always a certain (time-)unit cost associated to their realisation and such a cost is covered by the proposed CAMEL execution meta-model enhancement. By considering that an adaptation task takes a certain time period to execute, its respective overall execution cost $cost_i$ for a certain adaptation scenario can be computed as follows: $cost_i = unit\_cost_i * mean\_rt_i$., where $unit\_cost_i$ is the (time-)unit cost of the adaptation task. To be noted here that the above formula is simplified as it assumes that the unit cost for an adaptation task does not change for each realisation of it. However, it could be possible that this cost could vary. For instance, an adaptation task could migrate to a new IaaS service host or we could utilise a different adaptation service to realise the adaptation task at hand. To cover such cases and thus be generic enough, the above formula could be modified as follows: $cost_i = \frac{\sum_{i=1}^{N} unit\_cost_{ij}}{N} * mean\_rt_i$, where $unit\_cost_{ij}$ is the task's (time-)unit cost for the j-th realisation in terms of the same 'problematic' event.

5.2 Priority Computation Formula

The main idea for computing the priority pr_i of a certain adaptation task i is that such a priority should be an aggregation of the current measurements for the quality metrics of this task. To support an aggregation over measurements of different scales and value types, there is a need to conduct first normalisation. Depending on the preferred direction of values of the involved metrics, different mathematical expressions can be utilised for the respective utilify/normalisation function which can be unified by the following formula:

$$uf_{metr}(x) = \begin{cases} \frac{x - metr^{min}}{metr^{max} - metr^{min}}, metr \uparrow \\ \frac{metr^{max} - x}{metr^{max} - metr^{min}}, metr \downarrow \end{cases}$$

In this formula, uf_{metr} represents the utility function of metric $metr$ while $metr^{max}$ and $metr^{min}$ represent the maximum and minimum value that a certain metric takes across all adaptation tasks that are assessed and which are able to confront the same 'problematic' event. Further, the upper and down arrow signify the corresponding metric's positive and negative direction of values, respectively.

Once all metric measurements are normalised, the overall task priority can be computed by following the simple additive weighting (SAW) approach [9] as the weighted sum of these measurements. The respective formula below underlines the respective computation that should be performed.

$$pr_i = w_{mean\_rt} * uf_{mean\_rt}(mean\_rt_i) + w_{avail} * uf_{avail}(avail_i)$$
$$+ w_{succRate} * uf_{succRate}(succRate_i) + w_{succ} * uf_{succ}(succ_i)$$
$$+ w_{cost} * uf_{cost}(cost_i)$$

In this formula, the weight given to each metric (e.g., w_{mean_rt} for the $mean\_rt$ metric) represents its relative importance with respect to the other metrics. The sum of all these weights should then be equal to 1. In other words: $w_{mean\_rt} + w_{avail} + w_{succRate} + w_{succ} + w_{cost} = 1$. All these weights can be derived by following the Analytic Hierarchy Process (AHP) [22].

Cold Start Problem. In case that no recording exists for a certain adaptation task/rule, then its respective priority could be computed by considering values for the 5 selected quality metrics that might have been generated via testing or offline monitoring. This could enable to: (a) solve the initial situation where no adaptation task/rule has respective execution history recordings such that we can select the one that seems to be the most processing based on its stated/advertised quality values; (b) move from one adaptation task to another one (for which no recordings are yet available) when the respective need arises making the selection of adaptation tasks fairer.

5.3   Adaptation Rule Selection Algorithm

The adaptation rule selection algorithm that is proposed in this paper is quite simple but yet effective. In essence, it attempts to first compute each measurement per each metric and adaptation task/rule. Then, it concurrently computes the priority of each adaptation rule of an adaptation strategy (after normalising the measurements of each metric) as well as maintains the highest priority and the adaptation rule that exhibits it. In the end, either the latter two information pieces are returned or also the whole array of adaptation rules (which include their priority), if required by the user. Depending on the user preferences, the respective array can be sorted before being returned. This could be handy in the context of exception handling during adaptation enactment: instead of re-executing the current adaptation workflow that might have failed according to a certain aspect, we might choose to execute the next adaptation rule and respective workflow in order. The pseudocode of this algorithm is shown in the listing below.

```
function selectTask(AdaptationStrategy st, Prefs p){
   AdaptationRule[] rules = st.rules;
   init(params [5] [2]);
   //1st Phase - Measurement Computation
   for(AdaptationRule r: rules){
     computeMetrics(r); //Computes all metrics for r
     update(params,r); //Updates min, max values
   }
   //2nd Phase - Priority Computation
   maxPrior = 0.0;
   maxRule = null;
   for (AdaptationRule r: rules){
     //Normalise & compute priority
     double p = computePriority(r,params,p);
     //Check if maximum priority was obtained
     if (p > maxPrior){
        maxPrior = p;
        maxRule = r;
     }
   }
   //3rd Phase - Sorting rules array if needed &
```

```
//return results
Vector v = {maxPrior, maxRule};
//Only best rule must be returned
if (p.onlyRule) return v;
else{
 if (p.sort) sort(rules);
 v.add(rules);
 return v;
 }
}
```

Concerning the time complexity analysis of this algorithm, this depends on whether the array of adaptation rules is sorted or not. In any case, the first phase (measurement computation) takes $O(M * N)$ to execute where M is the number of adaptation rules and respective (composite) adaptation tasks in the current adaptation strategy at hand while N is the number of recordings per each task. In case the array sorting is not needed, then the time complexity becomes $O(M + M * N)$, which can be reduced to $O(M * N)$. Otherwise, it is $O(M * N + M * logM)$, where $O(M * logM)$ is the time needed to sort the adaptation rules array.

6   Running Example

To demonstrate our work's capability to dynamically compute the priority of adaptation rules of the same strategy and thus select the most suitable one over time, we rely on a city traffic management use case. This use case bases on a sequential workflow, which is repeatedly executed over time and comprises the following tasks:

- *monitor*: it monitors traffic and environment conditions over a certain city area and collects information concerning special events (e.g., concerts) that will take place in the city
- *analyse*: it analyses the current situation of a certain city area, as sensed by *monitor*, and produces a traffic regulation plan for it
- *execute*: it enacts the regulation plan derived (by, e.g., controlling the traffic lights frequency in a problematic sub-area).

The use case follows a micro-service architecture such that the above three tasks have been mapped to respective micro-services, which are called as S_1, S_2, S_3 for short, respectively. Service S_1 has been deployed in VM VM_1, which also hosts a time series data base (TSDB) for the storage of this service's measurements. Service S_2 has been deployed in VM VM_2, which also hosts a NoSQL database used to store important knowledge for supporting traffic analysis. Finally, service S_3 has been deployed in VM VM_3. All VMs reside in the city's private cloud and have a different size (e.g., VM_2 is wider than the other two both in terms of computation and storage). Figure 5 depicts the overall system architecture of this use case.

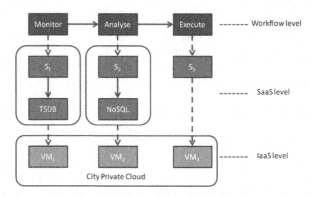

Fig. 5. The architecture of the use-case system [14].

To cover the adaptation behaviour of micro-service S_2 that realises the analysis functionality, the next (2) adaptation rules have been modelled:

$$down(S_2) \longrightarrow restart(S_2) \tag{1}$$

$$down(S_2) \longrightarrow reconfigure\,(S_2) \tag{2}$$

The first rule is utilised to overcome transient errors by restarting micro-service S_2. On the other hand, the second rule is employed to overcome permanent errors by redeploying S_2 (which can be considered as a SaaS component) on the same VM. Via this reconfiguration, it might be possible that such permanent errors are corrected by a new version of the micro-service's code.

As both rules address the same event (micro-service S_2 is down), we need to select the best possible one. Initially, no execution history recordings are available for them. To this end, we need to resort to their stated quality (e.g., produced via testing) in order to solve this cold start problem. Suppose that the priority of the first rule (1.0) is much higher than of the second (0.6) essentially as the former is much faster than the latter (which is also reflected on their *cost*). Thus, the first rule will be originally selected. This rule seems to operate well initially, as evidenced by Table 1 (indicating instances of the *TaskRealisation* class). This highlights that potentially only transient errors occur in S_2's code. However, after a certain time point, this rule is not successful at all, as permanent errors have occurred in S_2's code. As such, after two unsuccessful attempts to restart S_2, the dynamic priority of the first rule becomes lower than the original priority of the second. Thus, the second rule is selected and successfully solves the permanent errors by reconfiguring S_2 to its new, error-free version.

The overall adaptation execution history is covered through the information conveyed by Tables 1 and 2. The first table covers the raw information that is captured by the use case's execution model. The second table covers aggregated information which enables to dynamically compute the priority of the two adaptation rules, also shown in its content. In overall, these two tables showcase that the right information and knowledge is captured in our framework and the

Table 1. Instance information for *TaskRealisation* class.

Name	Task	startTime	endTime	adaptationResult
TR1	T1	1566454178	1566454200	SUCCESSFUL
TR2	T1	1566454320	1566454344	SUCCESSFUL
TR3	T1	1566454440	1566454464	UNSUCCESSFUL
TR4	T1	1566454500	1566454522	UNSUCCESSFUL
TR5	CT1	1566454600	1566454680	SUCCESSFUL

Table 2. Aggregated information for the use case's adaptation rules.

Task	Mean RT	Avail.	Rel.	Succ.	Cost	Priority
T1	22	1.0	1.0	1.0	0.11	1.0
T1	23	1.0	1.0	1.0	0.115	0.998
T1	23.33	1.0	1.0	0.666	0.116	0.9978
T1	23	1.0	1.0	0.5	0.115	0.598
CT1	80	1.0	1.0	1.0	0.4	0.9

right decisions are made with respect to which adaptation rule is more suitable according to the current situation. As such, our work is indeed able to correctly evolve the adaptation behaviour of the use case considered.

Please note that in Table 1, the first column maps to the name of the task realisation (a kind of identifier), the second to the name of the respective task involved, while the next three columns map to the three main attributes of the task realisation. On the other hand, Table 1 depicts the priority computation that has been performed each time a respective execution history record was captured for the two main adaptation tasks/rules at hand. In particular, it depicts the name of the task for which the computation is performed, the values that it takes for the 5 main quality parameters and its final priority value. The computation of priority is conducted by considering that the *successfulness* quality parameter is the most important and critical one. As such, it is weighed in a much higher degree (0.8) than the other four parameters (0.05 each). Finally, it is assumed that the unit cost for the adaptation tasks is the same as they map to methods of the same adaptation service.

7   Related Work

This section reviews related work on adaptation and scalability (rule) modelling for cloud applications as well as on application adaptation and its evolvability. It must be noted that we consider scalability rule modelling in the sense that scalability rules can be considered as a subclass of adaptation rules.

Most approaches in the adaptation of cloud applications do not consider the application execution history. As such, no execution DSLs have been suggested. In some cases, some execution-related information can be directly or indirectly collected in model-based approaches. However, full execution as well as adaptation histories are not captured yet. Which disables the respective approaches in evolving over time to incorporate new adaptation patterns as well as improve existing ones.

7.1 Scalability Rule Modelling

The adaptation meta-model we have proposed evolves the scalability meta-model of CAMEL [12]. In this respect, it is more expressive than most scalability rule languages offered as the latter are quite simplistic by associating single metric conditions to just one scaling action. Many of these latter languages were developed in the context of European projects, such as Reservoir [5] and Optimis [21].

[18] proposed a cloud elasticity language, capable of expressing simple scalability rules, including elements like the scope, the metric condition and sliding window, the scalability limit as well as scaling action details (e.g., scale type). Such a language has a moderate level of metric expressiveness as it complements a metric's name with additional details inside the scalability rule. Further, it relies on bad design choices, such as mixing scalability policies and rules. Its adaptation model expressiveness is also limited, as it is not able to specify complex metric conditions while it associates only one scaling action to each adaptation rule.

The SYBL rule language [3] attains a good expressiveness level by accounting (3) main layers: (a) application, (b) component and (c) programming, while it also enables specifying logical combinations of constraints on metric values. However, it is not as expressive as CAMEL's metric and adaptation meta-models in terms of specifying more complex conditions and complete metric definitions. Further, it does not cover unit modelling. Finally, SYBL just references via an ID the object to be adapted, while our adaptation meta-model introduces a full reference, from which all appropriate information can be fetched for this object, due to the full integration of CAMEL meta-models into a coherent whole.

Amazon's CloudFormation[2] is exploited for modelling horizontal scalability policies. Such policies specify conditions only on resource metrics, while their scaling actions concern a pre-configured VM image that must be manually mapped to the appropriate application component. Thus, compared to the proposed adaptation meta-model, CloudFormation has limited expressiveness in defining scalability rules.

---

[2] http://docs.aws.amazon.com/AWSCloudFormation/latest/UserGuide/Welcome.html.

7.2   Adaptation Rule Modelling

Most cloud application adaptation approaches restrain themselves at the resource level and attempt to derive resource-related adaptation actions by identifying the difference between the current and future application model. Only few approaches were devoted to cloud application adaptation modelling. Some of them do not even explicitly model adaptation rules but only parts of them. The rest are not rich enough to specify adaptation actions at all possible layers while they do not also enable modelling more advanced adaptation workflows. In this respect, our proposition is currently quite ahead from the state-of-the-art.

A modelling approach for cross-layer monitoring and adaptation was proposed in [23], supplying languages for system experts to specify the layers, their interrelations, as well as the constraints on each layer. For each individual layer, a run-time model depicts the current system state. Whenever the monitoring system detects a violation of a layer's constraints, a manual or semi-automatic adaptation takes places which may also affect the model of other layers, according to their interrelations.

A model-based approach to adapt cloud application topologies was proposed in [4]. Two Open Cloud Computing Interface (OCCI) models were utilized to derive the necessary adaptation steps to be implemented. The first is used to represent the current state of the cloud application topology, whereas the second the desired state. A comparison of the two OCCI models identifies the model mismatches and calculates the adaptation steps, required from transiting from the first to the second model, to be performed in the final step. As such, this approach does not directly model adaptation rules.

[17] introduces a conceptual model comprising the key entities related to adaptation inside a cloud environment. Two broader adaptation types are considered: (i) cloud application-specific adaptations; (ii) cloud resource-specific adaptations. This model's main contribution is the identification of direct and indirect relations among cloud entities, and of dependencies among adaptation actions. The main difference with our approach is that it does not account the dependencies in a cross-cloud environment. Further, it does not allow the explicit modelling of adaptation rules.

[16] presents an evolution of the models@runtime [2] pattern, providing the specification of adaptation plans, as well as a runtime environment to enact them. The adaptation plan specification relies on a novel DSL which enables designing adaptation plans as workflows. In contrast to our meta-model, this DSL is not rich enough to cover the necessary actions in all possible layers while it does not capture all basic (adaptation) workflow control constructs as in our work.

7.3   Application Adaptation and Its Evolvability

Only few approaches have focused on the adaptation of cloud applications. In fact, most of them concentrate mainly on scaling such applications, thus covering just one abstraction level, while the evolution of the cloud application adaptive behaviour is something that has not been researched before. Concerning cloud application scaling, the respective approaches can be separated into local or global reconfiguration ones, where in some cases, some approaches are able to exhibit both reconfiguration kinds [1,6,10]. Local reconfiguration is supported through the execution of scaling rules in the context of one cloud provider. On the other hand, global reconfiguration approaches are able to scale an application across multiple cloud providers. In this case, the scaling is performed by constructing and solving a constraint optimisation problem which attempts to assign each application component to one cloud offering from those matching it in such a way that particular user optimisation and SLO-based requirements are concurrently satisfied.

In the past, extensive research on service-based application (SBA) adaptation was conducted. The main outcomes were quite interesting, taking the form of cross-level research prototypes [7,19,25]. However, in most of the cases, these prototypes were not able to cover all possible abstraction levels and were not applied in the context of cloud computing, thus they do not have the ability to adapt an SBA by exploiting different kinds of level-specific cloud services. Further, they do not possess the ability to generate new adaptation rules. Some research work on SBA adaptation also focused on the adaptation evolvability [15]. However, that work focused mainly on just one abstraction level and not multiple ones to also account for their respective dependencies.

8   Conclusions and Future Work

This paper presented three unique contributions towards the modelling and evolution of the adaptive behaviour of multi-cloud applications. Concerning adaptation modelling, the paper has suggested two extensions to the state-of-the-art cloud application modelling language called CAMEL. The first extension concerns evolving CAMEL's scalability meta-model towards the capability to specify sophisticated adaptation rules as mappings from events (patterns) to adaptation workflows. The latter workflows are expressed in a language-independent manner. This enables their transformation to any workflow language which could be adopted by the workflow engine utilised to execute them in the context of the cloud application adaptation framework at hand.

The second modelling extension was performed over CAMEL's execution meta-model, originally designed to capture the execution history of multi-cloud applications. This meta-model was enhanced with the capability to record a multi-cloud application's adaptation history, covering information related to the respective adaptation actions performed, including their outcome as well as their start and end time.

The aforementioned information can be exploited for deriving quality metric measurements for adaptation actions related to their performance, availability, reliability, cost and successability. Such measurements can then be dynamically aggregated into a single, priority value which can enable to select one adaptation rule from those alternatives that can address the same problematic situation (i.e., event) that has occurred. This is the subject of the priority computation formula and the respective algorithm that applies this formula, both proposed in this paper, over all adaptation rules of the same adaptation strategy.

All these contributions provide support and realise part of the functionality of our envisioned multi-cloud, cross-level application adaptation framework. In essence, they facilitate the three main capabilities of that framework. The first contribution, apart from facilitating the modelling of adaptation rules, it allows to support any workflow execution engine that could be injected into our adaptation framework in order to enact the workflow part of these rules. The second contribution enables to record the adaptive behaviour of a multi-cloud application over time and constitutes the basis for the third contribution which is able to evolve this adaptive behaviour to be able to address the continuously changing application context and requirements. The appropriateness of our contributions was demonstrated via the use of a certain use case.

Currently, the following research directions are planned. First, the two CAMEL extensions will be validated via different use cases and a user study. Second, the proposed priority computation algorithm will be evaluated while it will be investigated whether it could be expanded to cover additional quality metrics. Third, the adaptation framework implementation will be finalised by filling in the missing gaps as stated in Sect. 2. Fourth, this framework will be thoroughly evaluated to assess its performance and suitability.

Acknowledgements. The research leading to this paper has received funding from the European Union's Horizon 2020 research and innovation programme under Grant Agreement No. 731664 (MELODIC project).

References

1. Ardagna, D., et al.: MODACLOUDS, a model-driven approach for the design and execution of applications on multiple clouds. In: ICSE MiSE: International Workshop on Modelling in Software Engineering, pp. 50–56. IEEE/ACM (2012)
2. Blair, G., Bencomo, N., France, R.B.: Models@ run. time. Computer **42**(10), 22–27 (2009)
3. Copil, G., Moldovan, D., Truong, H.L., Dustdar, S.: SYBL: an extensible language for controlling elasticity in cloud applications. In: CCGrid, pp. 112–119. IEEE Computer Society (2013). https://doi.org/10.1109/CCGrid.2013.42
4. Erbel, J.M., Korte, F., Grabowski, J.: Comparison and runtime adaptation of cloud application topologies based on OCCI. In: CLOSER (2018)
5. Galán, F., Vaquero, L.M., Clayman, S., Toffetti, G., Henriksson, D.: Deliverable D4.1, D4.2 and D4.3 - Scientific report. Reservoir project deliverable, January 2009
6. Horn, G., Skrzypek, P.: MELODIC: utility based cross cloud deployment optimisation. In: Proceedings of the 32nd International Conference on Advanced Information Networking and Applications Workshops (WAINA), pp. 360–367. IEEE Computer Society, Krakow, May 2018. https://doi.org/10.1109/WAINA.2018.00112
7. Guinea, S., Kecskemeti, G., Marconi, A., Wetzstein, B.: Multi-layered monitoring and adaptation. In: Kappel, G., Maamar, Z., Motahari-Nezhad, H.R. (eds.) ICSOC 2011. LNCS, vol. 7084, pp. 359–373. Springer, Heidelberg (2011). https://doi.org/10.1007/978-3-642-25535-9_24

8. Horn, G.: A vision for a stochastic reasoner for autonomic cloud deployment. In: NordiCloud, pp. 46–53. ACM, September 2013. https://doi.org/10.1145/2513534. 2513543

9. Hwang, C., Yoon, K.: Multiple Criteria Decision Making. Lecture Notes in Economics and Mathematical Systems. Springer, Heidelberg (1981). https://doi.org/10.1007/978-3-642-48318-9

10. Jeffery, K., Horn, G., Schubert, L.: A vision for better cloud applications. In: Ardagna, D., Schubert, L. (eds.) MultiCloud, pp. 7–12. ACM, Prague, Apr 2013. https://doi.org/10.1145/2462326.2462329

11. Kritikos, K., Magoutis, K., Plexousakis, D.: Towards knowledge-based assisted IaaS selection. In: CloudCom, pp. 431–439. IEEE Computer Society, December 2016. https://doi.org/10.1109/CloudCom.2016.0073

12. Kritikos, K., Domaschka, J., Rossini, A.: SRL: a scalability rule language for multi-cloud environments. In: CloudCom, pp. 1–9. IEEE Computer Society (2014)

13. Kritikos, K., Zeginis, C., Griesinger, F., Seybold, D., Domaschka, J.: A cross-layer BPaaS adaptation framework. In: FiCloud 2017, pp. 241–248. IEEE Computer Society, Prague (2017). https://doi.org/10.1109/FiCloud.2017.12

14. Kritikos, K., Zeginis, C., Politaki, E., Plexousakis, D.: Towards the modelling of adaptation rules and histories for multi-cloud applications. In: CLOSER. ScitePress (2019)

15. Leitner, P., Dustdar, S., Wetzstein, B., Leymann, F.: Cost-based prevention of violations of service level agreements in composed services using self-adaptation. In: S-Cube, pp. 34–35. IEEE Press, Zurich (2012)

16. Lushpenko, M., Ferry, N., Song, H., Chauvel, F., Solberg, A.: Using adaptation plans to control the behavior of Models@runtime, vol. 1474, pp. 11–20 (2015)

17. Marquezan, C.C., Wessling, F., Metzger, A., Pohl, K., Woods, C., Wallbom, K.: Towards exploiting the full adaptation potential of cloud applications. In: PESOS (2014)

18. Moore, L.R., Bean, K., Ellahi, T.: A coordinated reactive and predictive approach to cloud elasticity. In: Cloud Computing. IARIA (2013)

19. Popescu, R., Staikopoulos, A., Brogi, A., Liu, P., Clarke, S.: A formalized, taxonomy-driven approach to cross-layer application adaptation. ACM Trans. Auton. Adapt. Syst. 7(1), 7:1–7:30 (2012). https://doi.org/10.1145/2168260. 2168267

20. Rossini, A., et al.: D2.1.3–CAMEL documentation (2015). https://paasage.ercim. eu/images/documents/docs/D2.1.3_CAMEL_Documentation.pdf

21. Rumpl, A., Rasheed, H., Waeldrich, O., Ziegler, W.: Service manifest. Scientific report. Optimis project deliverable, June 2010

22. Saati, T.: The Analytic Hierarchy Process. McGraw-Hill, New York (1980)

23. Song, H., Raj, A., Hajebi, S., Clarke, A., Clarke, S.: Model-based cross-layer monitoring and adaptation of multilayer systems. Sci. China Inf. Sci. 56(8), 1–15 (2013). https://doi.org/10.1007/s11432-013-4915-5

24. Zeginis, C., Kritikos, K., Plexousakis, D.: Event pattern discovery in multi-cloud service-based applications. IJSSOE 5(4), 78–103 (2015)

25. Zengin, A., Kazhamiakin, R., Pistore, M.: CLAM: cross-layer management of adaptation decisions for service-based applications. In: ICWS, pp. 698–699. IEEE Computer Society (2011)

Author Index

Printed in the United States
By Bookmasters